The Windvane Self-Steering Handbook

The Windvane Self-Steering Handbook

Bill Morris

International Marine / McGraw-Hill

Camden, Maine • New York • Chicago • San Francisco
• Lisbon • London • Madrid • Mexico City • Milan
• New Delhi • San Juan • Seoul • Singapore
• Sydney • Toronto

The McGraw·Hill Companies

1 2 3 4 5 6 7 8 9 0 DOC DOC 0 9 8 7 6 5 4

Library of Congress Cataloging-in-Publication Data
Morris, Bill
The windvane self-steering handbook / Bill Morris.
    p.   cm.
Includes bibliographical references and index.
ISBN 0-07-143469-0 (hardcover : alk. paper)
1. Steering-gear. 2. Sailboats. I. Title.
VM845.M67 2004
623.8´62—dc22   2003025920

Questions regarding the content of this book
should be addressed to
International Marine
P.O. Box 220
Camden, ME 04843
www.internationalmarine.com

Questions regarding the ordering of this book
should be addressed to
The McGraw-Hill Companies
Customer Service Department
P.O. Box 547
Blacklick, OH 43004
Retail customers: 1-800-262-4729
Bookstores: 1-800-722-4726

Photographs and illustrations by the author unless noted otherwise.

For Angelica and Thomas

Contents

Chapter 3. Materials and Fabrication Methods 39

Chapter 4. Selecting the Right System 57

Preface and Acknowledgments

Mounted on a workbench in a machine shop, a modern servopendulum gear might appear to be just a bunch of stainless steel tubes or aluminum extrusions pointing this way and that, like some art nouveau rendition of Medusa. You dip the airvane to one side with your finger, the servo blade turns a little, and then you notice that the blade also swings freely back and forth, now rotating through two axes, even as you manipulate the airvane. "How the heck can this thing steer a boat?" was my naive response when I first set eyes on the Fleming steering gear I was about to purchase. It was early June, and my girlfriend and I had driven to San Diego to pick up the vane gear in preparation for my single-handed mini-shakedown cruise to Ensenada that summer. We looked in the shop, and seeing no one there, walked across the shop floor to a sparkling new windvane mounted on a workbench. As we studied the mysterious, shiny machine, an unshaven, weather-beaten gentleman walked up behind us. "G'day, mates. I'm Kevin Fleming, and that there is the vane gear you ordered."

In a deliberate, matter-of-fact style, he explained how the unit was constructed and how it worked, and then shared some of his own sailing experiences under vane steering. Later, when I deployed the gear for the first time just outside Los Angeles Harbor, the boat bashed about, sailing in circles, hopelessly at the tender mercies of a psychotic, stainless steel tyrant. I quickly discovered that I had turned the airvane the wrong way into the wind. The two-day sail to Ensenada was memorable: I knew then that I could sail forever with the vane gear at the helm. Since then, I have sailed nearly 20,000 nautical miles with the vane gear, and am still learning more about this fascinating machine.

In my conversations with Kevin and numerous other vane gear builders, all of them have expressed the same zeal—no, obsession—with their creations and with their lifelong search for the perfect vane gear design. They have spent years experimenting with gear mechanisms, push rods, hydrofoil lift characteristics, and construction in stainless, bronze, and aluminum alloys. So complex is the balance of forces in vane gear steering that the first successful horizontal-axis vane servopendulum did not appear until the mid-1960s, several years after astronauts had already orbited the earth! Since then, a small handful of truly original designs have established themselves in the vane gear industry, and variations of those designs have broadened the family of self-steering gears available for the cruising sailor.

My intention in writing this book was to express briefly and concisely, in simple, unbiased terms, the underpinnings of a science that has remained elusive and esoteric for too long. If I do have a bias, it is that windvane systems are the only reliable means of steering a small vessel, aside from crew taking turns at the helm, on long ocean passages. It is pure folly for shorthanded crew to depend exclusively on an electronic system. I am not in the business of building vane gears, nor do I formally endorse any of the products I discuss in the ensuing pages. My first goal here is to point out the mechanical and navigational advantages of a vane steering system. More than a mere option for shorthanded crew, vane gear steering is a natural extension of sailing itself. My second goal is to give sailors some idea of the range of windvane steering products available to them, including sizes, prices, and contact information. However, I have avoided proposing any formal rating system, since the vane gear each one of us selects depends on vessel size, transom configuration, type of main steering, and personal preference. Finally, it is important that cruisers learn how to install, maintain, repair, and modify vane gears for best performance—and even build a vane gear if they have the time and inclination. When we are hundreds of miles from modern repair services or an airport where we could receive shipments of parts, we learn to improvise with the tools at hand.

The research for this book has drawn from an assortment of sailing friends, windvane manufacturers, and secondary sources. First, I owe a huge thanks to fellow sailors Scott and Wendy Bannerot of *Élan* (Florida) for their explicit details on maintaining and modifying a vintage Aries vane gear, and ultimately convincing me to finish this book. Hans Faber of *Born Free* (Stockholm) explained the delicate engineering characteristics that make a servopendulum gear function while I smoked his cigars and drank his Scotch in French Polynesia; our conversations helped inspire me to write a book about windvane self-steering. It was serendipitous that I met Tony and Mitsuyo Williams on the Catalina 42 *Windriver* at the Balboa Yacht Club in Panama; they related to me the story of how they had helped bring about the creation of Scanmar International's "Swing Gate" Monitor mounting system. For their knowledge and experience with homebuilt trim-tab gears, I thank Bill Bailey of *Apollo* (Honolulu); David Webb, formerly of *Arcady* (San Pedro); and Bruce Wells of *Pyxis* (Queensland). Frank and Kaye Pearce of *Gingerbread Man* (Queensland) helped me get a close look at the process of rebuilding and customizing a vintage RVG trim-tab unit. I learned lots about the operation of Aries and Sailomat vane gears from David Berg of *Kismet* (Pago Pago) while he shared fun stories and poignant observations based on years of experience with those systems. David's wife Mary collected numerous articles on vane gear steering in cruising magazines, contributing greatly to my research. Laurent Clarot of *Banana Split* (New Caledonia) provided an opportunity to study the ins and outs of installing a Cape Horn vane gear to the sugar-scoop transom of a 42-foot ketch. Tom and Dee Bridgman showed me how to operate a Hydrovane aboard *Axe Calibre* (Axmouth, England), helping me to appreciate the inner workings of this incredible apparatus. Jack Dunn of *Fair Rose* (Queensland) gave me a copy of John Letcher's *Self-Steering for Sailing Craft* for my birthday—after I had spent two years looking for the book—and helped point me in the right direction for gathering more information on NACA foil profiles and rudder balance. I also deeply appreciate Charles Doane's technical review of the manuscript and providing me with valuable feedback that helped bring this book to fruition, and the work of legendary technical artist Jim Sollers.

The following individuals provided valuable technical advice, published materials, photographs, and insight regarding manufactured vane gear systems: Hans Bernwall, Scanmar International; John and Karen Curry, Hydrovane Self-Steering; Kevin Fleming, Fleming Self-Steering Systems; Peter Förthmann, Windpilot; Yves Gélinas, Cape Horn Marine Products; Dr. Stellan Knöös, Sailomat; and Peter Matthiesen, Aries Denmark.

Finally, Deborah Oliver, Jon Eaton, Molly Mulhern, and Janet Robbins of International Marine weathered the storm with their patience, guidance, and creative input while working around my sailing schedule; for all their efforts, I owe them great thanks.

Introduction

*T*he *Windvane Self-Steering Handbook* is exactly what the title suggests: a comprehensive manual to help you understand the practical aspects of sailboat self-steering based on power from the wind. A few other books dedicated to this subject have appeared in the English language over the last four decades, certainly the most widely known of which is John Letcher's *Self-Steering for Sailing Craft*, published by International Marine in 1974. Letcher gave us one of the best dissertations in existence regarding sheet-to-tiller steering, and prophesized a new generation of windvane steering devices. To would-be vane gear designers, he wrote, "Achieving successful windvane self-steering is not nearly as easy as it looks." Of his own attempt at designing and building a vane gear for his boat, he said, "My first satisfactory permanent installation took an astonishing 175 hours to design, build, and install—which is more than one-eighth of the time it took to design and build the boat!" In considering a vane gear design for our vessels, whether we buy a manufactured unit or build one ourselves, we should take to heart another of Letcher's memorable quotes: "Probably no installation will completely satisfy all the ideals; everyone has to make his own bargain with the devil."

In the last thirty years, true to Letcher's prophecy, countless new products have appeared on the windvane market, and vane gear designers have competed to offer stronger, lighter, and more efficient designs to cruising sailors. For this text I have taken great care to showcase products that have distinguished themselves as market leaders. The list of ten models, along with some of their variations, is based solely on my subjective judgment, not on any quantitative analysis of engineering specifications, durability, price, annual sales, or other objective criteria. I am sure there are other very fine vane gears available to sailors, and I encourage you to learn more about them.

I have tried to keep explanations in this book as simple and straightforward as possible. The descriptions of self-steering technology are from the point of view of a cruising sailor, not a marine engineer. Any theory you find in these pages is not meant simply to satisfy your intellectual curiosity, but to assist you on the practical level in selecting, installing, and maintaining a wind-powered steering system. To that end, the book is light on NACA lift principles, foil cavitation, and rudder balance, but heavy on sail rig balance and galvanic corrosion. In the last chapter are sketches and explanatory notes on the West End horizontal-vane auxiliary-rudder trim-tab system. Though of my own rough design, it is in truth an interpretation of other vertical- and horizontal-vane designs I have observed and studied over the years.

Even as I write about, say, balancing a sail rig or building an emergency rudder, I sometimes fail at controlling the impulse to tell a story. The anecdotes and bits of sardonic humor are meant to make a point, and to lighten up what otherwise could be some rather dry reading. Here and there you will encounter snippets of my sailing experiences and those of others as well. In this way you gain from the accumulated experience of other sailors who have found ways to solve difficult problems related to self-steering. The father of a childhood friend once admonished me, "Pain is the greatest teacher." For years I argued with that statement in my mind, putting faith in all the psychobabble I had learned in college. The wisdom of my elders began to make a lot more sense when I left Los Angeles Harbor in a 30-foot sailboat, cruised down the coast of Mexico and Central America, and headed out across the Pacific Ocean. When reflecting on mistakes made before and during a hellacious gale between Tonga and Fiji, I recall one of my grandmother's favorite sayings: "Once burned, twice taught."

Common sense tells us that when we open the toolbox to work on our boats, we are totally accountable for whatever job we undertake. By following the suggestions in this book, you assume full responsibility for any damage incurred by vessel or vane gear, or by any equipment you elect to use. You also assume full responsibility for any personal injury resulting from procedures followed in this text. Furthermore, I cannot guarantee the proper operation of any system or mechanical device covered in this book; there are too many variables involved for anyone except the manufacturer, installer, and skipper to answer for the functioning of a particular onboard system.

I have done my level best to ensure the accuracy of all the information in this volume. But even after extensive research and communication with individual vane gear builders, errors may have found ways to creep into the writing. For this I apologize. Changes in prices, measurements, design, construction materials, and other such details are inevitable, and may have occurred between this writing and the time of publication. Again, I encourage you to keep abreast of the most recent changes, especially if you are planning to buy a new vane gear.

The use of a few terms deserves some clarification here. Among sailors, *vane*, *airvane*, *windvane*, and *airfoil* are used as synonyms. However, there is some disagreement on the technical accuracy of using the terms interchangeably. According to the current *Merriam-Webster's Collegiate Dictionary* (11th ed.), the term *airfoil* denotes "a body (as an airplane wing or propeller blade) designed to provide a desired reaction force when in motion relative to the surrounding air." The same dictionary defines *vane* as "a movable device attached to an elevated object (as a spire) for showing the direction of the wind," or "a thin flat or curved object that is rotated about an axis by a flow of fluid . . . " Vanes, or airvanes, then, appear to be a subset of airfoils. To eliminate confusion, *airvane* and *vane* in this text refer to a tall, flat, or wedge-shaped object standing atop a self-steering apparatus for the purpose of harnessing the wind's power. Occasionally, you will find the word *foil* indicating a *hydrofoil*. Where the term *foil* appears alone, its application should be clear from the context.

To indicate the whole self-steering apparatus in a generic sense, I use the terms *vane gear*, *self-steering gear*, *windvane self-steering*, and similar combinations whose definitions should be, again, eminently obvious by their context in the paragraph. Submerged foils have varied purposes, and I have tried to be clear as to their discrete applications. In the self-steering literature, you will also see the terms *servo blade*, *blade*, *servo oar*, *servo paddle*, and *servopendulum* used as equivalents; for our purposes, however, the *servo blade* is the submerged foil essential to all *servopendulum* vane gears. The term *servopendulum* may refer to either the servo blade and shaft, or to the class of devices built on this principle.

WHAT YOU WILL FIND IN THIS BOOK

The following summary is meant to acquaint you with the contents of this text. As with many technical and quasitechnical books, you need not read every page of every chapter in order that the desired information gel and make sense. If you are familiar with the workings of vane gear systems, but want to learn more about purchasing a previously owned unit, you may elect to start with chapter 6, Purchasing a Used Vane Gear. If you need specific information on repairing your vane gear or would like to make some modifications to the unit, you might wish to consult chapter 9, Maintenance and Repair, or chapter 10, Customizing Your Vane Gear, and so on. Refer to the figures and illustrations as you read, pointing to the various components with a pencil as you follow the descriptions.

Chapter 1. An Overview of Sailboat Self-Steering
Which is the better type of steering for a sailboat: windvane or autopilot?

Sailors argue heatedly over this question, but for most, installing both systems on the average sailing vessel seems to be the preferred strategy. The chapter starts with a look at both sides of this question, while maintaining that a wind-vane steering gear is an essential system on vessels under roughly 45 LOA, regardless of whatever other self-steering arrangements are on the vessel. We will also take a quick tour through windvane self-steering history, highlighting major events and turning points over the last century that have led to the many fine windvane systems available on the market today.

Chapter 2. Wind-Powered Self-Steering Systems: How They Work

This chapter gives a quick summary of the main components and operating theory behind sheet-to-tiller steering and each of the several types of vane gear systems. The first of the vane gears is the vertical-vane trim-tab gear, generally homebuilt for either a transom-mounted main rudder or auxiliary rudder. The next is the horizontal-vane trim tab, a more complex evolution of the vertical drive, and available through at least one manufacturer. In the same manner as its predecessor, the horizontal-vane trim tab may be mounted on the main rudder or on an auxiliary rudder. More for history's sake than anything else, you will find a description of Blondie Hasler's vertical-vane servopendulum, which in its time was a groundbreaking innovation in modern mechanical self-steering. You will also learn how the contemporary servopendulum operates, combining Hasler's pendulum blade and Marcel Gianoli's horizontally mounted airvane to control a sailing vessel's main rudder.

Chapter 3. Materials and Fabrication Methods

For those who are curious about the alloys and polymers entering into the construction of different vane gears, this chapter will be of special interest. Topics covered include the galvanic series, or nobility scale, with special emphasis on bronze, brass, stainless steel, and aluminum alloys. The discussion will also look at the ways metals are manufactured and fabricated: casting, tubing, brazing, welding, and machining. Many parts, such as bearings and bushings, are made of plastics for their corrosion resistance. We will review the applications of nylon, Delrin, Torlon, and Teflon in marine hardware. Finally, we will look at different methods used by vane gear builders to construct vane steerers. The object here is to inform you rather than to endorse or denigrate a particular type of construction.

Chapter 4. Selecting the Right System

Assuming you have made the decision to purchase a windvane steering system, you must decide which manufacturer and model of vane gear best suits your needs. In some cases, as with a long, low, overhanging mizzen boom, or on a 120-foot, three-masted schooner, a vane gear is simply out of the question. You may find that a certain type of gear or a particular manufacturer offers more steering sensitivity in light winds, or that some model is more easily adapted to your vessel's swim step or stern rail gate. Other salient issues are vessel size, the steering unit's weight and size, materials and construction, the builder's reputation, and price. The author is not qualified to pass comparative judgment on the many different units available on the market. But a summary of things to look for can help equip you to make the best decision for you and your vessel.

Chapter 5. Vane Gear Specifications

Of obvious importance to anyone seriously considering the purchase of a new or used vane gear, this chapter covers construction details of ten of the best-known manufactured vane gears. Illustrations offer a conceptual idea of how each vane gear functions. You will also find notes on materials used in construction and a description of each vane system's internal gearing or transmission system. Other data include the approximate dimensions and weight of each model, along with its current price (in U.S. dollars). While reading this chapter, pay special attention to how each unit functions, how it would fit and look on your vessel (if you do not already own a vane gear), and what types of metals and plastics have gone into its construction. Some alloys and polymers require special care and handling to get the most service and longevity out of them.

Chapter 6. Purchasing a Used Vane Gear

For cruisers on a shoestring budget, a list of tips will assist in finding and purchasing a previously loved windvane. Some units may be so old that the manufacturers no longer provide the necessary repair parts; some companies may even have gone out of business. You will also find that there are various ways to locate these machines, which tend to be hot items in the used boat equipment market. Cruiser swap meets, marine newspapers, and Internet sites can help you get equipped at a considerable savings. We will also look at issues of quality, condition, repairability, and parts availability. Often, what you can no longer buy can still be easily fabricated by a machinist or welder.

Chapter 7. Installation

Naturally, this matter is best covered by the operator's manual included with each new unit. This chapter distills what has been gleaned from several of these manuals and includes a few pointers from experienced windvane owners. We will look at airflow, overhead clearance, placement of blocks and lines, alignment, and related topics. What may not be covered in your owner's manual is how to reinforce the hull to accept the weight and twisting action of the vane gear. Another matter the manufacturer will expect you to know in most cases is how to tame the recalcitrant, gyrating beast while you neatly mount it to your boat's stern—over the water. With determination, common sense, and some helpful hints, you should have little trouble mounting the unit properly.

Chapter 8. Sailing with Windvane Steering

Every time I sail with my vane gear or read a cruising article on windvane steering, I learn something new about this intriguing topic, half art and half science. The best way to approach it is with a quick review of sailing principles so that we are working from the same knowledge base and vocabulary. From there, we will move on to balancing the rig and then tweaking the vane gear to produce hours, sometimes days, of uninterrupted self-steering bliss. The chapter offers sailing suggestions for each type of windvane, including notes on self-steering in storm conditions.

Chapter 9. Maintenance and Repair

Your windvane unit, if initially calibrated and installed according to the manufacturer's specifications, will require little maintenance during its lifetime. If something breaks, it is probably covered for the first few years by a warranty against defective materials and workmanship. Some components of the system, though, are vulnerable to wear and tear, requiring attention once in a blue moon. This chapter covers lubrication, dealing with dissimilar metals, caring for aluminum, and other important details.

Chapter 10. Customizing Your Vane Gear

Whether you have a new or used vane gear, once you have installed the unit on the stern, the brunt of your work is done. But in some cases, you may find it necessary to make small modifications to the system in order for it to perform at its best. If the unit's mounting tubes have become loose from constant torsion, it may be advisable to reinforce the mounting structure. Perhaps your unit is in peril of excessive galvanic corrosion from the close proximity of dissimilar metals. A system for easy lubrication, especially in hard-to-reach spots, can make life easier on crew and windvane. The chapter also gives you tips on customizing airfoils for optimum performance in a variety of situations.

Chapter 11. Emergency Rudders

The chapter reviews a handful of emergency rudder configurations, some of which windvane manufacturers provide as optional kits with their stock vane gears. This is something to consider, especially if your vessel has a spade rudder or some other dubious rudder installation. Though a kit can be devised from one of the sketches included in the chapter, purchasing the emergency rudder offered with your vane gear will almost certainly yield a lighter, more efficient rudder assembly. Nonetheless, the indefatigable do-it-yourselfer who wants to save a few bucks can build an adequate system by following a few simple guidelines. Bear in mind it may need to be modified to fit the size and shape of the vessel and stern.

Chapter 12. Build a Horizontal-Vane Trim-Tab System

So you ask, "Why let the big guys make all that loot on a self-steering system that I can build myself?" That's what folks like Franklin, Knöös, and Bernwall must have asked themselves. If you intend to build a servopendulum gear, or perhaps invent the next generation of vane gears with your own creative engineering, you are on a quest that will devour several months, or several years, of your time, not to mention a tidy sum in machine tools and castings. However, this chapter does offer enough detail for the individual of average mechanical ability to build the "West End" horizontal-vane trim-tab vane gear. The conceptual drawings may be modified to follow the vessel's parameters and the builder's ingenuity.

In the Back of the Book

In the appendix is a list of manufacturers, distributors, and other services. A table of selected NACA four-digit profiles and the Beaufort Scale are also included for ready reference.

A glossary of terms specific to windvane self-steering follows the appendix. A glossary term is italicized at its first mention in text. The bibliography will help identify the books and websites I have referenced in the text. Finally, the index should help you quickly find what you want.

In closing, we can watch "Captain Ron" and read about other people's sailing adventures only so many times before we ourselves make the decision to go cruising. There is nothing else in this life that compares with seeing the world on our own terms, from our own sailing yachts. A properly installed windvane steering gear and a humble set of guidelines to install, maintain, and operate the system can make that dream come true.

The author's vessel, *Saltaire*, a 1966 Cal 30 built by Jensen Marine, at anchor in Port Boisé, New Caledonia. (Marilu Flores)

Chapter 1

An Overview of Sailboat Self-Steering

MECHANICAL VERSUS ELECTRONIC STEERING

Years of dreaming, saving, and preparing are about to come true: you're going cruising! The new triple-stitched main and roller-furling genoa are just waiting to take a bite out of the wind and send you sailing to paradise. The rebuilt diesel promises thousands of hours of faithful performance, and the navigation and communication equipment will keep you on track and in touch. But how about self-steering? Does your vessel have such a system, and if it does, are you satisfied with it? Or have you postponed selecting a self-steering apparatus until you learn more about what is on the market? The array of mechanical gadgetry dedicated to liberating the helmsman from the "tyranny of the tiller" is staggering, and when making the first purchase of a self-steering apparatus, downright intimidating. Before pulling out the checkbook and committing anywhere from several hundred to several thousand dollars for a self-steering system, you must first decide whether to purchase an electronic device, called an *autopilot*, a windvane system, or perhaps both.

The latest autopilots on the market combine an internal compass, a microprocessor, and a motorized assembly to direct the craft along the desired magnetic or true (if the autopilot is interfaced with GPS) course. More advanced models can adapt themselves to the vessel's steering behavior and even sail at an apparent wind angle. In general, autopilots require little practice or finesse from the user to achieve more or less satisfactory results. Hence their popularity. On the other hand, windvane systems are purely mechanical, using the combined forces of wind and water to keep the vessel faithfully on course. Vane gears require more practice and sometimes cost more, but as you will learn in the following pages, they have much to offer the blue-water sailor.

At first glance, a windvane system may appear to the untrained eye as an esoteric jumble of stainless steel tubing, blocks, and double-braided line undecipherable by mere mortals. The engineering is a bit complex, but the basic operational concept is really quite simple. When I told the wife of a fellow sailor I was considering a windvane for an extended cruise of the Pacific, she said such a contraption (she couldn't recall ever having seen one) would be "ugly." Later, when she saw the gleaming, new Fleming Global 301 mounted proudly on *Saltaire*'s transom, she gasped, "It's sexy!"

Most contemporary windvane systems generally fall under one of two categories: *servopendulums* and *trim tabs*. Servopendulums, comprising the majority of today's windvane systems, transmit changes in wind direction from an airvane on a nearly horizontal axis through a push rod and a carefully engineered set of gears to a submerged pendulum, also referred to in the industry as a rudder, oar, blade, or paddle. The servo blade turns on its vertical axis, simultaneously swinging to port or starboard as it is deflected by the rush of water. The blade's vertical angle gradually tapers back parallel to the vessel's keel as the boat resumes its correct course with respect to the wind. The pendulum transmits its force through a pair of double-braided lines, each of which alternately pulls the helm to adjust the heading. If this compressed explanation is a little confusing, don't worry—it will all come clear in chapter 2.

Trim tabs, so simple in design that they are often homebuilt, are also effective—but less so than servopendulums in heavy conditions. Mounted on the vessel's rudder or an auxiliary rudder, the trim tab receives the wind's signals from either a vertical- or horizontal-axis airvane, depending on the design, with the vane connected to the trim tab by stainless cables or solid linkage.

Wind-steering systems are said to perform better as the wind blows harder. That's at least partially true. As a rule of thumb, most units start producing consistent, accurate steerage at an apparent wind speed of about 8 knots. However, many sailors, including the author, claim their wind gears operate efficiently as soon as there is enough wind to fill their sails. What does increase with wind and boat speed is the amount of steering force generated and the speed with which the unit responds to fluctuations in the vane's angle to the apparent wind.

Electronic self-steering technology certainly has come a long way in the last decade or so, and some sailors say that autopilot performance can closely match that of a good vane gear. Still, many cruisers report that autopilots have difficulty performing in harsh conditions. A common practice is to use the vane gear in all conditions except for running downwind in light airs and motoring through calms. Autopilots and windvanes can easily be coupled to save on amperage and to reduce wear and tear on the autopilot. Exclusive dependence on autopilots can pose a huge challenge for smaller vessels with minimal battery storage and charging systems. Autopilots steal the life's blood from other vital systems, such as GPS, radar, weather fax, and radios. This is to say nothing of refrigeration, pressurized hot and cold water, microwave ovens, watermakers, color televisions, and the other electronic marvels folks install on their vessels these days.

A quick glance around any cruiser anchorage will show that on a large percentage of cruising vessels under 45 feet LOA (length overall), from the most sparsely equipped to the most high-tech, windvanes are still standard equipment. In a recent *Sail* article, retired 747 pilot and longtime sailor Joe Minick writes that he sees room for both an autopilot and a mechanical steerer on his Mason 43, *Southern Cross*. "But," he adds, "if I could have only one self-steering system, I would choose the windvane." This is a man whose life and profession have depended on autopilots for decades. Even the most advanced autopilots take time to learn a yacht's sailing characteristics, sometimes up to two or three hours. That's a long time when sailing through squalls with rapidly changing wind directions and speed. The downside of wind steering is the need to accommodate changes in wind direction with manual adjustments. With an autopilot, it may be preferable to hand-steer through such situations until the weather stabilizes. Recent technological advances are certainly closing the gap between mechanical and electronic steering devices, but no autopilot will ever be able to match the efficiency, dependability, and durability of a well-built vane gear.

The most common argument leveled against windvane steering applies to single-handed coastal sailing, where a wind shift during a long nap can spell disaster. Case in point: seven days out of San Diego and only 35 miles from Cabo San Lucas at the southern tip of Baja California, Mexico—and single-handed—I set the Fleming on a course that would have *Saltaire* passing about five miles below the cape. Snug in my little sleeping spot near the companionway, I swigged down half a bottle of merlot and passed out. "Ah hell," I thought to myself, retiring to the sheep pasture, "I'll wake up in a couple of hours." Six hours later, I awoke to the pounding of surf, and saw massive plumes of foam exploding less than a half mile off the bow. Had I not jumped to the cockpit at that moment to fire up the engine and quickly extricate my wee vessel from the rocks lying in her path, I wouldn't have lived to write these words. It wasn't the windvane that almost cost my life. It was the merlot. Carl Seipel, formerly of Scanmar International, manufacturer of the Monitor vane gear, writes, "If it is extremely important to sail a straight course while sailing, both an autopilot and a vane gear have to be supervised." Regardless of the type of self-steering system you choose, if you sail single-handed or short-handed within a hundred miles of land, it is imperative that you set the alarm clock for every half hour.

In addition to the issues already discussed are the matters of durability and ease of repair. Like virtually all electronic appliances, the autopilot is essentially irreparable by anyone but a trained technician, and the older systems are probably cheaper to replace than to repair. And remember, it's not *if* it breaks down, but *when*. Therefore, if you use an autopilot, it is wise to carry a spare unit. Most windvane manufacturers offer reasonably priced parts that can be switched with a meager set of wrenches and screwdrivers, though vane gears rarely break down. *Saltaire* has sailed nearly 20,000 miles with wind steering, much of it in rough weather, and the vane gear has yet to require anything more than occasional rainfall to keep its bearings clear of salt and grit. If you have ample reserve battery power, an aggressive charging system, and a preference for the push-button ease of electronic systems, then perhaps an autopilot is just what you need. But if you seek a robust machine that performs silently and damned near flawlessly on all points of sail, in all kinds of weather, while encouraging you to cultivate further the rarefied art of sailing, you will no doubt join the great number of ocean sailors who equip their vessels with wind-vane steering gears.

A BRIEF HISTORY OF WINDVANE SELF-STEERING

Captain Joshua Slocum

Wind-powered self-steering for oceangoing sailboats finds its earliest known roots in the famous voyage of Captain Joshua Slocum, who aboard his 37-foot yawl *Spray* made history by being the first man to sail solo around the world. When Slocum returned from his trip in 1898, casually tying up to

Captain Joshua Slocum. (*From Sailing Alone Around the World*)

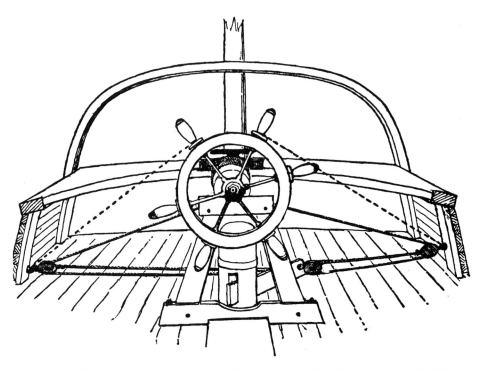

Figure 1-1. Self-steering arrangement on *Spray*. (From *Sailing Alone Around the World*)

the same mooring post in Newport, Rhode Island, from where he had embarked in April 1895, few could believe what he had achieved. After all, it was generally assumed that no one could steer an oceangoing vessel for very much time, aside from lashing the tiller or wheel long enough to prepare a meal or take a short catnap, without extra crew to alternate watches at the helm. Slocum gives us a glimpse at how he solved the steerage question in his book *Sailing Alone Around the World*, required reading for anyone contemplating an offshore passage under sail. The description of the steering arrangement is aided by a diagram in the book's appendix (see figure 1-1). The drawing shows lines running through three blocks, one block attached to what is apparently the rudderpost, all of this apparently comprising the vessel's sole steering, with no servomechanism in place for self-steering. Slocum boasted how *Spray*, with its well-balanced rig, self-steered, affording him ample time to read and meditate while the helm tended itself. Of his long journey from Thursday Island in the Torres Strait off northern Australia to Cocos Keeling 2,700 miles due west, he wrote: "During those twenty-three days I had not spent altogether more than three hours at the helm, including the time occupied in beating into Keeling Harbour. I just lashed the helm and let her go; whether the wind was abeam or dead aft, it was all the same: she always sailed on her course."

Early Experiments

The first windvanes appearing in the early twentieth century were nothing more than enlarged versions of airvane-controlled rudders used on model boats. The hobbyist attached a small piece of wood or framed cloth to a stem that was arranged to rotate in the direction opposite the rudder's axis. As the vane and rudder flicked a few degrees in either direction, the boat would entertain the owner with a few minutes of self-steered progress through flat water until a gust would overpower the tiny vessel and knock it off course. Except in very light airs, the water exerted greater pressure on the rudder than did the wind. Other model boat enthusiasts attached weights and elastic cords to tillers for course control, but constant weight changes and cord adjustments made the systems cumbersome. One model boat aficionado was the famous yacht designer Nathanael Herreshoff, who experimented with a rotating windvane connected by an arm to the tiller. Variations of this concept, with airvanes as large as mizzensails, eventually found their way onto full-size yachts. However, a large sail could not overcome a critical limitation of this system. Such an airvane could turn the rudder only until the vane was in line with the wind. Course correction usually requires some initial oversteering before the helm is trimmed for the proper heading. It is easy to see why experimenters in the early twentieth century had little luck with their self-steering arrangements on yachts.

Marin-Marie

French marine artist Marin-Marie was one of the earliest innovators to employ a device separate from the mainsheet or jib sheet to generate steering power. His system, which he installed on his motor launch, consisted of lashing the main rudder and using a small auxiliary rudder controlled directly by a large airvane. As the vane turned on its vertical axis, a line forced the rudder to rotate in the opposite direction, keeping the vessel on course. In 1936, Marin-Marie was the first to cross the Atlantic using a self-contained vane gear on his launch *Arielle*, and his approach would become the catalyst for future refinements in wind-powered steering. Although crude by contemporary standards, amateur inventors still experiment with variations of Marin-Marie's invention.

Trim-Tab Steering

An extensive search of self-steering literature has failed to reveal the name of an individual to whom we could attribute the earliest trim tabs. Someone, somewhere, realized that effective, wind-powered self-steering was possible, but only through some alternative means of exerting force on the rudder. Probably shortly after World War II, that unnamed individual devised the first trim tab for boat self-steering, a modified version of the rudder trim tabs used on aircraft. The trim tab, mounted to the vessel's transom-hung rudder, was connected to a vertical-axis airvane that swiveled 360 degrees, most likely atop the trim-tab shaft itself. Bernard Moitessier employed a variation of this simple system on *Marie-Thérèse* in the 1950s, and later on his 40-foot steel ketch *Joshua* as recently as the 1970s. The operator would first loosen the sleeve connecting the two shafts and trim the helm. After the airvane had swung around to line up with the wind, the operator would tighten the bolt on the sleeve connecting the upper and lower shafts. A counterweight extending forward of the vane would dampen the movement of the vane axis, guarding against oversteering. For the first time, a device was applying mechanical advantage to harness the water's force for steerage. This was a quantum leap in the art and science of self-steering, the *Homo erectus* of vane gears.

Blondie Hasler and the OSTAR

The decade and a half following World War II saw little advancement in yachting-related technology. Europe, at that time still rebuilding itself out of the ashes of six years' devastation, could show little enthusiasm for such leisurely pastimes, and in the United States, yachting was still viewed as a sport reserved for the wealthy. But by 1960, production fiberglass vessels had begun to make boating accessible to the middle class, and newer technology had made sailing easier for families and shorthanded crew. The time was ripe for a big event to give sailing its smashing debut in the eyes of the masses.

In 1956, on a bet of "half a crown," British Lieutenant Colonel H. G. "Blondie" Hasler challenged anyone who dared to a single-handed race across the North Atlantic from Plymouth, England, to Newport, Rhode Island. Hasler had achieved his first fame as a mariner by leading a ten-man team in two kayaks to bomb four German merchant ships in Bordeaux on the west coast of France. Map publisher and pioneer aviator Francis Chichester, who eight years later would be knighted for sailing single-handed around the world with just one stop, establishing a record speed for a solo circumnavigation in the process, was the first to accept Hasler's challenge. After spending the next two years scouting for competitors and sponsorship, Hasler persuaded the *Observer* newspaper to provide a trophy, and the Royal Western Yacht Club to sponsor the event.

On the starting date in 1960, five brave souls of the fifty who had sent letters of intent lined up at the starting point and began their historic dash across the pond in the first Observer Single-handed Trans-Atlantic Race (OSTAR). On his wooden Folkboat *Jester*, Hasler had installed his great contribution to sailing: a servopendulum blade controlled by a vertical airvane. A modified version of this design, the *Homo sapiens neanderthalensis* of vane steering, would later become the first commercially produced vane gear.

Chichester's 40-foot *Gipsy Moth*, named for the historic single-engine biplane he had flown as a younger man, was equipped with a rotating mizzensail functioning as a windvane. The cloth vane was so large it had to be reefed in heavy weather. This was essentially an adaptation of Marin-Marie's design, which still proved successful, as the fifty-eight-year-old Chichester won the 1960 OSTAR in 40 days, 12 hours. Ironically, it was the last hoorah for the old type of steering gear.

Though Hasler never so much as placed in any of the OSTARs, which he inspired, his pendulum oar remains to this day the standard for the bulk of commercially manufactured windvane systems seen on ocean sailing vessels. Moreover, Hasler's challenge to a brutal race ushered in a whole new era in sailboat design, construction, and equipment. Foam sandwich hulls, aluminum spars, ultralight multihulls, and numerous other innovations trace their beginnings to the OSTAR.

Marcel Gianoli

In preparation for the 1964 OSTAR, French naval officer Eric Tabarly wanted to employ a servopendulum vane design that would respond faster to wind changes and provide more steering power for the rough weather he would face in the grueling North Atlantic race. For this he sought the help of engineer and fellow countryman Marcel Gianoli, who retained the pendulum concept from Hasler's machine and coupled it with an airvane mounted more closely to a horizontal, rather than vertical, axis. Enter *Homo sapiens*. Gianoli's vane gear harnessed the wind's force gradually, feathering to one side or the other as apparent wind speed increased. This new, mysterious, gyrating windvane only enhanced the sinister profile of Tabarly's black, 44-foot, hard-chined plywood ketch *Pen Duick II*. At the start of the race that day in Plymouth, England, Tabarly, on special leave from the French navy, sent a prophetic message to his fellow competitors by raising a bright red spinnaker in a heavy blow. The next time anyone heard or saw Tabarly again was in Newport twenty-seven days later, where he finished first; in second place was Francis Chichester, who finished three days later. Though the new vane gear failed a few days short of Newport, it had played a critical role in maintaining Tabarly's healthy lead over the passage, and firmly established a new generation of self-steering technology. Most of the commercially produced vane gears, including such industry leaders as the Aries and Monitor, are based on the integrated Hasler-Gianoli design.

Nick Franklin

When the old-timers reminisce about the good ol' days of sailing and the larger-than-life sailing heroes of the late 1960s and early 1970s, they typically mention Nick Franklin and his Aries vane gear. Even among sailors who happily own and cruise with other vane gears, the Aries has managed to develop a cult-like following. This was the gear preferred by Tristan Jones, the eccentric Briton who by his own account sailed over 300,000 miles on small vessels during his lifetime and wrote sixteen books on his adventures. Perhaps most notable about the Aries is that it is probably the oldest servopendulum design in continuous production. Well, nearly continuous. In 1990, Franklin decided he'd had his fill of running a factory and closed the U.K.-based operation to go cruising. Peter Matthiesen of Denmark soon purchased the rights to the Aries and resumed production of the venerable vane, which has since undergone a few minor refinements in design and construction. Franklin's daughter Helen continues to sell spare parts for the U.K. Aries. The older Aries windvanes, particularly the original forty units built in 1968 and 1969 with bronze and stainless castings, are regarded as collectors' items. If you happen to own one, consider hanging on to it; a nice gesture would be to lend it to your local maritime museum.

Stellan Knöös, inventor of the Sailomat. (Sailomat)

Stellan Knöös

Swedish-American Stellan Knöös found a good way to put his doctorate in aeronautical engineering to work. After all, a hydrofoil is not much different from an airfoil, so why not apply his knowledge of both concepts to an integrated design? One major contribution by Knöös to the field of windvane steering was the combination of an angled servopendulum with an auxiliary rudder, which he introduced as the Sailomat 3040 in 1974. This is the machine Naomi James had on the stern of her 53-foot *Express Crusader* when she beat Sir Francis Chichester's record time for a single-handed circumnavigation. The Sailomat's servo blade was raked 30 degrees from vertical so the submerged blade could shake off accumulated seaweed and annoying flotsam. Knöös explains, "Unlike its competitors, the original Sailomat 3040, as well as the modern 536 and 601 systems, uses patented spherical-joint systems for the airvane-to-servo mechanical linkage, providing required 'toe-in' turning characteristics for the servo blade." In recent years Knöös has removed the auxiliary rudder from the servopendulum system, retaining the angled pendulum shaft. Also noteworthy is the Sailomat's compact mounting scheme, allowing plenty of transom space for a swim ladder or an overhanging LPG tank.

Hans Bernwall and Carl Seipel

Two of the biggest movers and shakers in the windvane industry over the last quarter of a century have been Hans Bernwall and Carl Seipel, cofounders of Scanmar Marine Products in Point Richmond, California. Bernwall and Seipel's ubiquitous Monitor servopendulum gear, one of the world's best-selling windvane steerers, can be seen braced to the sterns of cruising sailboats in every oceanic corner of the planet. The two Swedes originally had designed an auxiliary rudder trim-tab vane in 1970 to steer their 40-foot Alden cutter *Fia* during their circumnavigation. A handful of commercially built vane gears,

most notably the Aries in the United Kingdom, already had established themselves in Europe and North America. In those days, such units were difficult to come by in the United States, and were out of the price range of shoestring sailors. But by the time Bernwall and Seipel finished the tooling and fabrication required to build their windvane system, they had spent $3,000! (Dollar amounts throughout the book are in U.S. dollars unless otherwise indicated.)

The dynamic duo eventually went into business representing an eclectic range of marine products. In 1980, they bought the rights and tooling to the Monitor windvane and hired Gene Merwin, the retired aeronautical engineer who had designed the stainless steering device. Bernwall and Seipel later purchased rights to Saye's Rig from another aeronautical engineer, Roland Saye, and the Auto-Helm; both systems are now manufactured by Scanmar International. The company also imports the superlight Navik trim-tab servopendulum from Plastimo in France. Seipel sold his share of the business to Bernwall in May 1987 to pursue other goals. More recently,

Hans Bernwall of Scanmar International. (Scanmar)

Bernwall has overseen development of the SOS Rudder and MRUD (Monitor Emergency Rudder Conversion Kit).

A quick tour of any anchorage where long-distance sailing vessels congregate, such as the Panama Canal region, Tahiti, Cape Town, etc., will surely reveal that servopendulum vane gears with horizontally mounted airvanes are the overwhelming self-steering choice of ocean sailors on boats up to 45 feet (14 meters) LOA. In the space of four decades, single-handed and shorthanded passagemaking have migrated from the realm of the daring and adventurous, to the mainstream of offshore cruising and racing, owing largely to the windvane steering technology that grew out of the early years of the OSTAR.

Electronic autopilots, in all fairness, do have their place among all that anodized aluminum framing and shiny, stainless steel tubing. Most cruising vessels over 45 feet LOA are equipped with autopilots. The sheer size of some larger vessels would require a vane gear so large as to be excessively bulky and cumbersome. Larger vessels have space to carry huge battery banks and multiple heavy-duty charging systems, so the autopilot is just as giddily assured of its nourishment as a seaman recruit waiting in the chow line for eggs and black-eyed peas. Most servopendulums may be coupled with autopilots, joining the autopilot's input from a compass, wind-direction indicator, or GPS with the steering force of the vane gear in order to economize on battery usage. The zeal of competition, the humble needs of cruisers on small yachts, and marketplace forces will continue to drive refinements in self-steering technology. And certainly, we can expect vane gear design and use to remain a key component of offshore racing and cruising for many generations to come.

An ever-growing number of people are discovering ocean sailing as an endless source of passion and profound joy in their lives. The best way to keep that feeling alive and hold onto the dream is to keep onboard systems reasonably simple, allowing yourself some latitude to enjoy the raw beauty of sailing for what it is. A vane gear empowers you to enjoy the convenience of self-steering without defeating the very purpose of ocean sailing: freedom. You are not free when you are hand-steering your vessel through a gale in the middle of the night just because the autopilot decided it was ready for early retirement. If you choose a vane gear appropriate for your vessel's size and design, and maintain the gear for best performance, you will enjoy many years of ocean sailing while spending very little time at the helm. With minimal effort from the crew, the vane gear will be—this is not an exaggeration—at the bottom of the fix-it list every time you pull into port.

Chapter 2

Wind-Powered Self-Steering Systems: How They Work

Just about any well-designed sailboat will steer itself on a close reach in 10 to 15 knots of wind if the sail rig is balanced properly. As wind speed increases, the boat heels over, and the mainsail (along with the mizzen on a split rig) tries to draw the boat to weather, or toward the wind, producing an effect called *weather helm*. When this happens, the helmsman must steer the boat off the wind and slacken or reef the sails in order to restore balance. An opposite effect, *lee helm*, may occur when there is insufficient wind for balance, causing the bow to fall off the wind. This is corrected by turning the rudder toward the lee side of the vessel, forcing the bow back to windward. Split-rigged boats, most notably ketches and yawls, have a greater ability to balance themselves because they spread the wind's force more evenly along the length of the vessel. A typical ketch rig has a short mainmast, as compared to a sloop or yawl of the same size, and generally measures more on the beam. Split rigs spread the wind's effort over a wider sail area and are consequently more apt to self-steer. On my 28-foot, John Hanna–designed Gulfweed ketch *Circe*, I used to find myself dozing off for 10 or 15 minutes at a time while sailing to weather in 12 knots of true wind between Los Angeles Harbor and Catalina Island. As long as the wind held steady, that old, iron-fastened, mahogany-planked veteran— she was launched in 1945—would stay within five degrees of the correct heading.

The object of vane steering is to enhance a sailing vessel's natural tendency to self-steer. Even if you are able to trim the rig for zero helm, gusts and wave action will soon conspire to throw the boat off course, thereby requiring course correction. A windvane steerer guarantees the proper feedback so that the boat can stay "in the groove" between the *lift* created by the sails (except on a run) and the resistance to drift at the lee of the lateral plane, or keel. What follows in this chapter is a description of how vane gears function to keep vessels on course. Each type of windvane has its own unique operating principles, and the engineering within a particular category of gear may vary widely from one model to the next.

SHEET-TO-TILLER STEERING

Surprisingly, there are few descriptions of sheet-to-tiller steering methods in sailing books or periodicals. It is equally rare to hear of or see this low-cost alternative in an anchorage or marina. But for the sailor on a shoestring budget who has not the wherewithal for a manufactured self-steering system or the time to build the auxiliary rudder trim-tab system detailed in chapter 12, the sheet-to-tiller method may be a workable solution.

Al Gunther of Kingston, Washington, has outlined a modern version of sheet-to-tiller steering, based on that of John Letcher, in a website that gives a complete list of required equipment and a fairly good explanation of how to install and use the system. For anything but a dead run on his small Catalina sloop, Gunther runs a double-braided line through a block at the aft end of the boom, and through another block on the windward cockpit coaming approximately level with and perpendicular to the tiller, where he ties off the one line. The control line is also connected to a second piece of line cleated to some point along the middle section of the boat. On the leeward side, he attaches a neoprene hose snubber between the coaming and the tiller. He explains: "As a gust hits, tension on the main increases, pulling the tiller to windward, which keeps the boat from even starting to round up. This is an advantage over vane or autopilot steering. With vane steering, the boat first starts to round up, the vane or autopilot senses it, and then turns the tiller to correct." When running, Gunther uses the same setup, except that he tightens up the sheet on his servo-boom and slackens the snubber enough to balance the steering.

Gunther's system (see figure 2-1) is probably adequate for coastal sailing, allowing the single-hander freedom to make a sandwich, use the head, or get some quick shut-eye. But without further testing and refinement, I would not be the first to endorse it for offshore cruising, much less in a force 9 blow with 20-foot breaking seas. Particularly worrying is depending on the mainsail downwind, in which situation many sailors douse the main rather than risk an accidental jibe. Though reefing probably would not detract from the servo action of the boom, a properly employed vang, along with a preventer, would freeze the boom's movement, thereby making sheet-to-tiller steering impossible. If you wish to experiment with Gunther's method, refer to his accompanying list of recommended equipment (see next page).

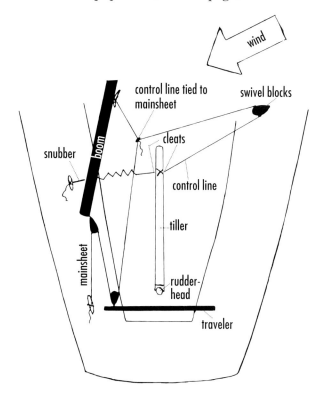

Figure 2-1. Mainsheet-to-tiller steering, based on Letcher and Gunther's designs.

Al Gunther's Sheet-to-Tiller Equipment List

- three ball-bearing swivel blocks with $1^{1}/_{4}$-inch sheaves
- six 3-inch bronze swivel snap hooks
- minimum 25 feet of $^{1}/_{4}$-inch, double-braided Dacron line
- 4 feet each of $^{3}/_{16}$-inch and $^{3}/_{8}$-inch OD surgical tubing and some coarse, waxed nylon thread for tying the tubing
- two C-cleats (a type of cam cleat), attached on either side of the tiller
- optional cam lever for easy attachment to jib sheet

Headsail steering configurations range from the simple to the very complex. One straightforward system, invented by Tony Skidmore, uses a backed staysail as a servomechanism for all reaching points of sail. Rather than providing any appreciable sailing power, the staysail is trimmed parallel to the boat's centerline, its sheet tied to the windward side of the tiller and a shock cord tied to a point on the lee deck. Richard Henderson, author of a well-known book on single-handed sailing, recommends routing the jib sheet so it can be attached to the windward side of the tiller. The shock cord is made fast to the leeward side. Theoretically, as the vessel comes off the wind, the shock cord pulls the tiller to leeward. As the bow turns into the wind, tension on the jib sheet increases, pulling the tiller to windward. This system may work on a beam or broad reach, but what happens when the boat is close-hauled? As long as the helm is trimmed to keep the vessel sailing at least 55 to 60 degrees off the wind, the system should work. But if trimmed any closer to the wind, it seems reasonable to expect this result: as the boat rounds up to the wind, the headsail will lose power, greatly reducing tension on the jib sheet. The shock cord will continue to pull the tiller to the lee, forcing the boat to round up. Unless corrected, this will allow the sails either to luff or to back, forcing the vessel into *irons*, or causing it to *heave-to*. In other words, the boat will be frozen in place, going nowhere. Heaving-to is a popular technique used by many sailors to stabilize their vessels in harsh storms, or to wait until sunrise before entering a poorly marked reef or harbor. Although an interesting topic and an important skill for blue-water sailors, heaving-to has zero relevance to self-steering. Notwithstanding my reservations about sheet-to-tiller steering in general, Henderson's book is a gold mine of valuable tips on virtually every aspect of single-handed and short-handed sailing, and has inspired many a sailor over the years.

Another sheet-to-tiller system, developed independently by Otway Waller, Frederick Fenger, Paul Hammond, Marin-Marie, and Wright Britton, could actually prove superior to windvane steering gears for downwind sailing. Their

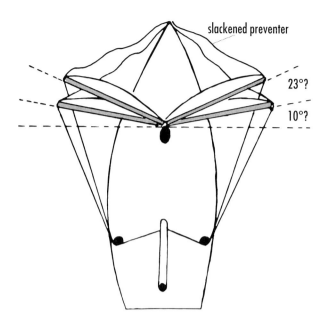

Figure 2-2. Twin headsail steering. Waller, Marin-Marie, Britton, and later, Letcher, never quite agreed which was the best angle for twin headsails, but they found it lay somewhere between 10 and 23 degrees forward of an angle perpendicular to the keel.

collective technique uses twin headsails, poled out into a wedge from the forestay, inner stay, or a point just forward of the mast for a balanced rig (see figure 2-2). The jib sheet from either side is made fast to its corresponding side of the tiller. When the vessel wanders to port, the port jib gathers more wind while the starboard jib loses wind. The port jib pulls the rudder to windward, nudging the bow back so that the vessel proceeds 180 degrees downwind. Britton actually marketed his system, comprised of two large headsails joined by a center seam hanked to the forestay. Because many sailors had reported heavy rolling while using twin headsails, Britton cut his sails with high clews to keep the sails out of the water. Waller found a quick solution for rolling on *Imogen*: raise an anchor a few yards up the mast to increase roll inertia.

Where Waller, Marin-Marie, and Britton disagreed was on the best trim angle for the two headsails. Waller used an angle of only 10 degrees, as measured forward of a line perpendicular to the keel. Fenger argued, based on a series of experiments with models, that 23 degrees guaranteed the best mix of balance and power. Letcher, who conducted extensive research in the field of wind-powered steering in the early 1970s, experimented with the 23-degree angle but said it forfeited too much power. On the other hand, he said the aerodynamic lift created at that angle might compensate for the lost windage. It would appear, judging from the extent of documented testimony regarding this system, that twin headsail steering might be the only true way to harness light airs for self-steering on a run. An autopilot would consume a lot of battery amperage to keep up with this utterly simple method.

Over the years, I have spoken with a handful of cruising sailors who have used sheet-to-tiller steering offshore successfully, or so they claim. Such conversations generally occur during Happy Hour at some yacht club bar or cruiser dive. We old salts tend to, shall we say, wax eloquently about our ocean sailing experiences when we are imbibing the nectars of the gods. I weigh the testimony of my fellow sailors accordingly. One of my reservations about employing the basic jib sheet-to-tiller method is that the servo action of the jib would appear to diminish as canvas is reduced. On the other hand, perhaps it is possible to offset the reduced canvas by closely calculating wind strength in order to adjust jib size. Skidmore's method seems to allow for a range of headsail canvas area, since the smaller servo-staysail provides the steering power. And though the mainsheet system proposed by Letcher and more recently by Gunther seems worthy, it precludes employment of a vang and preventer. The various jib sheet steering arrangements are totally independent of the mainsail and boom, except insofar as rig balance enters into the equation, so the helmsman is free to utilize a vang and preventer.

TRIM-TAB SYSTEMS

Both vertical-vane and horizontal-vane trim tabs have one main advantage over the more common pendulum gears: trim-tab systems are totally self-contained, working directly on the vessel's rudder or an auxiliary rudder, so there is no added deck clutter from lines wending their way around blocks to the helm. For some, this fact alone seems to outweigh any other argument in favor of the more popular servopendulum, which usually operates in conjunction with the vessel's own rudder—two exceptions are the Windpilot Pacific Plus and the discontinued Sailomat 3040, which combine a servo blade with an auxiliary rudder. Trim tabs are also more sensitive than servopendulums in light airs. In mild to moderate conditions, vertical-vane trim tabs are known to provide very smooth steerage. They do not tend to oversteer as much as horizontal-vane trim tabs because the vertically mounted airvane always receives wind to both sides of the panel or wedge. And though trim tabs generate less steering power than servopendulums, a high-quality, horizontal-vane trim-tab gear manufactured by a reputable firm can generally yield satisfactory results in most weather. An auxiliary-rudder trim-tab system offers one other benefit: the auxiliary rudder can easily be converted to an emergency rudder.

However, it would appear that the smaller, lighter auxiliary is weaker and more prone to breakage than the vessel's main rudder.

Vertical-Vane Trim Tab

By far the simplest self-steering device to comprehend and build is a vertical-vane trim tab (see figure 2-3). The same concept is easily incorporated with an auxiliary rudder. As long as the wind is comfortably below gale strength, you can go far and wide with this straightforward device. The vertical-vane trim tab

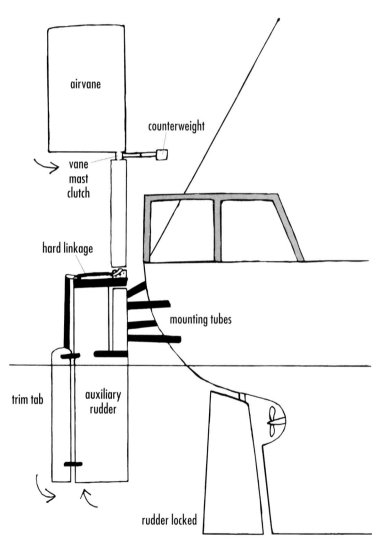

Figure 2-3. Vertical-vane trim tab.

Trim Tabs: Pros and Cons

PROS
- More sensitive than servopendulums in light airs
- Smoother steering
- Good alternative for center cockpits and hydraulic or stiff steering
- Totally self-contained; no conversion necessary for use as emergency rudder

CONS
- Less steering power than servopendulums
- If used with auxiliary rudder, remains permanently installed and vulnerable to collision
- Auxiliary rudder may affect steering when motoring in reverse or when maneuvering in a marina

is unmistakable with its large plywood or canvas panel. In a more refined version, such as that previously built by RVG, a cloth-covered airvane over an aluminum tube frame joins the trim tab by means of solid reduction linkage, which dampens the tab's movement and helps generate smoother steering action. The trim tab itself, resembling a trim tab on an airplane rudder, can be a narrow strip of wood, aluminum, or molded fiberglass connected to the trailing edge of the rudder. Its operation is as simple as its construction.

Having trimmed the sails to balance the rig, the operator first sets the helm for the correct heading and locks, or lashes, the helm. The helmsman then disengages the turret clutch at the base of the airvane, which can swivel 360 degrees around the top of the unit. The airvane should now turn automatically into the airstream, requiring the operator to do nothing more than reengage the clutch. If the trim tab is mounted on an auxiliary rudder, the helm remains lashed; if the trim tab is connected to a transom rudder, the operator then unlashes the helm so the rudder swings freely. Whenever the boat starts to fall off its point of sail, the airvane senses the change of wind direction and turns the tab, which catches the onrushing water; the tab then forces the steering rudder to turn in the direction opposite the trim tab's until the airvane is back in line with the apparent wind, and the trim tab is back in line with the rudder. My good friend David Webb, who now runs a charter boat out of New Zealand, renovated a homebuilt vertical-vane trim tab for his 40-foot schooner *Arcady*. A balanced auxiliary rudder and balanced trim tab comprised the vane gear, which worked quite well until the linkage failed halfway through a Pacific crossing.

Horizontal-Vane Trim Tab

The horizontal-vane trim tab (see figure 2-4) is a more powerful version of the vertical-vane trim tab. In the same manner as with the vertical vane, the trim tab may be mounted on either the main or an auxiliary rudder. A nearly horizontal airvane is mounted in a fashion similar to that of modern servopendulums. Its operation is like the vertical vane's, except that the horizontal-axis vane is turned on its swiveling turret until the vane stands as nearly vertical as possible. Tilting proportionally to changes in wind speed and direction, the angle-mounted air-

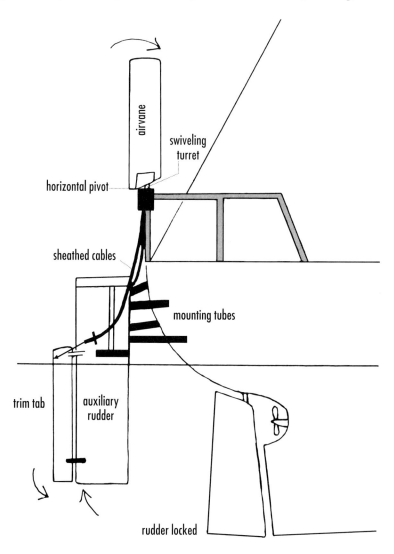

Figure 2-4. Horizontal-vane trim tab.

vane exerts more leverage than a vertical vane on the trim tab, and is therefore more appropriate for rough weather. Another advantage of the horizontal-vane trim tab is that the airvane and its mounting base may be mounted in a spot remote from the rudder, connected by steel cables. Such an installation must meet two requirements. First, the airvane, and most vane gear installations for that matter, must be located over the vessel's centerline, not to one side where its wind-sensing capability may be less efficient. Second, it must sit in a spot free of surrounding wind blocks, such as a radar dome or side-mounted solar panels. The same requirements obviously apply to all self-steering airvanes. Auto-Helm, one of the leading names in trim tabs, uses an airvane that may be mounted a considerable distance from the trim tab in order to achieve unobstructed airflow, even atop a 7-foot-high stern arch. The steel cables connecting the Auto-Helm's upper and lower units are similar to bicycle brake cables, except that the unit's cable sheaths are specially lined for low friction.

Bruce Wells, a Kiwi sailor who built his own trim-tab gear based on a design by Nick Skeates, used the gear to sail his 43-foot cutter *Oakura* in up to 60 knots of wind from Fiji to Australia with little trouble. Skeates's design, the Wylo II, incorporates a horizontal airvane, but the airvane's axis is absolutely horizontal, not raked as it could have been to prevent oversteering. Evidently this was not a problem for Bruce, who simply adjusted the counterweight for more righting leverage and switched to a shorter airvane whenever the wind got really nasty.

SERVOPENDULUMS

Servopendulum vane gears, in their various forms, offer several advantages over trim tabs. First and foremost is the pendulum's capacity to generate hundreds of pounds of force, overpowering even the strongest helmsman when the boat really gets moving. Another plus is the pendulum's anti-yawing tendency. When running before the wind under headsail or spinnaker alone, the center of force is toward the bow. As the vessel slides down a wave, the elevated stern tries to overtake the bow, which digs into the back of the previous wave, causing the boat to fishtail, or *yaw*. As the hull shifts to one side, the servo blade catches the water and automatically pulls the helm in the opposite direction. Another advantage over an auxiliary rudder trim tab is that most servopendulum blades can be folded up out of the water or removed when not in use. This is an important consideration when motoring in reverse or when maneuvering near submerged fishing nets and mooring lines. Most pendulums have shear pins, breakaway connectors, or collapsible tubes, making servopendulums less vulnerable to collision than auxiliary rudder trim tabs. Finally, some servopendulums may be modified for use as emergency rudders, but their smaller profiles make them a bit less efficient than auxiliary rudders for this purpose, even when the servo blade's size is enlarged. Several manufacturers sell optional emergency rudder conversion kits to be used with their standard servopendulum units.

Vertical-Vane Servopendulum

On the vertical-vane servopendulum (see figure 2-5, right), invented by Blondie Hasler for the 1960 OSTAR, the vertical airvane is connected to the servo blade via two gears. As the vessel in the sketch starts turning to starboard on the port tack, the vane turns counterclockwise, causing the pendulum, or servo blade, to turn clockwise on its vertical axis. The blade catches the water and is forced to starboard. A steering arm connected to the pendulum shaft pulls a line attached to the starboard side of the tiller or the equivalent side of the steering wheel. The helm turns the vessel, correcting the lee helm. In order to change course, the operator simply loosens the clutch, allows the vane to rotate into the wind, and reengages the clutch. One commercially produced vane gear, Saye's Rig, still uses a vertical airvane, but as you will read later, the application differs significantly from Hasler's prototype.

Horizontal-Vane Servopendulum

Unless your vessel's cockpit and stern are overcrowded with lines, blocks, antennas, jerricans, and a half-dozen solar panels on tilting swivels, you will probably install, if you have not already, a commercially produced servopendulum gear with a horizontal-axis airvane (see figure 2-5, left). Though we have already taken a cursory look at this type of apparatus, we go into more detail here and in later chapters, since much of the book is devoted to the horizontal-vane servopendulum developed by Marcel Gianoli. The transmission systems in these machines vary: some vane builders use bevel gears, others employ push rods, and the Cape Horn features a Z rod to transmit the windvane's impulses to the servo blade. All these designs do the same thing and are operated the same way; the differences are solely in the transmission systems.

The vane tilts on an axis lying roughly 20 degrees from horizontal. A counterweight extending below the airvane's axle resists pressure from the wind so that the airvane dips according to wind strength. A short arm extending 90 degrees from the airvane yoke connects to a push rod, which turns a pair of bevel gears or activates rod linkage. The gears or linkage connects with the top of the servo blade shaft. After the vessel has been trimmed for the specific point of sail, the airvane is aligned so it slices the wind edgewise at the selected angle.

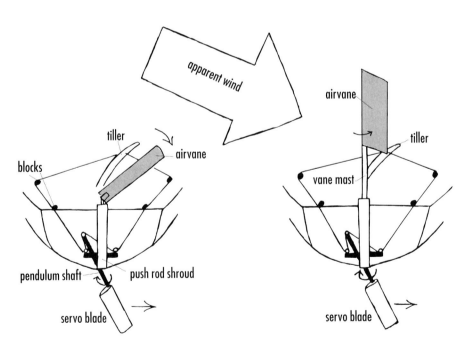

Figure 2-5. Servopendulums: horizontal vane *(left)* and vertical vane *(right)*.

When the boat starts falling off the wind on the port tack (figure 2-5), the vane dips to the lee, or starboard in this case, activating the push rod. The bevel gear or linkage movement rotates the servo blade clockwise to harness the water's force. The blade swings to starboard, its steering arm pulling the helm also to starboard, correcting the lee helm by steering the vessel to port. The helmsman may adjust the course by rotating the turret holding the yoke and counterweight. In rough conditions, the operator may switch to a shorter airvane or tilt ("reef") it back from the wind to prevent oversteering and to keep the wind from shearing the vane off at the yoke. Believe me, it happens.

Take a close look at a servopendulum gear, and you will know instinctively that a lot of very careful engineering went into producing it. The bevel gears or rod linkage, cast in either stainless or bronze, must mesh well but not too tightly, or caked salt and a thin film of corrosion will prevent the components from moving smoothly. While the boat is sitting still, you can amuse yourself by dipping the airvane to either side and watching the servo-rudder rotate on its vertical axis back and forth underwater. If you know someone with a Fleming vane gear, ask if you can try a little experiment. The later-model Flemings are handy for this lesson because their servo blade shafts have an extremely wide swing arc, but you can try this with any servopendulum. Make a line fast to the top of the lower pendulum shaft (see figure 2-6), that is, just below the connection to the upper shaft. Pull the line until the servo blade is at some angle, any angle, from the vertical and tie the line to the stern pulpit. Now dip the vane from side to side again. You will see that the servo blade rotates the same way it did in the vertical position. If there is an extra pair of hands to help you, untie the line from the stern pulpit, and then use the line to slowly raise and lower the blade a few times while someone else moves the airvane back and forth. The blade continues to rotate, irrespective of the shaft's angle or swinging movement. Cool, huh? You have just caught a glimpse of the servopendulum's magic.

Pendulum Trim Tab

In April 1984, the Contessa 32 sloop *Gigi* finished her journey from New York to San Francisco via Cape Horn. Then the smallest vessel to round the cape from east to west, she stayed faithfully on course with her Navik pendulum trim-tab vane gear (see details in chapter 5). Nearly all the participants in the Mini Transatlantic Race have been sailing with the Navik in recent years. Numerous other boats have carried this machine in ocean races, sometimes placing first in class. So what makes this little marvel tick?

The pendulum trim-tab vane gear, designed especially for boats up to 30 feet LOA, combines a trim tab with a servopendulum rudder. As you may have already surmised, the airvane does not operate directly on the servo-rudder. The horizontal vane turns the trim tab, which is hinged to the trailing

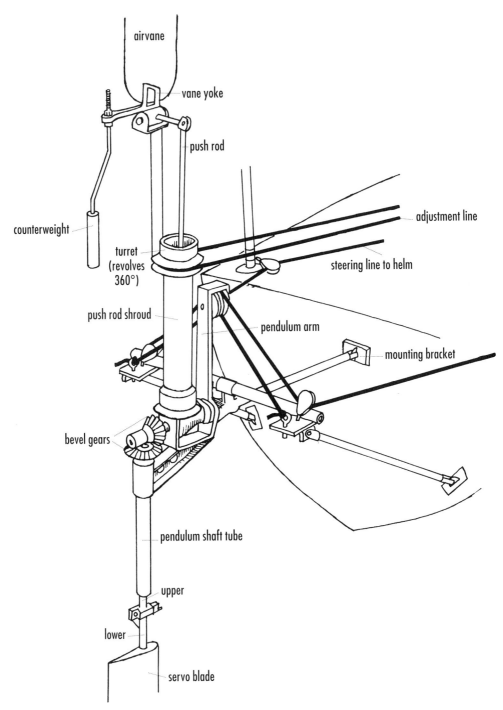

airvane

vane yoke

push rod

counterweight

turret
(revolves
360°)

adjustment line

steering line to helm

push rod shroud

pendulum arm

mounting bracket

bevel gears

pendulum shaft tube

upper

lower

servo blade

Figure 2.6. An overview of the Fleming Global 301, a standard horizontal-vane servopendulum. (Jim Sollers)

edge of the servo blade. After that point, the pendulum behaves just like the servo system described in the previous section. The servo blade turns and swings, adjusting the helm with lines running to the tiller or wheel. Trim-tab sensitivity allows self-steering in very light winds; as wind and speed increase, the unit responds with true servopendulum steering power. The helmsman operates the Navik in the same manner as a conventional servopendulum gear.

Though the Navik does not appear quite as rugged as some other servopendulums, it has proven up to the task in rough weather. The frame, supports, gear assembly, and pendulum shaft are constructed of stainless steel, which is heliarc welded rather than cast. Injection-molded Lexan (polycarbonate plastic) is used to manufacture the airvane, turret, control mechanism, and linkages. Lexan is light, corrosion proof, and extremely strong. The installed weight of the Navik is only 30 pounds, roughly half the weight of other pendulum vane gears, making this model popular for small, light displacement yachts. Plastimo of France manufactures the Navik, which is available for North American customers through Scanmar International and for the South Pacific region through Harken in Australia.

Pendulum Trim-Tab Tiller Arm

Just when you think you have heard of everything, along comes the "pendulum trim-tab tiller arm" from Scanmar. Known as Saye's Rig, it was designed for very large yachts. Retaining Hasler's vertical airvane, the servopendulum sends its steering impulses through a horizontal "tiller arm" attached directly to the trailing edge of the vessel's rudder (see chapter 5). The long pendulum shaft and tiller arm bypass customary self-steering arrangements, meaning no auxiliary rudder and no lines to the cockpit. The helmsman adjusts the vertical airvane—one of the very few in production—the same way he or she would a vertical-vane trim tab. The helmsman first sets the course, lets the vane swing into the wind, and then secures the airvane shaft. Scanmar advertises Saye's Rig as "ideal self-steering gear for very large boats with traditional transoms and/or boats with: hydraulic steering, high freeboard, center cockpit/aft cabin, transom davits, boomkin, mizzen boom, [or] transom-mounted swim ladder."

AIRVANE-CONTROLLED AUXILIARY RUDDER

This last type of vane gear is in a class all of its own and manufactured by only one company. Known as the Hydrovane, this auxiliary rudder system employs reduction linkage to convert impulses from a very large airvane into steering power at the partially balanced rudder without harnessing the water's force. Rather than embracing Marin-Marie's design, which was loosely based on the same broad concept, British inventor Derek Daniels found a more compact way to engineer a set of linkage that can be adjusted for different rates of mechanical advantage, depending on wind speed. The operator adjusts the horizontal-axis airvane in the same manner as with a horizontal vane on a trim tab or servopendulum system. When not in use, the ratio knob at the transmission is left in the neutral position. While sailing, the operator first trims and lashes the helm, then sets the ratio control knob at one of three settings to match wind speed. As wind speed increases, the auxiliary rudder requires more mechanical advantage, less deflection, to keep the vessel on course.

The unobtrusive Hydrovane can be seen mounted on many cruising vessels throughout the world, particularly on larger yachts with aft cockpits and hydraulic steering, where a conventional servopendulum would be difficult if not impossible to install, and a trim-tab system would not provide adequate steering power. Tom Bridgman and his wife Dee installed a 20-year-old Hydrovane on their Pierre Garroff–designed 40-foot center cockpit ketch *Axe Calibre*, which they built and launched in Axmouth, England. By the time I met the couple in Cochin, India, they had been cruising for eight years and were absolute fanatics about the Hydrovane's performance. The Bridgmans claim their vane gear steers in anything from 6 knots of apparent wind to a full gale with the same airvane. Tom said that on one occasion while the boat was at anchor, he tried to turn the auxiliary rudder manually with the airvane set in about 10 knots of wind. He was astonished to find that no matter how hard he tried, he could not budge the rudder; such was the force as amplified by the reduction linkage. "And one other really important point," added Tom, "is that I can use it as an auxiliary rudder."

NOTES ON RUDDER DESIGN

A lot more goes into the design of a rudder, servo blade, or trim tab than meets the eye. Aviation engineers and naval architects have long understood that the shape of an airfoil or a hydrofoil determines how the foil will behave when introduced to a fluid current. Well-designed rudders on boats are based on a similar shape, the specific proportions depending on the foil's application. Some boat rudders are flat, but as long as their speeds through water are fairly slow, the otherwise inefficient shapes render satisfactory service. In contrast, we depend on servopendulum blades to turn into the water at precisely the correct angle, sometimes at speeds greater than the hull's progress through the water. You will notice that the servo blade on a well-built vane gear is usually rounded at the *leading edge*, flaring out to a pair of symmetrical curves joining in a fine point at

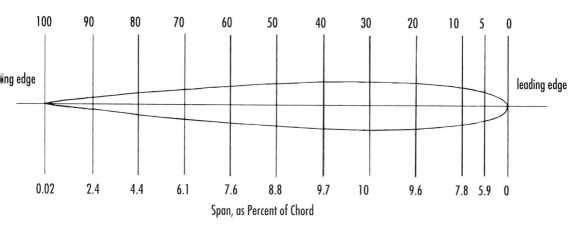

| 100 | 90 | 80 | 70 | 60 | 50 | 40 | 30 | 20 | 10 | 5 | 0 |

trailing edge

leading edge

| 0.02 | 2.4 | 4.4 | 6.1 | 7.6 | 8.8 | 9.7 | 10 | 9.6 | 7.8 | 5.9 | 0 |

Span, as Percent of Chord

Figure 2-7. The NACA 0010 foil, a common symmetrical shape used throughout the shipbuilding industry and in the design of some vane gears. The chord is the distance from the leading edge to the trailing edge, and the span is the foil's widest point.

the *trailing edge*. NACA (the National Advisory Committee for Aeronautics, later replaced by NASA) established a set of standard profiles for airfoils and hydrofoils during its operation from 1917 to 1958. The symmetrical shapes used for keels, rudders, and servopendulums are *four-digit foils*, one of the most common being a NACA 0010 foil. Two initial zeroes indicate a symmetrical shape, or no camber, while 10 refers to the *aspect ratio*. The foil's *span*, or widest point, is 10 percent of the *chord*, which is the distance from the leading edge to the trailing edge (see figure 2-7). The high-lift 0010 foil is a general-purpose shape used throughout the shipbuilding industry and in the design of some vane gears (see more data on NACA four-digit profiles in the appendix).

Naval architects and vane gear designers also take great care in positioning the hydrofoil's axis for optimum balance. They don't just stick the rudderpost or servo arm where it is mechanically most convenient. Figure 2-8 shows four ways to control a rudder's or servo blade's movement, each one with its own strategy for using lift. At top left, the turning axis is at the leading edge, with the center of lift (CL) well aft of the axis, making this rudder *unbalanced*. This foil will remain straight in the water's flow until considerable force is applied to change its angle of attack. In the *partially balanced* foil, the axis falls somewhere between the center of lift and the leading edge. This is used for many servo blades because only a slight amount of force is needed to activate the foil's lift potential. When the axis runs through the center of lift, the foil is *balanced*. Finally, the axis is located aft of the center of lift in an *overbalanced* rudder. This

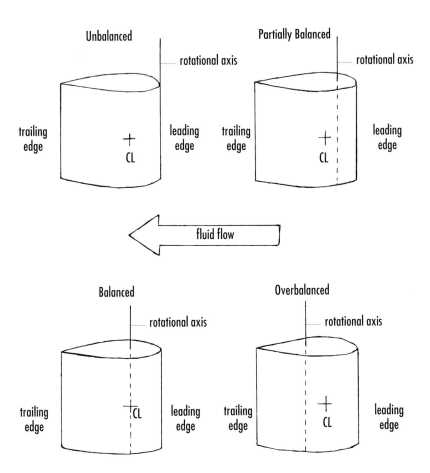

Figure 2-8. Rudder balance (CL = center of lift). These principles apply to all rotating foils, whether they are rudders, ailerons, and trim tabs on airplanes, or main rudders, auxiliary rudders, servo blades, and trim tabs as found on cruising sailboats.

is an inefficient design for self-steering purposes because it would take far too much effort to keep a servopendulum blade, auxiliary rudder, or trim tab pointed straight into the oncoming water. When you consider the vast number of possible foil shapes and the minute increments of distance from the leading edge where one could place a foil's axis, it is mind-boggling to imagine the infinite possibilities for foil design.

MECHANICAL-ELECTRONIC COMBINATIONS

A popular compromise between mechanical windvane steering and electronic autopilots is a coupling of the two systems. There are several advantages to this approach. First, this allows self-steering in very light winds, particularly while running under spinnaker. This also permits use of the servopendulum while motoring through calms. With the engine running, the batteries are gaining amps instead of losing them. Because such little force is needed to manipulate the vane yoke, a small tiller pilot may be employed with less wear and tear to the motor and worm gear assembly, saving the owner a tidy sum in initial cost and subsequent repairs or replacement. Finally, there is the safety factor. Single-handers and shorthanded crews will sail with less danger in coastal areas if they can follow a precise compass course, regardless of changes in the wind's direction. Headlands, promontories, canyons, and diurnal onshore and offshore wind shifts make coastal sailing far more challenging and exhausting than offshore, trade wind passagemaking. With a tiller pilot controlling the servopendulum, the watch will spend so much time trimming sails and readjusting the tiller pilot to keep the sails from flogging that it will be nearly impossible to doze off. How much safer can you get?

Articles written by sailors who have jury-rigged their own vane gear–autopilot couplers abound in the cruiser rags. Some are decidedly sturdier and more sophisticated than others, but reportedly they all work well. Each installation must take into account the type of autopilot, the vane gear's mounting configuration, and what materials will go into the autopilot brace. Some vane gear manufacturers now market an easily installed brace to connect the autopilot to the airvane yoke, though some of the homebuilt couplers are better constructed than commercially produced models. The airvane itself is dropped to the horizontal position or, even better, removed so it doesn't interfere with the autopilot.

Geoff Pack, editor of *Yachting Monthly*, was a serious ocean racer who set a new course record in the 1995 AZAB Race across the North Atlantic. Racing demands precision steering to prevent losing miles that would not matter much to the average cruiser. To keep his vessel *Kiskadee* on course, Pack used a combination of three main components. The center of this operation was a Monitor vane gear, which he claimed to use 75 percent of the time. The second component was a B&G Network Pilot, a heavy-duty, below-decks autopilot that he connected directly to the helm while changing sails or running hard under spinnaker. At first, he used the Monitor only as a battery saver, hooking the vane gear to the third part of his system, a small, above-decks Autohelm ST1000. He clamped a wooden block onto the stern rail, and then drilled a hole in the block for the small pivot bushing that comes with the Autohelm. He attached the other end of the autopilot to a thin piece of plywood locked in the vane yoke. This system worked well until he hit really heavy conditions, at which time "there was no substitute for the windvane itself when we pushed hard—it had such a sympathetic way of handling the boat in big seas."

We have covered seven types of windvane steering devices, plus the popular electromechanical hybrid technique preferred by some sailors, either because they are racing or motoring or perhaps simply because they just don't trust the windvane—yet. It takes practice and a certain amount of patience to get the confidence level up. The step-by-step procedures detailed in chapter 8, Sailing with Windvane Steering, will demystify this art and get you sailing successfully with the vane gear your first time out. If you can sail, you can operate a vane gear.

Chapter 3
Materials and Fabrication Methods

M ost sailors have at least an intuitive sense of the different applications of metals and plastics used in marine applications and some idea of their comparative quality. We have enough sense to install a zinc anode on the propeller shaft, and we know that sails or resin laminates unprotected from the sun's ultraviolet (UV) rays eventually will disintegrate. Because few of us are chemists, metallurgists, or naval architects (I was a liberal arts major), we implicitly trust designers and builders of boats and marine hardware to look out for the safety and efficiency of our vessels' onboard systems. Yet we learn that one stainless steel fastener stamped "316" will sometimes fail faster than another 316 stainless fastener under the same conditions. The difference is that two different companies produced them, perhaps in different countries, using slightly different alloy recipes and milling processes. We also learn that a number of lightweight, gray-colored alloys somehow qualify for the label "aluminum," but display very different characteristics when introduced to a marine environment. One will turn to cottage cheese faster than week-old milk even after steps have been taken to protect the alloy, while another will hold together indefinitely if properly manufactured and maintained.

This chapter covers the more salient aspects of the materials used in vane gear construction and methods of fabricating the systems. We look at the types of metals and plastics used in building vane gears, paying special attention to problems associated with the use of dissimilar metals. Nearly to the point of overkill, the chapter offers a comparison of metals based on their susceptibility to corrosion and other fundamental properties. Over the last three decades, major advances have taken place in metallurgy, particularly in the family of alloys known as stainless steel. Alloy recipes for marine hardware abound, and the better informed we sailors are of their applications and comparative quality, the better armed we will be when facing the harsh reality of ocean passage-making.

The descriptions will not be any more technical than is necessary for basic appreciation of the matter. The intent is twofold: first, to be able to spot potential problems in certain types of construction before we commit ourselves to one particular vane model; and second, to understand the potential consequences of repairs or construction that we make as vane gear owners or builders. Often there are several ways to approach problems, and we make the best effort, given our limited knowledge, to solve them. But it is reassuring to know, for example, that there are fasteners other than 304 or 316 stainless available to guard against potentially high-corrosion situations, though such specialized fasteners are often far more expensive and not always available at the corner chandlery.

CHARACTERISTICS OF METALS

Two hundred years ago, metals used in boatbuilding were few. Shipwrights fastened planks with black iron nails and affixed copper plating to the undersides of hulls to repel barnacles and teredo worms. Naval bronze served well for a variety of deck hardware and fittings. Yellow brass proved an excellent medium for sextants, telescopes, grog cups, and ships' bells, not to mention fancy nautical accoutrements adorning the officers' quarters. Later advancements grew out of aviation and submarine research, introducing lighter, stronger alloys, particularly newer types of bronze, stainless steel, and aluminum. When we say "aluminum," which is an element and the most abundant metal in our planet's outer crust, we usually imply an aluminum alloy.

Today, an impressive range of alloys enters into the construction of sailboats, rigging, and deck gear. For example, the American Boat and Yacht Council (ABYC) lists over a dozen copper alloys, known variously as bronze, brass, cuprous nickel, or Monel, depending on their composition. Some bronzes and brasses even contain aluminum. The Korean Friendship Bell atop Point Fermin, overlooking San Pedro Channel and Los Angeles Harbor, is cast in an exotic bronze containing, in addition to the standard ingredients, silver to help shape its hauntingly beautiful sound. Stainless steel has replaced bronze in many boat applications, though bronze is far more corrosion resistant. Sometimes what we think is stainless is actually bronze that has been chrome plated to look like stainless, a common practice with turnbuckles, which need to be highly resistant to crevice corrosion, a common problem with stainless. Through-hull fittings and even propellers are available in high-density plastics, but the prudent sailor still depends on the durability and strength of bronze for those critical pieces of hardware.

Some old salts decry what they view as the modern trend toward inferior copper alloys. One memorable example is a sailor in Los Angeles Harbor (we'll call him Hank), owner-skipper of an old 50-foot ketch first owned by a pair of well-known Hollywood actors, who used the boat to entertain movie celebrities at Catalina Island back in the 1930s. Hank's father used the vessel to hunt for pirate treasure along the California coast in the 1950s, and was featured in a couple of National Geographic films. Today Hank charters his boat and consequently needs to have the vessel inspected periodically by the U.S. Coast Guard. When the Coasties told Hank some years ago he had to replace all the original through-hulls, he at first tried to reason with the officials, showing them that the old bronze was still in top condition. The bureaucrats were not impressed, and Hank complied with the order. But instead of tossing out the venerable relics with their lovely green patinas, he stored them in a box in his garage. When the new fittings started failing some years later, he threw out their brittle, pink remains and replaced them with the original through-hulls! When I last talked to him three years ago, he was still running charters with the seventy-year-old fittings, which still looked good at the last annual haulout. Why the newer through-hulls failed is anyone's guess. Good bronze fittings are still available today and can be expected to last decades. The ones Hank purchased were evidently of dubious quality, containing some admixture of metal highly prone to galvanic corrosion. With all due respect to the old-timers, the marine industry has access to a variety of high-quality bronzes and brasses, each one tailored to a different role on seagoing vessels.

Melting Point

One measure for sizing up metals is their melting points (see the accompanying sidebar). Softer metals have lower melting points. Lead is heavy and easy to melt, making it handy to mold into fishing sinkers, sounding weights, or perhaps a counterweight for your homebuilt trim-tab gear after boiling the lead over an outdoor fire. If you try this, make sure you wear leather gloves, a heavy, long-sleeved shirt, and goggles; water and impurities in your lead pot (I use a tin can) will cause the lead to splatter, especially if it begins to boil. At the other end of the scale, titanium and chromium have extremely high melting points, making these metals ideal for high-speed drill bits. Thomas Edison discovered that the extremely high melting point of tungsten—6,170°F—made the metal eminently better suited than strands of carbonized bamboo to produce filaments for the incandescent light bulb. All the metals on the list, with the possible exception of silver, are important ingredients in marine hardware and electrical systems.

Melting Points of Base Metals, °C/°F

tungsten	3,410/6,170
chromium	1,890/3,434
platinum	1,773/3,223
titanium	1,660/3,020
iron	1,535/2,795
nickel	1,458/2,656
copper	1,083/1,981
silver	960/1,760
aluminum	660/1,220
zinc	419/786
lead	327/621
tin	232/450

Source: Chapman et al., *Working with Materials*

Malleability and Ductility

Malleability and *ductility* are two aspects of a material's plasticity, or ability to change permanently in shape without breaking or cracking. Malleability is the degree to which a material may be hammered, pressed, or rolled without rupturing. Highly malleable metal ingots can be rolled into large, thin plates for subsequent fabrication. Jewelers, welders, and sheet metal technologists bend, crease, cut, stamp, and fasten rolled metal to produce end-user goods.

Ductility is a measure of how much cold plastic deformation a material can withstand through stretching, bending, or twisting. One demonstration of a metal's ductility is its ability to be drawn into wire. Copper, a relatively ductile metal, can be pulled through a die into a long, even, cylindrical shape for use as electrical wire. This process is different from *extrusion*, the process of pushing a molten metal through a die to produce a long, consistent shape, such as aluminum spar stock.

Malleability and Ductility

ORDER	MALLEABILITY	DUCTILITY
1	silver	silver
2	copper	iron
3	aluminum	nickel
4	tin	copper
5	lead	aluminum
6	zinc	zinc
7	iron	tin
8	nickel	lead

Source: Chapman et al., *Working with Materials*

Tensile Strength, Hardness, and Toughness

Tensile strength is a measure of a metal's resistance to being pulled apart, as expressed in thousands of pounds per square inch. This quality is of special interest to vane gear builders because of the amount of twisting and pulling experienced by the mounting tubes. A 30,000-mile circumnavigation requires a servo blade and pendulum shaft to rotate literally millions of times through two axes, exerting a huge strain on the mounting structure and lower unit, particularly at the bolt holes of mounting brackets.

Hardness, commonly measured by the *Brinnell Method*, is also an important characteristic of metal. Vane gear bevel gears are constantly rotating while crunching salt crusts, dried flying fish wings, and other junk that falls into the gears' exposed teeth. Rod linkage must endure constant pushing and pulling, which strains clevis pins and eye connections. The vane's components must be flexible enough to resist breakage, yet they must have enough hardness and *toughness* to avoid bending or twisting out of shape, or even worse, breaking. A tough metal can withstand repeated applications of force without failing through permanent deformation or breakage.

Galvanic Corrosion

Several types of corrosion plague metals exposed to a marine environment. Ordinary surface oxidation, not a threat to boat hardware, is easily distinguished from harmful corrosion. Brass and bronze develop a green patina, aluminum produces a thin coat of white powder, and the ferrous content of so-called stainless steels leaves a reddish-brown stain. On aluminum and stainless, surface oxidation acts as a protective skin, curtailing further oxidation. Applying abrasive cleaners to polish either of these alloys only invites further oxidation, and in time could lead to a shortened life span for those pieces of hardware.

Serious structural corrosion takes the form of *electrolysis, galvanism, intergranular corrosion, stress corrosion,* or *erosion.* All of these boil down to two essential types of corrosion: erosion and electrochemical. Mechanical erosion occurs as a result of friction, either through the rubbing of a metal against another substance, or by attack from air bubbles, a problem experienced by high-speed propellers. In the context of vane gears, this type of corrosion is not a concern, so we will leave the matter aside. On the other hand, electrochemical corrosion is a curse to all metals on a boat, from masthead tangs to laptop computer components and rudder gudgeons. Electrolysis, galvanic action, stress corrosion, and crevice corrosion are all manifestations of this scourge.

Electrochemical corrosion occurs when two unlike metals are placed in close proximity within a shared *electrolyte,* a nonmetallic electrical conductor, in this case salt water. When salt is dissolved in water, the two substances form *ions,* which carry electrons from a negatively charged *anode* to a positively charged *cathode.* During the life of this DC (direct-current) battery, ions carry minute particles of the anode to the cathode until the anodic metal has totally disintegrated. Placing too many zincs below the waterline can cause your propeller to develop a grainy surface from the accumulated crust of zinc oxide, a consequence that can seriously hamper the prop's performance. Galvanic corrosion occurs from the mere presence of two dissimilar metals in salt water without any artificially induced electrical current. This can occur anywhere there is so much as a drop of salt water between two unlike metals, such as between a stainless screw and an aluminum mast. Electrolysis occurs when an outside electric current, particularly direct current, finds its way into the water, introducing or accelerating electrochemical corrosion. Although this stray-current corrosion might affect a metal servo blade if it is left submerged for long periods, most sailors pull the pendulum out of the water soon after setting the anchor. Trim tabs on main and auxiliary rudders permanently reside in seawater, so their submerged metal fittings must be inspected periodically for corrosion.

The great weight of discussion regarding corrosion in boat hardware, including vane gears, is on galvanism. And the principles learned here, insofar as metallic properties are concerned, are the same for all types of electrochemical corrosion. Most of our concern for galvanism on vane gears is focused on hardware above the waterline. Saltwater spray settles into linkage joints, gears, bearings, screws, and threaded rods. On some vane gears, cast aluminum, stainless steel, and bronze exist in close proximity, creating a constant maintenance challenge for their owners. Metals are rated on the galvanic series (see the sidebar on page 46), a table of the relative nobility of metals commonly used for industrial marine purposes. The noble classes of society have always been partial to gold, platinum, and silver, all of which are stable, inactive metals. Copper, iron, and tin, more active and hence less noble, were once regarded as metals of the common people, who could not afford anything better. A poor sixteenth-century peasant who wanted fancy dinnerware for the family acquired a few pieces cast in pewter, or "poor man's silver," a combination of tin and lead. The unfortunate consequence of prolonged use was lead poisoning, resulting in severe stomach pains, dementia, and finally death.

Theoretically, the closer two metals are in the galvanic series, the more electrically compatible they are when submerged in seawater. This rule, nonetheless, has its exceptions, as there are more variables to consider. The oxide films on stainless and aluminum alloys, for example, allow the two metals to coexist, as long as they are separated by plastic tape or some other dielectric. Copper-based metals, such as brass and bronze, are closer to aluminum on the galvanic series than passive forms of 304 and 316 stainless, but a copper oxide finish is still fairly active. Author-sailor Nigel Calder warns: "Copper alloys should never be used in combination with aluminum; passivated stainless steel or Monel is normally the appropriate choice for fasteners."

MARINE ALLOYS

Bronze and Brass

The Mesopotamians knew they were onto a good thing when they first started melting copper and tin together to produce bronze over 5,000 years ago. They developed methods of casting and hammering the grayish-yellow alloy into tools, cookware, and ornaments. Today, bronze may also contain lead, iron, zinc, manganese, silicon, nickel, aluminum, and trace amounts of other metals to give the alloy special qualities. Bronze is hard and corrosion resistant, but easy to work. If you have ever wondered why bronze fittings have such a rough texture, it is because bronze is usually cast in sand molds. However, it lends itself readily to soldering, brazing, and welding. Brass differs from bronze in several ways. The copper base is combined primarily with zinc, but may also contain smaller amounts of the same admixtures as bronze. Brass is a very malleable, ductile alloy, yellowish or reddish in color, used for wire, tubing, electrical fittings, and ornamentation, among other things. It is easily machined and may also be soldered or brazed. While brass is happier inside the cabin hanging prettily on the bulkhead, bronze finds its calling down in "shaft alley" or outside where conditions are harsh and forbidding. You will find cast bronze components in numerous commercially built vane gears, usually as bevel gears and solid linkages; bronze screws, bolts, and shafts are also good options for those wishing to build their own vane steerers.

Galvanic Series of Metals in Seawater

ANODIC/LEAST NOBLE

Magnesium and Magnesium Alloys

Zinc

Galvanized Steel or Galvanized Wrought Iron

Aluminum Alloys

Cadmium

Mild Steel

Wrought Iron

Cast Iron

13% Chromium Stainless Steel, Type 410 (active in still water)

18/8 Stainless Steel, Type 304 (active in still water)

Ni-Resist

18/8, 3% Mo Stainless Steel, Type 316 (active in still water)

Inconel (78% Ni, 14.5% Cr, 6% Fe) (active in still water)

Aluminum Bronze (92% Cu, 8% Al)

Naval Brass (60% Cu, 39% Zn)

Yellow Brass (65% Cu, 35% Zn)

Red Brass (85% Cu, 15% Zn)

Muntz Metal (60% Cu, 40% Zn)

Tin

Copper

50-50 Lead-Tin Solder

Admiralty Brass (71% Cu, 28% Zn, 1% Sn)

Aluminum Brass (76% Cu, 22% Zn, 2% Al)

Manganese Bronze (58.5% Cu, 39% Zn, 1% Sn, 1% Fe, 0.3% Mn)

Silicon Bronze (96% Cu, 0.8% Fe, 1.5% Zn, 2% Si, 0.75% Mn, 1.6% Sn)

Bronze, Composition G (88% Cu, 2% Zn, 10% Sn)

Bronze, Composition M (88% Cu, 3% Zn, 6.5% Sn, 1.5% Pb)

13% Chromium Stainless Steel, Type 401 (passive)

90% Cu—10% Ni

75% Cu—20% Ni—5% Zn

Lead

70% Cu—30% Ni

Inconel (78% Ni, 13.5% Cr, 6% Fe) (passive)

Nickel 200

18/8 Stainless Steel, Type 304 (passive)

70% Ni—30% Cu Monel 400, K-500

18/8, 3% Mo Stainless Steel, Type 316 (passive)

Titanium

Hastelloy C

Platinum

Graphite

CATHODIC/MOST NOBLE

Source: American Boat and Yacht Council, in Calder, *Boatowner's Mechanical and Electrical Manual*

Silicon bronze was once the standard choice among sailors for heavy-duty use as propeller shafts, rudderposts, keel bolts, and fasteners, but stainless steel and Monel have taken over these duties on many production boats since the 1960s. Nonetheless, silicon bronze, a popular brand of which is Everdur, is still the mainstay for through-hull fittings and turnbuckles, the latter commonly electroplated in chrome to match the silvery appearance of stainless standing rigging. The family of silicon bronzes is known for its hardness and resistance to crevice and surface corrosion. Everdur 651 and 655 are ideal for fasteners (including nails and rivets), U-bolts, and general marine hardware.

Developed primarily for aviation, aluminum bronze is also a useful alloy in many marine applications. It holds up well in anaerobic conditions that can cause crevice corrosion in stainless, making this bronze valuable for nuts, bolts, gears, and bushings. Its aluminum content, though, renders the bronze unacceptable for duty where it may be submerged in salt water with nobler metals for long periods, namely in the bilge or below the waterline.

Other copper alloys that you may find in marine hardware are manganese bronze, phosphor bronze, cuprous nickel, and Monel (70% nickel, 30% copper), an expensive but durable alloy used for keel bolts and fuel and water tanks. Actually a type of brass, manganese bronze contains a high percentage of zinc. Both brass and manganese bronze are susceptible to *dezincification*, the intergranular stripping away of zinc through galvanic action. Because of the low nobility of these last two alloys, they are inadequate for situations demanding high corrosion resistance and compatibility with other marine alloys.

Though marine-grade bronze is well suited to the demands of harsh marine conditions, it doesn't last forever. Bronze eventually succumbs to intergranular

Nominal Composition of Selected Marine Bronzes

INGREDIENT	TYPE OF BRONZE				
	Silicon	Manganese	Aluminum	Phosphor	Tobin
copper	96%	58.5%	81%	94.8%	60%
lead	0.05%	—	—	—	—
iron	0.08%	1%	4%	—	—
zinc	1.5%	39%	—	—	39%
manganese	0.8%	0.3%	—	—	—
silicon	2%	1%	—	—	—
nickel	0.6%	—	4%	—	—
aluminum	—	—	11%	—	—
phosphorous	—	—	—	0.20%	—
tin	—	—	—	5.0%	0.75%

corrosion as its mix of anodic and cathodic metals attack each other in a slow, galvanic war that can take a lifetime before showing ill effects. When bronze suffers from structural galvanic corrosion, its color turns pinkish and its texture crystalline and brittle. A seriously decayed through-hull typically announces its condition by snapping off when you are turning a seacock valve. Even high-quality silicon bronze will deteriorate quickly if left unprotected and exposed to an overdose of stray electrical current. Placing sacrificial zinc anodes on the propeller shaft and other strategic places on the undersides of the hull provides a hedge against serious galvanic action. Bronze fittings on a vane gear are unlikely to suffer serious corrosion unless they are electrically connected to a stainless servo blade hanging in salt water while the boat sits in an electrically "hot" marina.

Stainless Steel

One of the most versatile alloys available to us is stainless steel. Though yachties still insist on tough, marine-grade bronze for through-hull fittings and propellers, stainless has replaced bronze and brass in much of the other hardware found on oceangoing sailboats. All steels, including stainless steels, contain iron and carbon in varying proportions. In addition to these two metals, stainless steels contain 12 to 25 percent chromium, which forms a thin, protective oxide coating on the surface. There are four families of stainless steel: *martensitic, ferritic, austenitic,* and *duplex.* The low carbon and nitrogen content of martensitic and supermartensitic alloys makes them ideal for chemical processing plants and the oil and gas industry. Ferritic stainless, containing a greater percentage of carbon and iron, includes the common 400-series stainless we see in pots and pans, flatware, and inexpensive hose clamps. Austenitic stainless, comprising the bulk of common marine stainless, includes grades 304 and 316. Grade 304 is what we get in fasteners and standing rigging if we forget to demand grade 316, which has a higher molybdenum content for greater tensile strength and corrosion resistance. The stainless known as 316L is low in carbon and therefore less susceptible to corrosion than regular 316.

A recent arrival to the marine industry is duplex stainless steel, combining the higher tensile strength of ferritic stainless with the corrosion resistance of austenitic stainless. The result, though, is more than a sum of the two alloys. Higher chromium content makes this steel more resistant to *crevice corrosion,* a form of intergranular corrosion occurring when salt water attacks stainless steel's oxide skin and forms hairline cracks; the intruding electrolyte provides a medium in which minute particles of anodic metals succumb to cathodic metal particles. More molybdenum spells greater resistance to pitting corrosion, which invades the surfaces of stainless objects left in stagnant, oxygen-starved water. Finally, the added nitrogen promotes structural hardening and tensile strength. The overall result is a stainless that is lighter and stronger than grades 304 and 316.

Duplex is divided into four groups: lean duplex, possessing little added molybdenum; 2205, the workhorse grade, containing moderate amounts of chromium, molybdenum, and nitrogen, plus 5 percent nickel; 25 percent chromium duplex; and superduplex, containing the greatest portions of chromium, molybdenum, and nitrogen. Grade 2205, accounting for more than 80 percent of duplex sales, is used by at least one vane gear manufacturer, Fleming Self-Steering Systems, to produce castings for high-stress components. Expect to see more vane gear builders and other marine industries adopt duplex stainless alloys in the next few years. Duplex stainless is a truly exotic alloy. Imagine a stainless casting so tough and corrosion resistant that after thousands of miles of constant exposure to salt water, it is absolutely free of any visible surface oxidation, while the electropolished grade 316 stainless tubing attached to it is starting to show a few light brown stains. Now try to believe this: if you place a magnet next to the 2205 fitting, the magnet sticks! Incredible, but true.

Gleaming 316L stainless steel Cape Horn parts await final assembly. (Cape Horn Marine Products)

The lower grades of stainless, particularly 304 and 305, are notoriously prone to pitting and crevice corrosion, occurring when metal is left in stagnant water from which dissolved oxygen has escaped. The oxygen-starved water eats the oxide skin, leaving the metal vulnerable to further corrosion. Swaged stainless wire and tightly packed propeller shafts are common victims of crevice corrosion. Low-grade stainless has less nickel, which is expensive. Some manufacturers of 304/305 and 316 stainless fasteners and wire like to cut corners, diluting the nickel content to unacceptable levels. Unfortunately, mill operators in some countries sometimes skimp on expensive metals in favor of quick profits. When we shop for stainless merchandise at the chandlery, we naturally check the rating stated on the wire spool or stamped directly into the item, and then we place our trust in the vendor. Other than that, experience and dockside advice are our best guides.

Aluminum

Aluminum is one of the great paradoxes of our postindustrial society. We in the marine world have sort of a love-hate relationship with this metal. On the negative side, it ranks very low on the nobility scale, just above magnesium, zinc, and wrought iron (see sidebar on page 46), and has very low tensile strength when compared to other marine alloys. On a boat, even the best aluminum alloys turn to white powder if mated to stainless, bronze, or brass fasteners without adequate protection.

On the positive side, aluminum is very light and very cheap, and it has a higher strength-to-weight ratio than stainless. Otherwise, we would have stainless booms and masts, right? Aluminum is also less susceptible than stainless steel to crevice corrosion and work hardening. The noncorrosive properties of aluminum remain intact as long as it is isolated from nobler metals. Of all metals, aluminum is the best for diesel fuel tanks; the sulfur in diesel gradually dissolves stainless steel tanks, especially at the welds.

Though aluminum mills produce alloys in literally hundreds of grades, the U.S. Coast Guard warns us that we should trust only those alloys labeled "marine grade—corrosion resistant" for marine fabrication. Confusion over this matter has led to near disaster in the shipbuilding industry. In a recent case, the USCG issued a warning to all purchasers of 5083 H321 aluminum alloy produced at a mill in Ontario, Canada. The company could not guarantee the metal's quality because it had been cold rolled to nonmarine specifications. Some of the approximately 270 vessels built of the alloy were showing signs of exfoliation corrosion (flaking of surface material) and intergranular corrosion within a short time after construction.

If your vane gear contains aluminum, you should be especially careful to remove the servo blade from the water when the vessel is in a marina, close to stray current. With a servo blade of plastic or fiberglass construction, be careful not to let the servo arm come into prolonged contact with the water, since current travels throughout all directly connected metal parts. AC is not nearly as harmful to marine metals as DC, unless the AC is somehow converted to DC. An AC-to-DC power supply, or rectifier, like the one in my laptop computer, employs a diode to eliminate electrical flow in one direction, yielding pulsating DC current in the other direction. Crystalline forms of metallic oxides breed naturally occurring diodes, and one very effective diode for converting AC to DC just happens to be aluminum oxide. This opens up the potential for accelerated galvanic corrosion if adequate measures are not taken to protect aluminum fixtures from stray current. Don't panic! Several highly regarded vane gear models with aluminum castings have performed faithfully for their owners over tens of thousands of miles. Two of the oldest commercially produced servopendulum windvanes, the Aries and the Sailomat, are largely composed of aluminum castings and tubing, but even many of the mid-1970s models are still plying the oceans. Their dedicated owners lubricate the aluminum moving parts regularly and pull the servo blades out of the water as soon as they throw down the hook or tie up to a dock.

There are three ways to protect aluminum in a marine environment: *anodiza-*

tion, *isolation*, and *insulation*. In practice these break down to several different techniques. Manufacturers of nautical equipment often cover their aluminum products with a sacrificial anodic finish that can last many years. This finish, applied through electrolysis, is an attractive, efficient way to protect roller-furling foil sections, light-duty winches, and various cast and extruded aluminum components of a vane gear. Though it is best not to paint aluminum, many sailors spray a light coat of zinc chromate primer on masts and booms, and then quickly follow up with a couple coats of two-part polyurethane paint with fairly good results. The anodic primer forms a sacrificial barrier against corrosion.

Isolation may be achieved by leaving the alloy bare and out of contact with nobler metals. This strategy works well for large surfaces, particularly the topsides of aluminum boats, which are best left unpainted. Surface corrosion at first occurs quickly, but then stabilizes, leaving an unsightly yet stable oxide patina. Beautifully painted aluminum boats and ships do exist. But practical-minded cruisers generally leave all aluminum unpainted, except perhaps for spars. A large area of cathodic material can concentrate galvanic action on a small anodic spot exposed by a scratch or pinhole, causing far

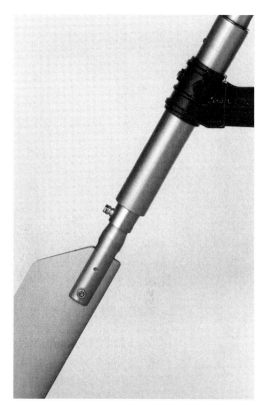

Anodized aluminum shaft and servo blade of Sailomat 601. (Sailomat)

more serious damage than if the galvanism were spread across a much larger surface. A small hole can become larger in time, seriously compromising hull or deck structure if not repaired. Another method of isolation is using a *dielectric*, or insulator, to prevent electrical flow between aluminum and the offending cathodic metal. You can insulate stainless fasteners from aluminum vane gear parts with plastic bushings or other protective barriers. The latest West Marine Master Catalog lists at least eight aerosol lubricant and corrosion inhibitors that should work well on aluminum. Other anticorrosive treatments, such as Never-Seize, Anti-Seize, Loctite, and Duralac, are good dielectrics for fasteners.

METAL PROCESSING AND FABRICATION

In order to own, operate, and maintain a vane gear, we don't need to be metallurgy experts. A few readers will build their own vane systems, putting to use with their own hands some of the fabrication techniques outlined briefly in the next few pages. Only a few of us will ever have occasion to perform any foundry work, yet soldering, brazing, and welding are handy skills for any serious sailor. At the very least, we should have a fundamental understanding of these various forms of metal processing and fabrication methods. The industrial practices discussed here are only those relevant to the manufacturing of vane gear pieces and other marine metal hardware. Libraries, websites, and trade schools offer great opportunities for those who wish to learn more about, or acquire skill in, the various applied metallurgical arts.

Casting

After the initial stages of smelting base metal ores and combining them into their myriad alloys, the first manufacturing process is *casting*. Actually, this is the final step for some items, which are used as they are, such as cast-iron skillets, or assembled with other parts, as with some bevel gears and other vane gear components. Casting is the practice of pouring molten metal from a crucible into a mold, where it cools and from which it is then released in its final form. Four techniques are used in molding cast metals: sand, permanent-mold, die, and centrifugal. Traditional sand casting, which still produces the largest volume of "cast-to-shape" pieces, uses sand, ceramic, or slurry to form the mold. A pattern carved in wax, metal, wood, plaster, or plastic is pressed between either side, the *cope* and *drag*, of the mold. In the lost-wax method, molten metal is poured directly into the wax pattern, which quickly melts out and is displaced by the metal. Permanent-mold casts are produced in cast iron, steel, or bronze molds; the casts are then disassembled and reused for repeated castings. This type of casting allows closer tolerances and cheaper, higher-volume production. In die-casting, molten metal is forced into a mold at extremely high pressures—up to a million pounds per square inch for some high-melting-point alloys. The method achieves a much finer finish and permits the shaping of thin sections. In order to form round, symmetric objects, such as engine flywheels and vane gear turrets, it is better to pour the molten metal into a spinning mold, a process called centrifugal casting. Some of the advantages to casting, regardless of method, are shape control, low production costs, and consistent granular structure throughout the cast.

Rolling

Cast ingots may be converted into plate and sheet through repeated hot and cold *rolling*. An ingot starts as a brittle, porous, and coarse-grained structure, which is first rolled into a wrought structure, then in order of decreasing thickness, a billet, slab, plate, sheet, strip, and foil. The application of extreme pressure and alternating temperatures eventually transforms the metal into a thin, fine-grained, ductile material suitable for a variety of subsequent fabrication processes.

Seamless Tubing

The 304 and 316 stainless tubing we use for stanchions and vane gear mounting tubes is milled through the *Mannesmann process*, the rolling of a rod billet under high compression until the center of the rod shears open into a narrow opening along the full length of the newly formed tube. This is similar to what happens to a pencil eraser if you roll it back and forth between a rule and a desktop: the center crumbles into a long hole. Repeated passes through a pair of rollers on slightly opposed axes further expands and refines the metal tube. There are several levels of quality in stainless tubing. The one needing the least amount of cleaning is electropolished, grade 316L marine tubing. Its tighter surface grain structure puts up a stronger defense to attacks by saltwater ions than the more porous surfaces of lower-grade tubing. It is expensive, but it will keep its magnificent mirror shine while brown splotches of oxidation mar the lesser grades.

Brazing and Welding

It is doubtful that we will find many vane gears assembled through brazing or *braze welding* because both techniques usually involve joining metals with a dissimilar metal. But this method is handy for quick repairs, provided you have the required tools. When brazing, one heats the two parent metals to a point above 800°F with an *oxyacetylene* torch. The other hand runs a brass or bronze rod next to the flame along the joint, where the rod melts and seeps into the joint by capillary action. This can be done only if the parent metals are closely joined with no gaps. Braze welding is a technique for joining two metals that cannot take advantage of capillary action. Adjoining edges may form a groove or some other type of seam that fills up with rod material, ensuring the filling and bonding of gaps and fissures along the seam. A copper-based metal intended to bind stainless steel will soon corrode after being introduced to salt water, so the two methods are at best temporary, emergency fixes for vane gears.

Welding takes on a variety of forms, all of which apply to marine construction. In the most traditional practice, the welder uses an oxyacetylene torch to cut metals or to fuse them either with or without a welding rod. The particular method depends on the metal, its thickness, and the shape of the two edges to be welded. While torch cutting may be applied to many different metals, torch welding is preferred for iron and mild steel. *Arc welding*, also for iron and mild steel, is the process of joining metals with electric current flowing through either a nonconsumable electrode or a metal filler rod to the joint of the parent metals. In order to avoid welds contaminated by oxides in the atmosphere, some applications require tungsten inert gas, or *TIG*, welding. This is a form of arc welding that uses the inert gas as a shield around a nonconsumable electrode; in other words, the welder melts the parent metals, not a rod, for fusion. TIG welding is the preferred method for fusing stainless and a number of nonferrous metals, including manganese and aluminum. Gas metal arc *(MIG)* welding is suitable for the same alloys as TIG, but MIG is the better choice for metals more than $1/4$ inch thick. Carbon dioxide gas forms the shield around the electrode, in this application a continuously fed bare-metal filler wire.

Machining

All vane gear manufacturers use at least some machined parts in their products. The advantage of machining over casting and welding is closer tolerances. However, good-quality machine work is labor-intensive and therefore costly. And unlike casting, machining leaves open a bigger window for mistakes if the machine operator is not working exactly to specifications. If some part of your vane gear has incurred permanent damage, in most cases, you can depend on the manufacturer to send you a replacement part, as long as you are near a shipping service. Barring that possibility, you may need the services of a machine shop to build you a one-off copy of the part. Furnish them with the old part, if possible. If not, supply the machinist with a sketch of the part with precise measurements. For low-grade bronze, stainless, and aluminum parts, you can probably depend on the shop to procure a metal that will serve your needs adequately until you can order the Real McCoy. You will find these alloys virtually anywhere there is human habitation. Verify that the metal is *not* mild steel, which will start oxidizing as soon as the ocean air hits it and will resemble a crumbled oatmeal cookie within a few weeks. As you can see from the galvanic series, contact between bronze and stainless should be OK, at least until your next major port. Where circumstances force you to place dissimilar metals in close contact, coat the contact surfaces with a dielectric, or at least marine grease, to forestall galvanic corrosion.

The basic, multiservice machine shop generally has a drill press, a bench grinder, a polishing machine, a milling machine, and a lathe, along with assorted other pieces of equipment reflecting the shop's area of specialty. Assuming you know what the first three are, a *milling machine* is somewhat similar to a drill press, except that the cutting bit can turn in different directions and cut laterally, not just vertically. This machine can cut gear teeth, noncircular holes, grooves, and so on. High-volume production shops sometimes have programmable CNC milling machines, which can be set up to cut a one-off, multifaceted piece, or endless copies of the same part. The lathe, much like the one furniture builders use to form spindles for chair legs, spins a piece of metal horizontally so that it may be cut with a fixed cutting tool. In the hands of a skilled operator, a machine lathe can cut the outer surfaces of bushings and other cylindrical fittings to very high tolerances.

POLYMERS

Plastics used in vane gear construction include nylon, Teflon, Delrin, and polycarbonate plastic, known to mariners as Lexan and Hyzod. While the first three products are recognized for producing high-quality marine hardware, polycarbonate is the mainstay for plastic sheet and injection-molded parts used on boats.

Nylon, Teflon, and Delrin

Nylon, developed in the 1930s, is a strong, high-stretch, abrasion-resistant plastic popular for dock and mooring lines, bushings, and washers. It has fairly high compressive and tensile strength, but is still smooth and flexible. If you need to insert a bushing into a corroded or roughly finished space, you will have more luck with nylon than with a rock-hard material. Teflon (polytetrafluoroethylene) has "the lowest coefficient of friction of any solid material," according to AP Technologies, a major plastics vendor. This plastic is resistant to friction, chemicals, and heat (we fry bacon on it), making it a superior material for bearings and other high-wear applications. However, Teflon has low tensile and compressive strength, so we cannot depend on it for heavy loads.

Manufacturers of vane gears, roller furlers, and deck hardware generally prefer the acetyl polymer Delrin for bushings, bearings, and races. DuPont developed Delrin in the early 1950s as a substitute for nonferrous metals. Frank McGrew, assistant research director for DuPont, dubbed the formaldehyde-based plastic "synthetic stone" for its hardness and durability. A patent dispute during the 1960s hindered the project for some years, but DuPont prevailed, and Delrin has remained a leading engineering polymer ever since. Though Delrin's compressive and tensile strength is similar to that of nylon, Delrin is harder and more easily machined. If your vane gear has Delrin bearings and races, you will find that they never freeze up. You will find maintenance hints for Delrin in chapter 9, but in all honesty, such parts should be fine if you do nothing at all.

Polycarbonate

We know polycarbonate plastics by the well-known brand name Lexan, or its lower-priced competitor Hyzod. The main advantages of this plastic are high impact strength and high softening temperature. Most sailors recognize the superiority of polycarbonate over Plexiglas acrylic sheet, which tends to fade and crack easily. Polycarbonate will also fade and suffer from shallow surface crazing, but I have never heard of it breaking. Plastimo uses injection-molded Lexan parts to build major sections of its Navik vane gear, including the servo blade and trim tab. These components are strong, UV resistant, and light, making the overall vane gear package potentially very attractive to owners of boats under 30 feet LOA.

Injection Molding

It is fair to assume that more vane gear manufacturers will turn to injection-molded plastics, most notably polycarbonate, to promote lighter weight and far greater corrosion resistance. Plastics do oxidize, but centuries, perhaps millennia, will pass before a thick piece of molded plastic will break down in salt water. UV light is the archenemy of plastic, but the addition of reflective and opaque solids can significantly enhance a plastic's lifetime in the sun.

Injection molding is a process in which plastic pellets or granules are melted and then forced into a split mold. This technique produces the majority of end-user plastic items that we see around us in everyday life, including ballpoint-pen barrels; cups and bowls; computer, television, and stereo housings; and every size and shape of plastic bottle imaginable. Injection molding can produce thin- or thick-walled sections, but the process favors uniform wall thickness. Another engineering challenge is shrinkage, which grows commensurately with wall thickness. Those who intend to design injection-molded plastic servo blades or trim tabs must take shrinkage into account if the two foils are to conform to a strict hydrodynamic shape.

You should now have a fairly good idea of the alloys, plastics, and fabrication techniques that together produce windvane steering gears. Vane gear builders must find the best fit among all these production options in order to yield a machine that is soundly built and economically feasible to manufacture. At the same time, the final product must turn out a respectable profit after the builder has written checks for rent, payroll, advertising, insurance, etc. Considering the potential obstacles to success, the vane gears cited in chapter 5 appear to fit all the requirements, those of both builder and customer. In all my discussions with vane gear owners, I have never heard sailors refer to their vane gears as "lemons." To the contrary, all the vane gear owners I have met have beamed with pride over the durability and operating ease of their wind-powered steering systems.

Chapter 4

Selecting the Right System

You would think that the beginning of a chapter on such a critical piece of cruising equipment as self-steering gear should start with a scare tactic—something like, "The vane gear you select will mean the difference between life and death." Such a contention might be appropriate if we were talking about the hull-and-deck structure or the rigging. But all the commercially produced vane gears presented in chapter 5 are solid, sound pieces of equipment that have undergone years of testing and refinement. Some are more expensive than others, or lighter, or less prone to corrosion, or designed more for one type of boat rather than another, but they are all good systems. I do not extol the virtues of one model at the expense of another. The decision to buy a particular make or model comes down to personal choice, hopefully based on a realistic assessment of the vessel's needs, the applicability of the vane gear models being considered, and the prospective buyer's pocketbook. However, where appropriate, I mention specific features of models that may render them more appropriate in certain situations.

Some information that would be helpful in evaluating vane gears is not available to us, possibly because it is not practical to calculate. For example, how convenient it would be if each manufacturer published the amount of steering power produced at a given speed through the water. We the consumers could easily make a comparison among the different models by asking, "Say, what's your unit's 15-knot, maximum thrust rating?" The measurement could be taken with the steering lines disconnected and the vane fully tilted to one side so the servo blade is rotated to its maximum angle. Some companies have no doubt made such measurements, but I have never seen such data published. Perhaps there are too many uncontrollable variables, rendering it impossible to make objective measurements of a vane gear's performance. After all, the same servo blade may extend farther below the waterline, submerging the blade over a greater portion of its pendulum arc and producing more force as weight is added to the stern. The presence of two crew members at the stern of a small vessel to make the necessary measurements could place enough weight aft to cause a measurable increase in steering leverage, effectively invalidating their data. Even if we could exact such measurements, the variety of vane gear designs and their adaptability to certain types of vessels outweigh whatever quantitative observations we could make along one measure of performance. Basing a vane gear's suitability on a narrow set of outputs is like judging an individual's worth as a skipper by how much that person can bench press.

Unlike the automobile and aircraft manufacturers, boatbuilders and marine equipment manufacturers must contend with the joining of two fluid worlds, air and water. Vessels floating on that shiny film border are subject to a more complex set of ever-changing variables than their land and air counterparts. Boats move along at relatively slow speeds, bobbing about as they respond to the vicissitudes of wave and current in the two fluid masses. Windvane steerers are no doubt the world's only mechanisms powered exclusively and simultaneously by the forces of wind and water. Can you think of another? We must appreciate the passion, intuition, experimentalism, and entrepreneurship of those who have toiled to produce these marvelous machines. Beyond what you read here, you will do what the rest of us have done, relying on the builders' advice and the collective experience of fellow cruisers as to what kind of unit to acquire for your vessel.

TYPE OF MAIN STEERING

Paramount among the factors affecting your selection of a vane gear system is the vessel's main steering. A tiller will accept any type of vane gear design, the most appropriate usually being a conventional servopendulum. When we talk about wheel steering, we must specify which type because the mechanisms vary tremendously from one design to the next. Rack-and-pinion steering and cable steering are easily adapted to servopendulum steering by means of a control line drum attached to the wheel. Each of the servopendulum manufacturers offers a wheel drum as an option.

A few steering arrangements dictate a solution incorporating an auxiliary rudder. Hydraulic steering tends to be "mushy" because of a check valve that protects the rudder from sudden impact. Well-greased, heavy bronze castings in worm gear steering are often too stiff for a servopendulum, and any wheel with more than four turns is geared too low for effective course corrections from a servo blade. Center cockpits, regardless of their main steering mechanism, generally place the helm too far from the transom to enjoy the benefits of a servopendulum. The Hydrovane, Saye's Rig, the Windpilot Pacific Plus, and auxiliary rudder trim tabs are all effective self-steering solutions where conventional servopendulums are not practical. However, in the case of a center cockpit, a below-decks Cape Horn servopendulum lets you have your cake and eat it too, since this system works directly on the vessel's steering quadrant.

VESSEL SIZE

The next thing to consider when shopping for a new windvane is the size of vessel on which the gear is to be mounted. A Navik, built in France by Plastimo, would be ridiculously small for a 60-foot, 25-ton boat but perfect for a Cal 25, Santana 27, or Columbia 28. The 60-footer would be better served by a Fleming Global 601, a Saye's Rig, built by Scanmar, or some other make or model specifically designed for big boats. For really big boats with lots of reserve battery power, it may be more practical to install a below-decks autopilot rather than a slightly scaled-down replica of the Eiffel Tower on the transom.

The majority of vane gear models appearing on the market today are designed for vessels ranging from 30 to feet 50 LOA, which comprise the vast majority of cruising vessels. Some vane gears are slightly modified to fit a particular size or design of boat. Fleming, Sailomat, and Windpilot match boat size to one of several vane gear models, each one differing in length and weight. On the other hand, the Aries and Monitor are sold in only one size for 30- to 50-foot yachts, with mounting tubes cut and arranged to accommodate the specific hull design. Rather than designing a giant Monitor or Auto-Helm,

Scanmar International decided to offer Saye's Rig for boats over 50 feet LOA. Manufacturer-recommended size limitations appear with each model in the technical data listed in chapter 5.

STERN AND RUDDER CONFIGURATION

Some people have been led to believe that no vane gear could ever be designed to accommodate their boomkin or transom-mounted rudder, though I have seen several vane gears adapted for either scenario. If you need graphic evidence of this, virtually all vane gear builders have extensive files of vessel designs and corresponding sketches of steering units. The manufacturers enjoy boasting of their ability to tackle engineering challenges. One memorable case involved British sailor Tony Williams, who had purchased a brand-new Catalina 42, *Windriver*, for the purpose of sailing from San Francisco to Panama, then doing the Milk Run to Queensland, Australia. The Catalina 42 has an elaborate swim step and ladder down the middle of a sugar-scoop transom, making the prospect of a vane gear very unlikely. This vessel was designed for daysailing and weekend coastal cruising, and few Catalinas venture far offshore. Consequently, Tony could not find a sister ship with a vane gear installation that he could emulate. When Tony first approached Scanmar with his

Monitor Swing Gate in open position on a Catalina 470. The gate's tube framing blends nicely with the vessel's stanchions and stern pulpit. (Scanmar)

idea of mounting a Monitor on a swinging brace, the company told him it was impossible. The extreme stresses on the unit in offshore conditions required that the vane gear be bolted firmly to the stern. *Finito,* end of discussion. Not one to accept defeat easily, Tony persisted with his plea. He and his fiancée Mitsuyo did not wish to forfeit the convenience of boarding the dinghy from the swim step. As a sheer coincidence, Keith and Susan Levy of the Catalina 470 *C'est La Vie,* which has a similar transom, approached Scanmar with the same request soon after Tony and Mitsuyo made their initial query. By this point the folks at Scanmar obviously could predict the emergence of a new trend in vane gear design, fueled entirely by customer demand. Scanmar's engineering team finally produced a set of plans that would have the Monitor mounted on a vertically hinged brace, allowing the entire vane gear to be swung open, intact, as a box-shaped gate. The finished product was incredible. The vane gear gate and vessel blended so well, they looked as if they had been designed and manufactured as one fully integrated system. *Windriver* finished the Pacific crossing under vane gear steering without incident. So proud is Scanmar of its achievement that it advertises its unique Swing Gate design on its website.

The easiest, most straightforward vane gear installation is, of course, on a relatively flat and vertical, or slightly raked, transom. It took me only a few hours to drill the six holes into my Cal 30's transom from my dinghy, cut the two stainless lower mounting tubes with a hacksaw, drill holes at the ends for the fasteners, and bolt the Fleming vane gear to the transom. For the final fitting and alignment of the tubes, I turned the boat so the stern faced the dock. Tying the vane turret to the stern pulpit made it possible to measure the tube lengths within a close tolerance. I easily bolted the unit together with two box-end wrenches. It was that simple. My biggest challenge was figuring out where to drill the lower bracket holes to avoid bolting through the vessel's name while keeping the tubes safely above the waterline. A number of other pendulum gears are mounted pretty much the same way, with three or four mounting tubes and swivel brackets fastened with 316 stainless $1/4$-inch or $5/16$-inch bolts. Others, such as the Sailomat and the Windpilot Pacific, have one central mounting bracket that carries the whole unit. If you have not the time or inclination to install the vane gear yourself, you may wish to contract the services of a rigger or boatwright. Your vane gear manufacturer or distributor should be able to recommend a rigger who has experience installing the company's products.

Skippers tend to worry when they want to mount a pendulum vane gear to a canoe stern or where there is some obstruction, such as a boomkin or transom rudder. There are plenty of Tayanas, Babas, Hans Christians, and Westsails—all of which are heavy-displacement double-enders—out there with stock self-steering gears. Since all these vessels are popular, well-established cruising boats, you can rest assured that all the vane gear manufacturers have complete drawings for mounting their products to those vessels' canoe sterns. Obscure or one-off designs can be accommodated if the vessel's owner submits copies of plans, along with a few photographs of the boat itself and whatever measurements the builder may require but cannot extrapolate easily from the plans.

Transom rudders are less common than canoe sterns, but are no more difficult for the vane gear installer. Since the 1960s, many production fiberglass boats under 30 feet LOA have been built with transom rudders hung by stainless pintles and gudgeons. Most of these small boats, such as the MacGregor Venture series and the smaller Catalinas, are daysailers and gunkholers not meant to sail offshore. Don't expect vane gear builders to carry mounting plans for those vessels. An exception would be the Catalina 27, which has made numerous major ocean passages. Five bucks says Scanmar has mounting plans available to marry a Navik pendulum trim tab to a Catalina 27. Larger vessels with transom rudders can be seen in cruiser anchorages with all manner of mounting systems. One method is to extend the deck a foot or so aft of the rudder's trailing edge, creating a platform for scuba and propane tanks, personal flotation devices, fishing rod holders, and a vane gear. Scott and Wendy Bannerot, who coauthored *The Cruiser's Handbook of Fishing*, have an Aries mounted to a deck extension to get around the transom rudder on their 41-foot aluminum sloop *Élan*. Another method is to extend the mounting tubes beyond the rudder and proceed as one normally would with a conventional transom. Let's not forget the trim-tab option. The airvane and turret of an Auto-Helm can be adapted to operate an owner-built trim tab mounted on a transom rudder. This is an inexpensive alternative, since there is no need to purchase the auxiliary rudder and trim tab normally included in the system.

Mounting a vane gear to a boomkin demands a bit more creativity from the installer. If the boomkin doesn't extend too far from the transom, mounting tubes need only to be lengthened to clear the tip of the boomkin. Where the boomkin extends farther, say more than two feet from the transom, the boomkin will need to be incorporated into the vane gear's mounting system. Provided the wooden or metal structure is strong enough, either welded to the hull or supported by the backstay and a bobstay, mounting tubes and brackets may be affixed directly to the boomkin.

OBSTACLES, OR *GERÜMPEL*

There is a rapidly accelerating trend toward more stuff on small boats. And much of that stuff ends up at the stern because there is no other practical place to put all this extra gear. Binfried and Ute, a German couple cruising on the Moody 38 *Anna Maria*, taught me the most wonderful word for this crap: *gerümpel*, meaning "stuff." Remember comedian George Carlin's routine on the topic of "stuff"? About needing more and bigger places to store our stuff so that we have more room to buy even more stuff? I wonder if Carlin is a sailor. LPG tanks, stern anchor, throwable PFD, barbecue, fishing tackle, swim ladder, jerricans, surfboards, and other *gerümpel* choke the rear deck. Looming over this mess on some boats are what I call monkey bars, upon which rest a radar dome, assorted vertical and mushroom antennas, a huge wing of solar panels and not one, but two wind generators. This monstrous cage imbues the owner with dual illusions of shelter and dominion. To top it off, a huge steering wheel, the dreaded Stainless Steel Curtain, ostensibly intended to save room, denies passage to all but the most agile. As for the second-story electric generating plant, don't get me wrong. Those who aim to cultivate renewable, nonfossil energy sources have my deepest admiration. But let's not forget that this is a *saaa*ilboat. If you are contemplating the installation of a windvane, you will need to carve a large enough hole in that hardware matrix to allow the free flow of air around the airvane. Large solar panels are the most egregious offenders. They should be mounted horizontally above or below the airvane. If mounted vertically to catch late or early sunlight, solar panels should be located low, preferably secured to either side of the stern pulpit. Not only does this strategy ensure proper action of the vane, it keeps the center of the wind's effort closer to the hull.

There are, as mentioned in the first two chapters, vane gears that accommodate rear-deck encumbrances. The Auto-Helm is a trim-tab system with a remote airvane, which is sometimes mounted at the center of the equipment arch, often between banks of solar panels. Shading of the panels by the airvane is the only potential problem here. Given this arrangement, the only time the panels are all working together is at high noon. As long as there is no significant air blockage from equipment below the arch, and no low-hanging boom interfering with the airvane, there should be no reason not to install a pendulum vane gear.

Some skippers have an almost irrational fear of permitting steering lines to invade their cockpits. Lounging comfortably in their chic Banana Republic outfits at their home marinas, sipping umbrella drinks, and listening to Jimmy Buffett, these well-meaning weekend sailors, concerned for safety and aesthetics, uphold the sanctity of the cockpit with religious zeal. As they prepare for an extended cruise, they imagine themselves continuing the party offshore. Within the first 24 hours of slipping their dock lines and waving good-bye, they learn that life offshore is spent in the cabin, lest they burn to a crisp from direct or water-reflected sunlight, or get thoroughly drenched by a mischievous little wave slapping against the hull. Those steering lines leading to the wheel or tiller are not a hindrance while on passage. If a steering line is in your way, step over it. Before entering your next anchorage, you will disconnect the lines, coil them aside, and forget about them.

If circumstances preclude a conventional servopendulum, you may select among the few trim tabs or auxiliary rudder servopendulums on the market, or perhaps construct your own trim-tab system. You still have to make allowance for clear airflow around the airvane, but at least an auxiliary rudder or trim-tab arrangement keeps the deck clear of extra running rigging. Saye's Rig, sort of a cross between a servopendulum and a trim tab, is mounted directly to the vessel's rudder and therefore offers the same benefit as a standard trim tab: no lines to the cockpit. The key difference is that Saye's Rig is intended for vessels in excess of 50 feet LOA.

DESIGN FEATURES

Having read the previous chapter, you should have a good sense of what materials and general types of fabrication enter into vane gear building. In chapter 5 you will find notes on specific design and construction methods for each model presented. Choice can be daunting, more so when lots of different products do pretty much the same thing and are more or less within the same price range. Certain design aspects, though, may appeal to you more than others, especially if you have used a vane gear before. If you have not, find an opportunity to sail under vane steering on a fellow sailor's boat. As you adjust the unit and watch its steering action, you will develop some sense of its effectiveness and limitations. Examine its condition. How old is it? How much has it been used? Does it show any serious signs of corrosion? Check welds for signs of cracking or previous repair. Take a walk around the local marina and study vane gears from dockside, comparing their designs and looking for signs of damage. If breakage or excessive corrosion is visible on a particular model, try to discern, if possible, whether it is the fault of the builder or of the owner. Poor craftsmanship or substandard materials might be good reasons to avoid a particular model. Following are a few tips on what to look for in a new vane gear system.

Servopendulums

All servopendulums operate in the same manner, producing similar results with different engineering. The most obvious difference is in the transmission connecting the vane yoke to the servo blade. For example, some builders join the upper and lower ends with two bevel gears, which are cast or machined in stainless or bronze. Others join the two ends of the unit with stainless or bronze rod linkage. Sailomat converts the wind's energy into servopendulum rotation via "spherical joints." The various systems appear to function amply well. The operator calibrates the bevel gear system by adjusting a bevel gear, generally held in place by a thrust bearing. One calibrates rod linkage by means of threaded, telescoping rod ends.

The vane turret is another obvious feature, which can be either a notched

Sailomat 601—a servopendulum vane gear system with a raked servo blade—on Quest 33 *Troll-Fjord,* overall winner of 1999 Bermuda One-Two Race. (Sailomat)

turret or a drum turret. The surest way to keep the airvane from accidentally rotating is with a notched turret. Notches are separated every 5 to 7 degrees around the adjustment wheel, which is secured by a pin or a spring-loaded pawl. Despite the notched wheel's advantages, you should be aware of two potential limitations. First, if you cannot achieve the precise steering you desire with the vane turret, you must fine-tune the helm. The Aries compensates for the notches with a piece of chain that you connect to the steering line ends and hook onto a clip attached to the tiller. You fine-tune the helm by changing the position of the chain across the clip. It is not always necessary to make the extra adjustment at the helm, and moreover, I have never heard anyone complain about steering adjustments with notched turrets. David Berg, a well-known delivery skipper in the Caribbean and South Pacific, used to leave the helm to his Aries windvane while sailing *High Flyer* up and down the Intracoastal Waterway in southern Florida. Dave easily tacked the 36-foot, full-keeled, teak-planked, heavy-displacement sloop through channels 150 yards wide by clicking the vane turret back and forth with the remote steering line. Incidentally, this is not something Dave recommends for the novice. Close-tacking in narrow, shoaly channels is difficult enough under hand steering. The only other potential disadvantage with notched turrets is weight, a concern for vessels under 30 feet LOA. Notched turrets tend to be large in diameter; the bigger the turret's diameter, the more notches there are for finer steering control—and the more the wheel and support structure weigh.

A drum turret is a narrow cylinder with a horizontal sheave. The operator adjusts the turret with a piece of line running once or twice around the sheave and back through a remote block held tight by a shock cord. The advantages are infinitely fine vane adjustment without retrimming the helm, and less weight. For the builder, a drum turret means less metal to be purchased and lower production costs because the piece is cast ready for assembly, rather than machined, as in the case of some notched turrets. The only possible drawback for the user is the tendency toward accidental rotation when the adjustment line becomes slack; you can prevent slippage by making sure the turret adjustment line is always tight.

Since the servopendulum itself is the heart of this class of vane gear, it merits special attention in the selection process. A servopendulum blade should be based on an appropriate NACA four-digit profile, easily identified by a wide, rounded leading edge and a sharp trailing edge. The span, or widest point, should be forward of the midpoint of the chord. Most servo blades are suspended 180 degrees to the water from their gearing, a straightforward approach that works for most boats. For a sugar-scoop transom, one way to fit a vane gear is with a raked servo blade, such as that found on a Sailomat. The diagonal pendulum shaft is less likely to accumulate seaweed, fishing nets, and plastic bags. On the other hand, most vane gear builders can tailor the mounting tubes to extend beyond the sugar scoop's edge, so you have many options from which to choose.

There should be some means of either removing the pendulum shaft or folding it up out of the water while not in use. Absent this capability, the servo blade will be left to the mercy of the brine. Another important feature is a shear pin, break-away connector, or collapsible tube somewhere along the pendulum shaft. This is the vane gear's only defense against collision with a submerged object that somehow is not deflected by the vessel's keel. Unfortunately, auxiliary rudders and trim tabs are no less vulnerable than the vessel's main steering. Finally, you may wish to consider the servo blade's capacity for an emergency rudder conversion. Some builders market optional conversion kits. If you wish to have a separate emergency rudder, you may elect to build or purchase such a unit. For more information, see chapter 11, Emergency Rudders.

Trim Tabs

My research reveals four trim tabs currently in commercial production. They are intended for different purposes, so your choices are limited. The Auto-Helm and AutoSteer are conventional trim tabs, both of which may be fitted to

Matching Vane Gear to Vessel

MAIN STEERING
- Tiller: any vane gear system serves well; conventional servopendulum most preferred
- Cable or rack and pinion: any vane gear system; servopendulum most preferred, except with center cockpit
- Hydraulic: auxiliary rudder system, such as trim tab (e.g., Auto-Helm), Hydrovane, old Sailomat 3040, or Windpilot Pacific Plus

COCKPIT
- Aft: any vane gear system; auxiliary rudder system in case of hydraulic steering
- Center: trim tab, Cape Horn (inboard), Hydrovane, Sailomat 3040, or Windpilot Pacific Plus

TRANSOM
All transoms accept all systems; in case of canoe stern or boomkin, customized bracing and mounting surface(s) will be required for all vane gear designs.

VESSEL SIZE
- Under 30 feet LOA: many systems will serve well, but the Fleming 201, Navik, and Windpilot Pacific Light are specifically designed for smaller boats
- 30–50 feet LOA: encompasses the vast majority of cruising yachts; vane gear depends on considerations listed above
- Over 50 feet LOA: a number of vane gears will work satisfactorily, but the Fleming 601, Saye's Rig, and Windpilot Pacific Plus II are specifically designed for yachts up to roughly 65 feet LOA.

the vessel's main rudder. The Auto-Helm is also available as a complete kit with auxiliary rudder and stainless control cables. Two pendulum gear hybrids complete the list. The Navik, a pendulum trim tab intended for small vessels, is basically a conventional servopendulum with a trim tab on the trailing edge of the rudder. Finally, Saye's Rig is a "pendulum trim tab tiller arm," designed specially for vessels over 50 feet LOA. Because of the uniqueness of the Navik and Saye's Rig, the only room for variety is in the mounting architecture, which is tailored to your vessel's transom configuration.

If you plan to build a trim-tab system, such as the "West End" detailed in chapter 12, your main choice is between a vertical airvane and a horizontal airvane. Most do-it-yourselfers select the vertical vane for its simplicity and straightforward operation. It does not produce the same steering power as a horizontal vane, but it generally serves its purpose well in winds below gale strength. If you choose to build a horizontal-vane trim tab, decide whether you want cable or hard linkage. Cables may eventually suffer more friction, but they are certainly easier to install. Hard linkage takes more time to customize and install, but it is less prone to friction and wear than cable linkage.

EVALUATING THE MANUFACTURER

Reputation

Small start-up vane gear companies with innovative engineering and construction techniques will sprout up from time to time, some surviving, some not. Nearly all of the vane gear builders and suppliers presented in chapter 5 and in the appendix started out being operated by one person, gradually emerging from the garage or back patio to become well-established companies. Some builders fold before they even scrape up enough money for an ad in the local marine directory. This is not necessarily because they offered an inferior machine. A successful business requires capital resources, advertising, long-range financial planning, and solid management. The typical vane gear manufacturer is a small, privately owned company operated by a fiercely individualistic, iconoclastic entrepreneur who would rather be tinkering with some vane gear refinement or spending a day sailing than yammering away on the telephone with bankers and advertising executives. If you want a fascinating, informative discussion on the physics of sailing and self-steering, spend an hour talking to a vane gear builder on the telephone, or better yet, stop by the shop.

Peter Matthiesen of Aries. (Aries Denmark)

Intuition and common sense figure highly in assessing the overall reputation of a vane gear. If you are focusing on one of the builders cited in this book, it is easy to find information that will aid you in the selection process. Most of them have extensive websites and advertising literature. You can contact the builder by mail, tele-

Hydrovane's new owners, the Curry family, in Tenacatita, Mexico, 1997.

phone, fax, or e-mail; to purchase a new unit, you will likely use all four to exchange technical information about both the vessel and how the builder will customize your vane gear and mounting system. You may find that only two or three people run some of the smaller shops, and none of them is a full-time receptionist. If you attempt a telephone call to inquire about purchasing, they may have their hands full trying to get a couple of units built by their deadlines and simply don't have time to talk at that moment. The person answering your call may be a welder, a machinist, or just a sailing buddy who has popped in for a visit. Instead of eliminating that builder from your list, ask when someone will be able to return your call.

As you wander around the local marina studying vane gears, if you have a chance, strike up a conversation with a windvane owner about the model and the person's relationship with the builder. After purchasing the unit, new or used, has the owner ever needed to contact the builder to order parts or ask for assistance regarding maintenance or repair? Did the builder respond with the parts or assistance requested? In the owner's communication with the builder, has the contact person shown a sincere desire to provide help or service?

Find out how long the firm has been building vane gears. We can expect a company that has been operating for a long time to continue operating for many more years. For us, the consumer, this equates to long-term access to parts, service, and technical support. Someone may come along and buy the company out, as we have seen happen in this industry, but if the company has been reliable in the past, it will more than likely continue to be reliable under new ownership. That is the only way the firm can maintain its credibility with the consumer, particularly in a small niche market where word of mouth accounts for a large percentage of sales.

With a relatively new company, you obviously take a greater risk. The vane gear has not been subjected to the same extensive blue-water testing as the more established models. The more widely known models have been refined over the years, incorporating feedback from owners who have made ocean crossings in every kind of weather. These sailors have been in a position to assess the windvanes' strengths and liabilities, and have been able to point out ways the units can be improved. Purchasing and installing a model that has been on the market only a short time turns your vessel into a test platform, and the builder will wait anxiously for feedback in your postcards and e-mails. If you attempt to contact the company for parts or advice and find that the little start-up has folded, you will need to arrange for repairs on your own.

Price

The old adage "You get what you pay for" does not necessarily apply to vane gears. Though all the gears mentioned in this book are good pieces of equipment, some require more maintenance and occasional repair than others. However, and I mean this sincerely, I have found no correlation between durability and price in the many conversations I have had with owners of different windvane models. A less expensive unit might outlast and outperform a more expensive one, and vice versa. The price for a new vane gear ranges between roughly $2,000 and $4,500, depending on manufacturer or distributor, model, and size. Some builders will charge a little more for oversized or unusual mounting structures, but the extra costs are generally minimal, and you can expect the builder to inform you of such costs before accepting your deposit. If you are concerned about cost, you will find ocean-proven models at the low end of the price range. Then again, some sailors with big bankrolls may feel they are buying better performance and durability with a more expensive vane gear. If money is less of an object, let the vane model's quality and adaptability to your vessel, along with the builder's reputation, be your sole guides. This liberates you to finding the best match, which can be anywhere in the price spectrum.

Warranty

Each manufacturer has its own unique kind of warranty. The range of warranty coverage is from one to ten years for materials and workmanship under normal load conditions; in other words, builders do not cover groundings on coral reefs or rear-end collisions with supertankers. Perhaps the most creative warranty is the one carried by the Cape Horn Integrated Self-Steering System, obviously written by a true sailor: "Each Cape Horn is guaranteed for one circumnavigation, 28,000 miles, or four years against damage done by the sea or the wind." Some manufacturers place a shorter warranty period on bearings, even the best of which are prone to wear. Do not expect any warranty coverage for blocks, double-braided line, or airvanes. As a matter of fact, regard such items as "consumables," and pack spares, especially double-braided polyester line.

You should find a warranty card inserted in the operator's manual with your new vane gear. Complete and return the card soon after you purchase the unit. In addition to your name and address, the card will ask for your vessel's name and state registration number or national documentation number, the vane unit's serial number, and the date of purchase. That information is necessary to identify you as the original owner, a standard proviso for warranty coverage. Scanmar stipulates "warranty photos" of the vane gear installation as a condition to warranty coverage. This practice may seem petty, but if you think about it, photos make good sense. An installation that ends up unintentionally raked, or too low in the water, or improperly reinforced will place undue strain on the whole assembly, resulting in poor performance and a short life span. Photos give engineering staff a chance to verify correct installation before approving the warranty. Scanmar has a reputation for living up to the letter of its warranty, providing quick, cheerful service to its clients in far-flung ports the world over.

Repair

Possessing a warranty printed on an official-looking piece of paper is one thing. Invoking its protective power may be quite another. Before commissioning a new windvane, ask how the builder covers repair situations. Let's face it, some vane gears do occasionally break down, and of course, it will happen at the least opportune moment. The most common causes of failure are frayed or broken steering lines and snapped airvanes, both of which you can replace easily while under sail. In rare cases, a weld breaks or some other structural damage occurs to force the unit out of service until it is repaired. If the gear has suffered a weld failure and you are a long distance from the manufacturer, the repair kit is of no use. So what do you do? Send the entire unit back in a box by airfreight all the way from Zanzibar? Probably not. It is easier, and eminently less expensive for both parties, to take the gear to a nearby welding shop for the necessary repair. You probably will want the builder to reimburse you if damage occurred under

New Vane Gear Checklist

The following questions are a condensation of the major issues in purchasing a new vane gear. This is a proposed list; surely, you will want to ask more questions during your selection process.

1. What type of stern does your vessel have? Canoe? Sugar scoop? Boomkin? Conventional (vertical or slightly raked)?
2. What type of vane gear are you considering, servopendulum, trim tab, or other? Why?
3. Does this model fit your stern and allow for obstacles mounted near the transom? Will the airvane receive unobstructed airflow from all directions?
4. If you prefer a particular windvane model, how heavy is it? Does it fit within the manufacturer's recommended vessel size limits?
5. If you have wheel steering, does the builder offer an optional steering drum to be fitted to the wheel?
6. Of what types of metals is the vane constructed? Are they corrosion-resistant, marine-grade alloys?
7. If dissimilar metals are used, are they separated by appropriate dielectrics, such as nylon or Delrin bushings and washers?
8. If you prefer a servopendulum, can the servo blade be easily raised or removed when not in use?
9. Does the pendulum shaft have a shear pin, breakaway connector, or collapsible tube to protect the unit in case of underwater impact?
10. How long has the manufacturer been in business? Have you learned anything about this company's reputation and its vane gear models from other sailors?
11. What have you learned about this vane gear from other cruisers? Does the model hold up in long periods of heavy weather, or does it have a greater tendency than other gears to break down?
12. Does the manufacturer provide a spare parts kit? If not, is the vendor willing to assemble a kit to be purchased separately?
13. Is the vane gear covered by a warranty? How long is the warranty period? What are its provisions and limitations?
14. Does the vane gear come with an operator's manual, complete with exploded diagrams, a parts list, maintenance and repair instructions, and an explanation of the warranty?
15. Have you asked the builder how you may order spare parts or receive authorization for repair if you are at a great distance from the builder or vendor?

normal operating conditions, but receiving the builder's authorization before proceeding with the repair will make your request a lot easier to process. After sailing off over the horizon, you will sleep more soundly if you have specific instructions on how to arrange warranty repairs. Without an advance agreement, or at least a verbal understanding, there is no guarantee the builder will agree to reimburse repair costs.

Parts Availability

When sizing up a windvane builder, check into its means of supplying spare parts. Most vane gear manufacturers offer an optional repair kit containing replacement parts. Likely candidates for a repair kit are fasteners, bearings, bushings, sheaves, and other items exposed to constant wear and tear. If the vendor does not make a standard kit available and you are planning a major passage, ask the salesperson to recommend a kit selected from the parts list, even if the items are covered by warranty. One big, tyrannical dictator over your cruising life is weather. When it's time to sail, it's time to sail. This fact far outweighs your rights under warranty. Having your own repair parts will save you valuable time down the line, when you otherwise would be calling long-distance from a foreign port trying to arrange shipping and customs clearance.

While you are asking the builder about warranty coverage, inquire about company policy on shipping parts. Does the company pay for airfreight, or will you have to wait until the island trader anchors off your coral patch on its monthly copra run? Life in the South Pacific has two speeds: *slow* and *stop*. Parts in a surface cargo container can take two to three months to arrive at outlying ports, and then longer to reach your particular location. You need to clarify before your voyage exactly how the builder ships parts. Fortunately, DHL, FedEx, and UPS services are available throughout much of the developing world, but in some cases you will have to pick up shipments and walk them through customs at the local airport.

Chapter 5
Vane Gear Specifications

Aries (Denmark/Post-1993) (servopendulum)

Auto-Helm (auxiliary rudder horizontal-vane trim tab)

Cape Horn (servopendulum)

Fleming Global 201 and 301 (servopendulum)

Hydrovane (airvane-powered auxiliary rudder)

Monitor (servopendulum)

Navik (pendulum trim tab)

Sailomat 601 (servopendulum)

Saye's Rig (pendulum trim tab on main rudder)

Windpilot (servopendulum and servopendulum-powered
   auxiliary rudder)

The best way to cover this kind of material is with numbers, illustrations, and brief descriptions. It is beyond the purpose and scope of this book to list every lock washer, bushing, and clevis pin that goes into the assembly of the various models. Each vane gear manufacturer publishes an owner's manual, generally including detailed diagrams, installation options, operator instructions, a parts list, and ordering information for spares. The Manufacturers, Distributors, and Online Services section in the appendix contains contact information for companies cited in this book.

This chapter furnishes you with a general description of each of the ten vane systems selected, including the vertical length of each major section and a list of materials used in constructing each unit. All weights and measurements entered here are as reported by each builder or distributor. Most builders publish metric measurements, so for those Americans and Burmese still on the Imperial system, centimeters have been converted using the equation 0.39 inch = 1 centimeter. Where necessary, weight has been converted using 2.2 pounds = 1 kilogram. In a few cases, measurements of certain components, along with overall length and weight, are totally dependent on custom design. Even a model that comes in one size may vary widely in its tube mounting structure to fit different transom shapes. Therefore, weight is the uninstalled weight, except where indicated. For specific details applying to your vessel, please contact the manufacturer.

For the sake of conciseness, I have selected only one or two models from each company to give you an idea of the builder's product line. The exception was Cape Horn; each of the two basic models is available in an above-decks version with double-braided lines leading straight to the tiller or wheel instead of to the vessel's steering quadrant, as with the below-decks versions. Other manufacturers, including Fleming, Sailomat, and Windpilot, build larger, smaller, or intermediate sizes not listed in this chapter. Most vane gear builders try to capture the widest range of boat size possible with one design, and then perhaps modify the concept where necessary at either end of the spectrum. Exceptions to this rule are the Navik, designed specifically for vessels measuring 30 feet or less from stem to stern, and Saye's Rig, for which there are no standard, published measurements because each vane gear is essentially a one-off design to fit a very large yacht.

Bear in mind that each manufacturer in this field, except Plastimo, is a small firm headed by one or two individuals who typically divide their time between making windvanes and messing around with their own boats. The principals are generally die-hard sailors who always seem to be refining their designs for enhanced performance. At the same time, they need to make enough profit to make the whole operation economically viable. Designs and materials change, and so do the appearance, size, and weight of the vane gears.

Builders do listen to feedback from their clients for design improvements. After all, we're the guinea pigs out there pushing the envelope in extreme weather and daunting sea conditions. If you find a particular weakness in your vane gear, pass the information along to the manufacturer. A dedicated builder keeps a record of accumulated feedback from users and applies the information to new designs, gradually refining the product over time. If you will indulge me yet another digression, this is a dialectical process: thesis, antithesis, and synthesis. The end product is not totally a reflection of our responses to the manufacturer, but a mutual adaptation, or synthesis, between old and new. Or we can take the general systems theory approach: GIGO, or "garbage in, garbage out." Our input helps to get "quality in, quality out."

The prices you encounter were in effect at the time of writing and are, naturally, subject to change. Most builders list prices in U.S. greenbacks, though you may be ordering a unit from Europe, Australia, or Canada. If currency fluctuations are substantial, we can expect U.S. price equivalents to change commensurately. A few sections include summaries of published warranties in cases where they were readily available. I emphasize that the omission of warranty provisions in other cases is by no means a reflection on the builders—manufacturers or distributors will be happy to supply this information.

ARIES (Denmark/Post-1993) (servopendulum)

The Aries windvane has undergone a number of refinements since Peter Matthiesen bought the company from Nick Franklin in 1990. Matthiesen's vane gear is a bit more trim and elegant-looking than the original, but it is still basically the same time-tested design. It still weighs roughly the same, and it has retained the notched-wheel turret that has been the Aries signature since

Under double-reefed sails, a modern Aries makes easy work of beating to weather on *Caroline Torekov*. (Aries Denmark)

Franklin placed his first Aries ad in the August 1968 issue of *Yachting World*. Recommended vessel size limits are 28 to 55 feet LOA, but Franklin installed the unit on vessels up to 60 feet with good results. There is currently only one model of Aries, regardless of vessel size, except in the length of the pendulum shaft. This is acceptable if we compare a windvane's strength to that of an average adult, which is sufficient to steer any size of vessel in most conditions, as long as the vessel is not overcanvased. Any servopendulum system can produce several times the force of a helmsman and maintain that force interminably.

Aries Specifications

CONSTRUCTION
Tubing: Anodized HT30 aluminum
Castings: Stainless die-cast bevel gears and mounting brackets; all other castings are AC5 (LM5) aluminum, some from sand patterns, some die cast
Bearings: Nylon
Solid shafts: 316 stainless
Airvane: Marine plywood
Servo blade: Foam-cored fiberglass

COMPONENT LENGTH, INCHES (CM)
Airvane	46 (117)
Main body	21 (53)
Center mounting tube (diameter)	1.5 (4)
Mounting tube to waterline	43 (109)
Servo blade (length below waterline)	30 (76)

Maximum total length: depends on length of servo shaft

WEIGHT: 75 lb. (35 kg)

COLLISION PROTECTION: Breakaway tube on servopendulum shaft

PRICE: Tiller steering: $2,800; Wheel steering: $3,080

AUTO-HELM
(auxiliary rudder horizontal-vane trim tab)

Scanmar makes its Auto-Helm available to those who cannot fit a Monitor (servopendulum) to their vessels or who are adamant about keeping extra lines out of the cockpit. Circumstances warranting a trim tab and auxiliary rudder include hydraulic steering, excessive play or friction in the vessel's steering, wheel steering with more than four turns, high freeboard, too much weather helm, and a low mizzen boom. Recommended vessel size limit is 45 feet LOA, but the Auto-Helm has been fitted to vessels up to 50 feet. This windvane sys-

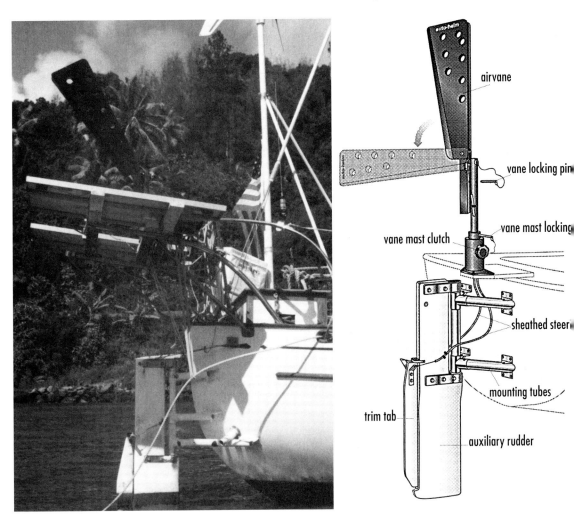

airvane

vane locking pin

vane mast clutch

vane mast locking

sheathed steer

mounting tubes

trim tab

auxiliary rudder

Auto-Helm horizontal-vane trim tab, manufactured by Scanmar. (*Right:* Scanmar)

tem is unique in that it comes in two units, the combined auxiliary rudder and trim-tab assembly and the vane mast, which controls the lower unit from a remote location via Teflon-sheathed stainless cables. The vane mast and connecting hardware may also be purchased separately to fit a transom rudder and an owner-built trim tab. As with many servopendulums, the operator can "reef" the airvane in heavy weather by tipping it down to the horizontal position. The Auto-Helm rudder may also be used as an emergency rudder. An autopilot may be connected to the airvane yoke for motoring or downwind sailing, but the unit's acute sensitivity will probably be sufficient for ghosting in light airs. The sample measurements are for a Fantasia 35.

Auto-Helm Specifications

CONSTRUCTION

Tubing: 316 stainless steel
Bearings: Delrin
Solid shafts: 316 stainless steel
Airvane: Anodized 6061-T6 aluminum
Auxiliary rudder and trim tab: Hand-laid fiberglass filled with closed-cell, high-density polyurethane foam

COMPONENT LENGTH (FOR FANTASIA 35), INCHES (CM)

Airvane   36 (92)
Vane mast   48 (122)
Auxiliary rudder   68 (173)
Note: Vane mast may be shortened for custom fit

WEIGHT (INSTALLED): Without rudder/trim tab, 32 lb. (14.5 kg); rudder/trim tab, buoyant (no significant weight in water)

PRICE: $3,695 (upper unit only: $1,650)

CAPE HORN (servopendulum)

The Cape Horn is a strongly built, stainless steel system available as a permanent, below-decks installation or a removable outboard system. The central mechanism of this line of servopendulum gears is a unique Z rod, replacing bevel gears or ball joints. The Z rod, lying inside the mounting tube, rotates with impulses from the airvane and drives the servopendulum, which in the below-decks models turns a quadrant located inside the lazarette. Double-braided lines run from the quadrant through blocks in the lazarette to jam cleats in the cockpit for instant connect/disconnect and trim. In the outboard models, the servopendulum drives a steering arm connected to the tiller via control lines. The owner installs the mounting tube by cutting a hole through the transom and bonds the two with epoxy and fiberglass. The forward end of the tube is supported by a pair of stainless steel struts bolted up to the deck or down to pads epoxied to the hull. Inventor-founder Yves Gélinas warrants the

Cape Horn Joshua outboard model. The Varuna and Joshua models provide the same Cape Horn steering characteristics in a conventional, outboard version of the Cape Horn. (Cape Horn Marine Products)

Cape Horn Spray below-decks model. The Jean-du-Sud and Spray models are permanently installed with the mounting tube running through the transom. (Cape Horn Marine Products)

Cape Horn for one circumnavigation, 28,000 miles, or four years against damage under normal use. The component lengths listed here are only sample measurements, as they can be modified for custom fit.

Cape Horn Specifications

CONSTRUCTION
Tubing: 316L stainless steel
Steering quadrant: Welded 316L stainless steel
Bushings: Teflon and UHMW polyethylene
Solid shafts: 316L stainless
Airvane: Nylon cloth over stainless wire for standard foil; aluminum for storm foil
Servo-rudder: Teak

DIMENSIONS (LENGTH ONLY), INCHES (CM)	JEAN-DU-SUD AND VARUNA	SPRAY AND JOSHUA
Airvane		
Standard	24 (61)	24 (61)
Storm	17 (42)	17 (42)
Main body	53 (135)	65 (165)
Center mounting tube (diameter)	2.5 (63)	3.25 (83)
Mounting tube to servo blade	13.5 (342)	20.5 (52)
Servo blade	32 (81)	42 (107)
Overall length (with standard foil)	123 (312)	152 (386)

WEIGHT: Jean-du-Sud, 32 lb. (14.5 kg); Spray, 57 lb. (26 kg)

COLLISION PROTECTION: Full swing of pendulum shaft out of water; breakaway servo blade attached by shock cord

PRICE: $2,150 to $2,450

FLEMING GLOBAL 201 AND 301 (servopendulum)

Fleming Global 301 on Cal 30 *Saltaire*. After nearly 20,000 miles of sailing, the Fleming still steers faithfully on all points of sail, through all kinds of weather.

Often accused of being overbuilt, the Fleming servopendulum is a straightforward, no-frills approach to self-steering with no knobs to adjust, no aluminum parts to be lubricated or fussed over, and no dissimilar metals waiting to attack each other. A shiny, new Fleming vane gear is not only attractive, but relatively inexpensive, brutally strong, effective from 8 knots of true wind to a full gale, and lighter than you would expect from an all-stainless windvane. Kevin Fleming, an Aussie who has returned home after many years in San Diego, California, builds his vane gears from duplex stainless castings and thick-walled 316 stainless mounting tubes, rendering the machines virtually indestructible. So confident is Fleming of his products, he covers the machines with a ten-year warranty against defective materials and workmanship and a five-year warranty on bearings. The Global 201 and 301 both use a pair of bevel gears with an adjustable thrust bearing. Fleming also offers an optional emergency rudder, which is assembled onto the servo blade and operated with the pendulum shaft lashed. Fleming gears come in five sizes, covering a boat size range from under 30 feet to 65 feet LOA.

Fleming Global 201 and 301 Specifications

CONSTRUCTION

Tubing: 316L stainless steel
Castings: 2205 and 17-4 PH stainless steel alloys
Bearings: Stainless steel rollers and Delrin ball bearings
Bushings: Delrin
Solid shafts: 316L stainless steel (Global 201: $^3/_4$ inch;
   Global 301: $^7/_8$ inch)
Airvane: 4 mm thick aluminum or marine-grade birch plywood
Servo blade: 316L stainless, 18-gauge sheet bent over solid rod and tube

COMPONENT LENGTH, INCHES (CM)	GLOBAL 201	GLOBAL 301
Airvane		
Standard	32 (81)	32 (81)
Storm	24.5 (62)	24.5 (62)
Main body	31 (76)	31 (76)
Center mounting tube (diameter)	$1^1/_8$ (3.2)	$1^1/_8$ (3.2)
Mounting tube to rudder	16 (41)	22 (54)
Rudder and shaft	30 (76)	34 (83)
Overall length (with standard foil)	109 (277)	119 (294)

WEIGHT: Global 201, 40 lb. (18 kg); Global 301, 43 lb. (20 kg)

COLLISION PROTECTION: Shear pin for fore-and-aft protection; full swing of pendulum shaft out of water

PRICE: Starting from $1,900

HYDROVANE
(airvane-powered auxiliary rudder)

This is a unique design, achieved by some brilliantly simple engineering that harnesses the direct force of the wind to power an auxiliary rudder. The secret is a specially balanced rudder that responds easily to impulses from the airvane. Unlike experiments with airvane-controlled steering a century ago, the Hydrovane gets its power from a particularly long horizontal-axis airvane. The operator sets a controller at one of three settings, then inclines the airvane to

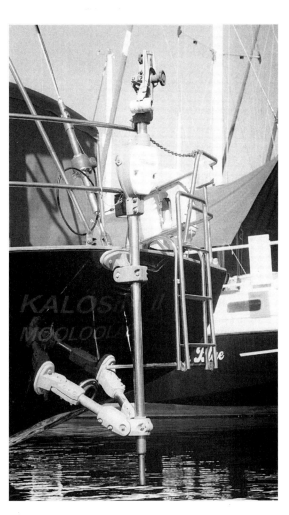

Close-up of Hydrovane transmission with string loop for remote course steering. (Hydrovane)

Hydrovane mounted on stern of 45-foot vessel. The airvane is stored below when not in use.

compensate for changing wind strength, thereby modifying the vane's leverage on the rudder. In case of main rudder failure, the Hydrovane doubles as an emergency rudder. The builder recommends this sleekly designed vane gear for any sailing vessel up to 20 tons or 50 feet LOA. Designer and founder Derek Daniels recently sold the company to Karen and John Curry, who handle marketing and customer relations from their Vancouver, British Columbia, office. Production manager Geoffrey Town, who personally has assembled each of the 4,000 units from Hydrovane's inception, still oversees the small factory in Nottingham, England. Hydrovane also provides a rebuild service for older, worn units.

Hydrovane Specifications

CONSTRUCTION

Tubing: 316 (EN58J) stainless
Castings: LM5 anodized aluminum alloy and silicon bronze
Bearings and washers: Delrin bearings; nylon ball race on rudder shaft; Teflon washers
Solid shafts: 316 (EN58J) stainless
Airvane: Reinforced nylon cloth on anodized alloy tube frame
Auxiliary rudder: Cast nylon

COMPONENT LENGTH,

INCHES (CM)	SMALLEST	LARGEST
Airvane	56.5 (144)	56.5 (144)
Main body	25.5 (65)	25.5 (65)
Rudder and shaft assembly	64.5 (164)	93.5 (238)
Overall length	146.5 (372)	175.5 (446)

WEIGHT: Ranges from 96 to 135 lb. (43.5 to 61.5 kg)

PRICE: $3,990 to $4,550, depending on mounting brackets

MONITOR (servopendulum)

The Monitor, manufactured by Scanmar International of Sausalito, California, is one of the best-selling vane gears on the market. Its light stainless steel construction and one-size-fits-all design make it popular with many yachties. The Monitor uses a pair of cast bevel gears, and depends on welded, thin-walled tube framing and a floating servo blade to achieve its low weight. The operator adjusts the yoke by pulling a control line connected to a sheave, chain, and reduction gear sprocket for infinite course control. This method prevents accidental airvane rotation. Scanmar also markets the Monitor Emergency Rudder (MRUD) and the SOS Rudder, a separately installed emergency rudder that mounts onto its own transom brackets when needed. The Monitor plainly reflects the philosophy of CEO Hans Bernwall from the point of view of both

Monitor on Westsail Fair Weather 39. The servo blade on this Monitor, which has steered through many thousands of miles of offshore sailing, is kept in like-new condition by staying in the raised position when not used. (Jack Dunn)

manufacturer and sailor: "I don't want anything on the boat I can't fix myself or can live without." Bernwall backs up his servopendulum with a three-year warranty against defective materials and workmanship. Monitor owners with whom I have spoken agree that Scanmar gives great care to its clients, responding quickly with advice and parts wherever there is a pay phone and an international airport.

Monitor Specifications

CONSTRUCTION
Tubing: 316L stainless
Castings: 316L stainless
Bearings: Delrin
Solid shafts: 316L stainless
Airvane: Birch plywood for standard vane; plastic sandwich for light-air
    vane
Servo blade: High-lift profile; 316L stainless steel sheet filled with
    closed-cell polyurethane foam

COMPONENT LENGTH, INCHES (CM)
Airvane
    Standard   37 (94)
    Light air   45 (114)
    Mizzen (optional)   26 (66)
Main body   24 (61)
Servo blade only   24 (61)
Overall length: varies, depending on mounting tubes

WEIGHT: 53 lb. (24 kg)

COLLISION PROTECTION: Quick-release connector on pendulum shaft

PRICE: $3,395 (steering connection package sold separately)

NAVIK (pendulum trim tab)

The Navik, manufactured by Plastimo, weighs only 30 pounds but generates surprisingly powerful steerage.

This amazing, lightweight gear, built by Plastimo of France, is popular among owners of boats measuring 30 feet LOA or less. However, Guy Bernardin chose a Navik for his 38-foot entry in the 1982 BOC single-handed around the world race. The Navik is a unique design combining the light-air sensitivity of a trim tab with the steering power of a servopendulum. Another distinguishing feature is the extensive use of injection-molded polycarbonate plastic, even in the gearing mechanism components, making the unit extremely light. Heliarc-welded stainless steel comprises the frame, supports, vane mast, and rudder shaft. The Navik is available in North America through Scanmar International, and in Australia from Harken.

Navik Specifications

CONSTRUCTION
Tubing: Heliarc-welded 304 stainless
Castings: Injection-molded Lexan
Bushings and sleeves: Delrin
Solid shafts: Injection-molded Lexan
Steering quadrant: Teak
Airvane: Injection-molded Lexan linkage
Servo blade: 304 stainless shaft with injection-molded Lexan blade

COMPONENT LENGTH, INCHES (CM)

Top of airvane to mounting bracket	56 (140)
Mounting bracket to bottom of servo blade	56 (140)
Overall length	112 (280)

WEIGHT: 30 lb. (13.6 kg)

COLLISION PROTECTION: Quick-release connector on pendulum shaft

PRICE: $1,995 (Scanmar International)

SAILOMAT 601 (servopendulum)

The Sailomat is one of the few truly unique design concepts to occur in the field of vane gear design since Hasler's and Gianoli's prototypes of the early 1960s. If you see a vintage Sailomat from dockside, you may wonder at first why the rig has three appendages. The original 3040 design had its own auxiliary rudder, along with the airvane and servopendulum, all geared together, eliminating steering lines. Stellan Knöös, who founded Sailomat in 1974, changed the design in recent years, eliminating the auxiliary rudder but retaining the raked servo blade. Operation of the modern system is essentially the same as for other servopendulums. The modern 536 and 601 systems use "patented spherical-joint systems," rather than common bevel gears for the airvane-to-servo blade linkage. The central framing and mounting base for current Sailomat systems are made of light alloy castings. Airvane and pendulum shaft "tubing," to use the term loosely, is not tubing in a strict sense, but extruded, thick-walled, anodized, marine-grade aluminum. The mounting base makes a relatively small footprint, 170 mm high and 300 mm wide (approximately 7 by 12 inches). The raked servo arm accommodates sugar-scoop transoms, swim ladders, and off-center mounting—up to 400 mm, or nearly 16 inches, from the centerline. Seven sizes of this model cover boat lengths from 23 to 65 feet LOA.

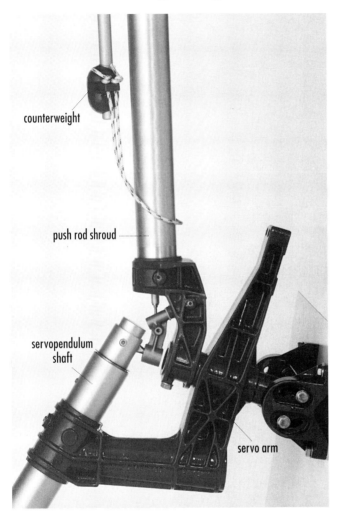

counterweight

push rod shroud

servopendulum shaft

servo arm

Close-up of Sailomat 601. The Sailomat employs "patented spherical-joint systems" to transmit the airvane's impulses to the servopendulum shaft and blade. (Sailomat)

Sailomat 601 Specifications

CONSTRUCTION

Tube extrusions: Anodized, marine-grade aluminum alloy
Servo blade shaft and pendulum shaft: Aluminum 6082 T6
Castings: Marine-grade aluminum alloy for main sections; bronze for
  other castings
Bearings: Composite plastic
Fasteners: 316 stainless, including Helicoils in castings
Airvane: Polycarbonate plastic
Servo blade: NACA 0012 profile; aluminum alloy extrusion

COMPONENT LENGTH, INCHES (CM)

Airvane	
Standard	39 (100)
Light air	45 (115)
Storm	31 (80)
Mast tube length	depends on vessel requirements
Mounting base	7 (17)
Servo blade and shaft	depends on vessel requirements
Overall length	
Minimum	110 (280)
Maximum	150 (380)

WEIGHT: Ranges from 51 to 64 lb. (23 to 26 kg), depending on custom size

COLLISION PROTECTION: Raked servopendulum shaft with collapsible tube;
full swing of pendulum out of water

PRICE: From $3,400, depending on options

SAYE'S RIG
(pendulum trim tab on main rudder)

Saye's Rig on Sampson C-Breeze 50. (Scanmar)

This is one gear you won't see everyday, even though it has been in production for thirty years and has made numerous circumnavigations. Saye's Rig, invented by Roland Saye and now manufactured by Scanmar International, operates as both a servopendulum and a trim tab, connected directly to the vessel's main rudder by a long, U-shaped stainless pipe. A particularly interesting feature of this gear is the vertical-axis, wedge-shaped airvane, which gives the vane broader wind-sensing range. Measurements are tailored to fit the requirements of very large sailing vessels with widely varying stern configurations. Hans Bernwall points out that most of the installations have been on boats with hydraulic steering, which usually does not allow a servopendulum system. Here you will find measurements for a Sampson C-Breeze 50 as an example. Saye's Rig is intended for vessels approximately 50 to 65 feet LOA and can easily accommodate high freeboard, transom davits, a boomkin, a mizzen boom, or a transom-mounted swim ladder. In addition, it can be controlled by an autopilot. This system carries a one-year warranty against defective materials and workmanship.

Saye's Rig Specifications

CONSTRUCTION
Tubing: 316L schedule 40 stainless steel pipe
Castings: Bronze
Bearings: Torlon
Solid shafts: 316L stainless
Airvane: Synthetic fabric on stainless steel tube framing
Trim tab: Solid fiberglass

COMPONENT LENGTH (FOR SAMPSON C-BREEZE 50), INCHES (CM)

Airvane mast	72 (183)
Trim tab and shaft	60 (152)
Tiller arm	120 (305)
Overall length	132 (335)

WEIGHT: Depends on customized size and installation

PRICE: $2,895 (rudder/tiller assembly ranges from $350 to $550)

WINDPILOT
(servopendulum and servopendulum-powered auxiliary rudder)

The Windpilot was first designed by John Adams and entered production in 1968. Peter Förthmann, who took over the operation in 1976 and also published his own book on windvane steering, now manufactures the Windpilot product line in Hamburg, Germany. The Pacific Plus I, for boats under 40 feet

The Pacific Light, for boats under 30 feet LOA.
(Windpilot)

The Pacific Plus I "double rudder" system, for boats under 40 feet LOA. (Windpilot)

LOA, and the Pacific Plus II, for boats under 60 feet LOA, combine a servopendulum with an auxiliary rudder, eliminating steering lines from the deck. Windpilot also makes available two conventional servopendulums: the Pacific, for boats under 60 feet LOA, and the Pacific Light, for boats under 30 feet LOA. A unique and highly convenient engineering feature of the Pacific Plus is a "quick-in, quick-out" lever for the easy engaging and disengaging of bevel gears between the pendulum and auxiliary rudder. In addition, the Pacific and the Pacific Plus both come with a pin fitting that accepts an Autohelm or Simrad tiller pilot.

Windpilot Specifications

CONSTRUCTION
Tubing: Marine-grade aluminum
Castings: Die-cast AlMg5 aluminum
Linkages: Machined silicon aluminum bronze
Bearings: POM and PTFE
Solid shafts: Marine-grade aluminum
Airvane: 6 mm marine plywood
Servo blade: Epoxied western hemlock
Auxiliary rudder (Pacific Plus): Polyethylene skin and PE foam filling
  with stainless shaft

COMPONENT LENGTH: Component lengths on all Windpilot models are dependent on specific vessel requirements (each model is available in eight different shaft lengths); contact the manufacturer for details

WEIGHT: Pacific Light, 28 lb. (13 kg); Pacific, 44 lb. (20 kg); Pacific Plus I, 100 lb. (45 kg); Pacific Plus II, 110 lb. (50 kg)
(Note: Buoyant auxiliary rudder yields lighter net weight in water)

COLLISION PROTECTION: Full swing of pendulum shaft out of water; servo blade hinged for fore-and-aft protection

PRICE: Pacific Light, $1,700; Pacific, $2,700; Pacific Plus I, $4,400; Pacific Plus II, $4,900

Chapter 6

Purchasing a Used Vane Gear

One way to save money on a windvane is to buy a previously loved unit. That is, if you can find one! When someone sells a boat, one of the things the owner might remove from the vessel, along with books, binoculars, and other personal gear, is the vane gear, destined for either another vessel or a quick sale to raise badly needed funds for some other noble enterprise—like eating. Generally, the vane gear raises a boat's value, particularly among potential blue-water sailors. But every now and then, either someone who has sold a cruising vessel, or someone who has bought one with a vane gear but has no intentions of cruising, puts a used vane gear on the market. A handwritten notice on the yacht club bulletin board generally guarantees a quick sale if there are members outfitting a boat for an extended cruise. If not, the seller must go beyond the circle of yacht cronies to reach potential buyers.

On the other side of the equation is you, the skipper who aims to save anywhere from $1,000 to $3,000 on a vane gear. If the unit was built by a reputable company and has not been damaged, it will probably serve you as well as a new vane gear. You may need to replace bearings, and you probably will need to cut new stainless steel or aluminum mounting tubes to make a perfect match between your vessel and the vane gear, but these are trivial matters. One more thing: you might need to cut a couple of airvanes out of $1/8$-inch marine plywood (see chapter 11), since these are expendable items not included usually with the purchase of a used windvane. For less than a hundred dollars, which includes the price of a cheap hacksaw and a bottle of stainless steel polish, you should have everything you need to spruce up the gear and mount it securely to your vessel's transom. This is barring broken or missing parts, which you will have to order from the manufacturer, or in the worst-case scenario, fabricate on your

A vintage Aries, built by Nick Franklin in the United Kingdom.

own. In most cases, the unit is complete; if there are pieces broken or missing, the seller will probably know how to locate and order the parts.

Selecting a used vane gear invokes most of the same issues as buying a new vane. In addition to age and wear and tear, parts availability and technical support will tend to be more immediate concerns. Bargaining with the seller is a lot easier if you know what you are looking for, and are aware of what you could be getting into if you buy the wrong unit. The checklist at the end of this chapter is a companion to the one on page 72. Your acquisition must meet transom and space constraints, match the vessel's size and weight, and fulfill whatever other requirements you impose on likely candidates. Once you have found a vane gear that meets the parameters you have established, bargaining for a mutually acceptable price should be a straightforward matter.

WHERE TO LOCATE USED VANE GEARS

As with most consumer items in a laissez-faire economy, there are many ways to locate a used windvane. Cruiser swap meets, nautical publications, the Internet, and the marina bulletin board are effective means of bringing seller and buyer together. Oddly, one place where you will not find many used vane gears is a used boat gear shop. Now and then, one will pop up, but the price is usually higher because of the consignment fees paid to the shop owner. For some reason, most sellers of vane gears prefer to sell the units on their own, opting instead for the lower fees charged by marine rags and swap meet promoters. Perhaps this is because, of all the high-ticket items a skipper has left over after a decade or two of cruising, the vane gear is the only piece of equipment still functioning like new and guaranteeing a significantly longer duty life. A thoroughly used autopilot, radio direction finder, Loran-C, refrigerator, stove, GPS, SSB, radar, or bag of sails has little value. Poke around your local used boat junk shop and take a look for yourself. The skipper, well aware of the vane gear's resale value, sees little reason for handing over 10 to 20 percent of the sale price to the chandler.

Cruiser Swap Meets

A couple of months before the start of each cruising season, the coastal sailing meccas of North America blossom with cruiser swap meets. In southern California, most of the swap meets occur in early fall, two or three weeks before the Baja Ha Ha, which is scheduled for the end of October. Similar gatherings are held in early spring for local sailors and for the stragglers who missed the opening of cruising season in the fall and want to make a quick run for the South Pacific before hurricane season starts in the northern tropics. Sponsors include marinas, yacht clubs, and, in at least one case, a major vendor of used marine hardware. Catalina Island, lying 20 miles from Los Angeles Harbor, invites marine equipment suppliers to give free seminars on inflatable lifeboats, first-aid kits, diesel fuel filters, HF and SSB radios, sails, and other cruising paraphernalia. These gatherings are great places to network and exchange cruising cards (listing crew names, vessel name, call sign, etc.) with other blue-water sailors.

Get there early—swap meets usually open at six o'clock on a weekend morning. You might find someone selling an old Aries or Monitor that will fit your boat well with some new mounting tubes cut to fit the transom. If you are unsure about some aspect of the unit, ask a few people standing around what they know about the particular brand, size, and condition of the unit. Do not be shy, and do not feel as if you are being obnoxious. The windvane is a vital part of your boat's essential systems, ranking in importance immediately below the rudder, mast, stays, shrouds, and sails. While you inspect the unit, refer to chapter 5 and other portions of this book, which you thoughtfully stuffed into your knapsack, along with sandwiches and a thermos of coffee, having anticipated a long morning of equipment hunting and haggling.

The year before starting my extended cruise on *Saltaire*, I visited a few cruiser swap meets to look for used anchors, fishing tackle, nautical books, and a vane gear. At Minney's Cruiser Swap Meet in Newport Beach I stumbled across an old Aries, for which the seller demanded $1,000, not a penny less. I offered him a $300 deposit and promised him the other $700 later in the morning. It was a simple matter of making a quick run to an ATM for some extra cash. As he was about to respond, another gentleman—actually, I had another name for him—jumped in front of me, whipped out ten $100 bills from his pocket, and walked off with the vane gear. The seller looked at me apologetically and stuck the loot in his wallet. "Sorry, buddy," he shrugged. Another case of raw capitalism.

This 1980s-era Fleming Major steered Don and Joy Lloyd's 32-foot steel sloop *Anita* (Melbourne) around the world.

Minney's biannual swap meet, by the way, is quite an affair. The event, a carnival-like gathering of sellers, buyers, and curious "looky-loos," beckons every type of sailor and nautical eccentric imaginable. Ernie Minney is a well-known, colorful character on the West Coast cruising circuit, operating what must be one of the largest used boat gear stores on the planet, Minney's Yacht Surplus in Costa Mesa. Having completed a six-year circumnavigation earlier in life, Ernie hosts a free cruiser barbecue every October, and gives away door prizes of books and boat gear, not to mention loads of advice to novice cruisers. His website lists hundreds of used sails, and he ships merchandise to sailors around the world. When sailors cannot sell their merchandise at the swap meet, Ernie sometimes shoves a few bucks into their hands and drags the gear over to his own shop, where he sells the stuff dirt cheap. If you are starting your cruise from anywhere along the west coast of North America, you are absolutely nuts if you miss this major cruising event. Check your local sailing periodicals for details on nautical flea markets and swap meets in your region.

Nautical Classified Ads

A sure place to find used vane gears for sale is in the classified ads of boat magazines and nautical newspapers. Another place is in the "boat equipment" section of your local community newspaper if you live near the ocean. Posing specific questions over the telephone can be a difficult chore, made more frustrating if the person on the line is unfamiliar with the apparatus or is witnessing the ignominious defeat of a favored football team on ESPN.

"Rrrring."

"Yeah, whuddaya want!"

"Uh, I noticed your ad for a wind . . . "

"Yeah, yeah, it's my mom and dad's, it's out back in the garage, and I don't know squat about sailing stuff. Sorry, gotta get back to my game."

"Yes, well, perhaps you could tell me if all the parts are there."

"Look, I told you I don't know. Why don't you just come over here and take a look at it yourself?"

"OK, where do you live?"

Pierre Bieri slips the auxiliary rudder onto his Sailomat 3040 in preparation for a sail from Queensland to New Caledonia aboard 45-foot *Panacea*.

"Geez! We live at [too fast to write down], so we'll see ya later."

"Click."

The only part of the address you got was the city, 200 miles away. Do you risk making the trip to meet some disagreeable person who knows nothing about the vane gear, which may or may not be complete? If there are no other used windvanes in your area, and the price is irresistible, the answer is yes! Call the next day, get the right address, and visit as soon as you can. Indifference will have transformed itself into effusive hospitality as the sellers' progeny desperately looks for money to pay off a football game bet. As long as the person collecting the money is a legal adult, enjoy the bargain! You now own a vane gear!

As a general rule, there is a strong correlation between prices of used items and prices paid for advertising. Magazines charge more for advertising because each issue lies on the coffee table a whole month or even longer, while a weekly tabloid has a life span of only two or three days. An example is the *Log* newspaper, found in every yacht club, marina office, sailor dive, and boat cabin from Santa Barbara to San Diego. As a matter of fact, I found *Saltaire* in the *Log*. I paid so little, I am too embarrassed to put it in writing. The paper routinely carries ads for all sorts of used boat gear at very competitive prices; windvanes are often listed at under $1,000. In a magazine, the seller pays more money for the ad, and thus normally demands a higher price for the equipment advertised. Obviously in less of a hurry, the seller waits patiently for a serious, qualified buyer who does not mind paying a bit more for good quality. The upshot is the likelihood of a vane gear that has received lots of TLC during its tenure on the seller's yacht.

The Sailomat 3040 ready to go.

Internet

As part of your search, you may wish to surf the Internet for a used vane gear. E-bay and other online services are likely places to find a unit. Some chandlers advertise new and used items in their online catalogs, and a few nautical publications have online versions with classified ads, such as the Classy Classifieds in *Latitude 38*. It is also possible to buy online through such services as AuctionSail. The one obvious problem with buying online is your inability to see merchandise before buying it. After having paid another small fortune for shipping, you might end up with an incomplete or even severely damaged machine. You place your trust in the seller to send the item in the advertised condition after you have kissed your money good-bye. If the seller is a private individual, you could be taking an undue risk, ending up with nothing at all—in such cases, protect yourself by using an online payment service, such as PayPal, which will hold monies in escrow until you have inspected the goods and approved payment. To put it plainly, there is no substitute for seeing and running your hands over such a vital piece of equipment as a vane gear before laying down a large sum of cash.

Marinas and Yacht Clubs

I have already mentioned marinas and yacht clubs as sources of used boat gear, but the matter deserves a few more words. Your fellow yachties are infinite sources of wisdom, garnered from untold years of combined experience. I learn important new lessons about boat gear and the art of sailing from other mariners in virtually every anchorage and marina I visit. At times I am shocked by what I don't know. Before you start looking beyond the marina gate for a vane gear, inquire among your friends. If you are long on dreams but short on money, someone may have a line on an inexpensive, used windvane from one individual and access to parts from someone else. This is not meant to insult your intelligence. It is just that many new cruisers unnecessarily spend a lot of money on things that do not work or do not meet their needs adequately as they climb the learning curve. Invariably, all they had to do was ask. That gruff, weather-beaten, old sailor sipping vodka from a broken coffee mug on a Tuesday morning may have the answers you need. Take the time to ask and listen. Glean what others have learned about self-steering gears, taking everything with a grain of salt rather than jumping to quick conclusions.

Naturally, you already have checked the notices on the marina bulletin board and called the used vane gear sellers, if any. Spend some time walking around the local marinas, learning about self-steering systems and putting out word that you are looking for a used system. Posting a "wanted" notice on the marina bulletin board and handing out small cards or flyers to sailors no longer using their vane gears are effective ways to drum up responses. Finally, well-established marinas and yacht clubs commonly publish a monthly newsletter, a great place to post an ad with the alluring title, "Wanted: windvane steering gear." If the newsletter is mailed to boatowners' homes, inactive sailors will also have a chance to respond. Happy hunting!

WHAT TO LOOK FOR

Matching a Unit to Your Vessel

Once you have found a unit that seems appropriate for your vessel, make certain the gear is the right size for your boat. If your vessel's LOA and the boat LOA of the seller are in the same size range, chances are the unit will fit well. The average size for offshore cruising yachts, despite what you read in the mainstream sailing magazines, is roughly 30 to 40 feet LOA. A six-pack of Coronas says the top of the bell curve is 35 feet, give or take a foot. Knowing this, vane gear builders target their designs for that range of boat size, although the models may actually fit a wider range, say 27 to 50 feet LOA. Another thing to consider is that many of the vane gears on the market were built in the 1970s, when cruising boats were smaller, averaging closer to 30 feet LOA. The new self-steering product lines cater to a much wider range of boat size than before in order to keep pace with the increase in cruising boat size. One can expect the 1970s-era windvanes to be good for vessels under 50 feet LOA and ideal for boats 28 to 40 feet LOA. The Aries and the Monitor are, and always have been, designed for boats in the 28- to 55-foot range. The older Flemings, ubiquitous in their native Australia, are generally found on boats measuring 28 to 45 feet, though the newer models cover a wider size range.

Other than size, you will need to verify the vane gear's adaptability to your vessel's transom. Refer to chapters 4 and 5 to get an idea of what will and will not fit. Constraints could be a boomkin, a low mizzen boom, solar panels, a low radar dome, or a cluttered equipment arch looming over the rear deck. Different vane gears have unique ways of accommodating such obstructions. You need only to identify which models and mounting strategies promise satisfaction, given your vessel's stern configuration and obstacles.

Common Problems with Used or Discontinued Vane Gears

- Missing or broken parts, possibly not available from manufacturer or distributor
- Possible unseen damage, such as hairline cracks in light-gauge stainless steel tubing
- Missing documentation, such as owner's manual
- If discontinued, possible lack of technical support, parts, and documentation from manufacturer
- Lack of warranty coverage

Price

In the United States, the going price for used vane gears in good condition currently ranges from approximately $700 to $1,500. Variables affecting price are the manufacturer, model, age, and condition of the unit, plus the seller's geographic region. The older the windvane, the more difficult it is to source replacement parts. A recent version of the vane gear may still be in production, but some pieces of the vintage models may have been discontinued. To ensure the machine is complete, first refer to chapter 5 of this book or to the builder's website for an idea of the vane's overall appearance. Also compare the unit with the diagrams and photographs in the owner's manual, if it is handy. The presence of an owner's manual is, in itself, a good indicator of a unit's completeness and of the kind of treatment it has received. A skipper who meticulously stores operators' manuals in waterproof folders is more likely to take care of everything else on the vessel as well. The manual will show specific sheaves, bearings, bushings, fasteners, washers, circlips, etc., all of which need to be in place for the unit to be "complete." An incomplete unit is not necessarily a reason not to purchase; being aware of the missing hardware puts you in a better position to bargain for a lower price.

Price is also a function of the seller's geographic region, which probably will be your general region, too, unless you are willing to pay for shipping. For example, prices on boats and marine gear in the Pacific Northwest and southern Florida, for reasons I have never fully understood, are significantly higher than in the Los Angeles area. Prices in the San Francisco Bay Area and San Diego are somewhere in between. If you are in Australia or New Zealand, favorable exchange rates could yield a nice bargain if you are carrying U.S. dollars, British pounds, or Euros. On the other hand, shortages of sailboats and sailing gear in general keep Australian prices on those items high, even after allowing for currency exchange.

Condition and Repairability

During your prepurchase inspection of the unit, jot down a quick list of things that appear to be missing or damaged. This is especially important if you have the luxury of choosing between two or more used vane gears. Is the unit missing a major component, such as a casting for a vane turret or a ball joint linkage? Expect those items, if they exist, to be quite dear. Are there mounting brackets for the tubes connecting the unit to the transom? Do not worry about the tubes themselves; there is a chance that you can recut them for your vessel, but don't count on it. Aries mounting tubes are thick-walled anodized aluminum, so you will want to reuse them if possible, but even they can be replaced if necessary. Do you see any solid shafts extending from larger tubes? Try rotating and shaking the shafts to see if they are frozen or have too much play. A frozen shaft might need new stainless bearings and races, or perhaps just some cleaning and lubrication. Verify that any resistance to rotation is not due to a bent shaft. A loose shaft might need new Delrin or Teflon bearings; the old races may be reusable if they are not cracked. Is there a broken or cracked weld? A MIG welder can easily restore a stainless joint to like-new condition, but find out what conditions led to the damage. Breakage under normal operating conditions could indicate a poorly designed vane gear and the likelihood of repeated failure.

Parts Availability

Each vane gear model is comprised of both standard and custom-made parts. "Standard" does not always mean "easy to find." Injection-molded polymer hardware, especially bearings, races, and bushings, may demand a vigorous search among some specialty fastener suppliers, but you will find them. Brass, silicon bronze, and stainless fasteners are available at virtually any chandlery or neighborhood hardware store. Bolts over $^3/_8$ inch in diameter may require a little extra driving around town, but they are readily available in silicon bronze and 304, 316, and 18/8 stainless steel. You will also find circlips, loose ball bearings, and oversized washers in marine-grade alloys.

If the windvane is missing castings or custom-machined parts, you will need to purchase them from the manufacturer or from a designated parts distributor. Your only alternative is to fabricate the parts as closely as possible to their original specifications. The cost and time required to build a pattern and cast the alloy in marine-grade stainless, bronze, or aluminum is probably not worth the money you save on the purchase price of the vane. On the other hand, producing a one-off part on a lathe or milling machine is a far less complicated matter. Machining is a quick, cost-effective means of producing nonstandard bushings and various small parts that would normally be cast, such as linkages and thrust bearings.

DISCONTINUED MODELS

Vane gears no longer in production can pose some special challenges, to say the least. If it is merely a phased-out model from an extant manufacturer, as in the case of a Sailomat 3040 or a Fleming Major, the obvious solution to locating an owner's manual or spare parts is to contact the builder. Even if an original of the manual is no longer available, the company can no doubt send you a photocopy. In addition, you can expect the builder to send you a complete parts list with current prices and ordering instructions. If you have found an old Atom's Rig, RVG, Gunning, or other vane gear that has fallen into obscurity, you will

Frank and Kaye Pearce of Sydney sort out the pieces of a discontinued RVG trim-tab unit they picked up for a bargain.

have to be a bit more diligent in your search for a manual and spare parts. The Internet is a wonderful source of detailed technical information on vane gears. Dedicated fans of an obsolete vane gear model might have an online owners' group, which could be an extremely valuable source of the kind of information not published by businesses. One such group exists for owners of the discontinued RVG trim-tab vane gear. Owners of both discontinued and currently manufactured vane gears will tend to be straightforward about design flaws and questionable fabrication methods, and may offer advice on solving technical problems.

Though important, the absence of a manual does not automatically disqualify the vane gear from a meritorious career on your vessel's transom. Before you decide that a discontinued windvane is not worth the hassle, check around the marina to see if anyone has the same model. If no one else nearby has a similar machine, or if another owner does not possess an owner's manual, you may be getting in over your head. Then again, the vane gear's shortcomings may have fairly clear repair solutions. As far as operating the windvane is concerned, chapter 2 explains how the unit functions in principle, and chapter 8 tells you how to sail with the unit, be it a trim tab, a servopendulum, or some combination of those basic forms of self-steering. Of course, each model has its own method of operation. At a price of perhaps one or two hundred dollars, the mysterious vane gear may be worth the trouble of repairing the unit and discovering how it works. From time to time, you will stumble across a home-built trim-tab windvane, knocked together by some quixotic dreamer with a stick welder, some mild-steel tubing, and a pile of coat hangers for welding rods. Who knows? You might find one properly designed for a boat roughly the same size as yours and fabricated in a professional manner. The odds weigh heavily against that possibility. It is best not to accept a homebuilt windvane, not even as a gift, unless you have sailed with the vane gear and are satisfied with its operation. If you want a homebuilt unit, you can build it yourself with equal or better results.

A particularly frustrating hypothetical situation would be to purchase a windvane built by a now-defunct business, only to discover that the machine lacks an important doohickey between this thing here and that thing there. What is it? Who knows? Let us hope you didn't buy the mysterious machine in the first place. If your senses tell you it is a good unit for the price, and your mechanical intuition suggests the missing part is not a major obstacle, you may have found yourself a bargain. Some experience in a machine shop will go a long way in producing or supervising the fabrication of any missing parts. Though exploded diagrams do not list measurements to high-precision tolerances, the information you glean from an operator's manual or even from sketches in old advertising literature will guide you in the right direction. Your willingness to experiment with machine tools, welding, and perhaps a bit of pattern making and sand molding could yield workable results. Machine shops and small foundries are accustomed to taking on small jobs from inventors and hobbyists. The artisans take pride in their work and often enjoy sharing the finer points of their crafts with clients and curious visitors.

This is all hypothetical, of course. All the builders featured in chapter 5 were still in business at the time of this writing, most of them having entered the industry in the late 1960s or early 1970s. Other reputable builders also exist, but for the sake of concision were not included in this volume. What of other builders, no longer in existence, having left in their wake engineering marvels composed of high-quality materials? The absence of technical support and spare parts will be at times frustrating, but perhaps a worthwhile sacrifice if the vane gear looks promising. It's your call.

Used Vane Gear Checklist

Use this list in tandem with the New Vane Gear Checklist on page 72. Most of the topics we covered with respect to new vane gears apply equally to used vanes. A used piece of equipment naturally raises questions about wear and tear, parts availability, and the possibility of having to fabricate new sections for the unit. Do not expect the former owner of your vane gear to help you ferret out these issues after you have gratified that person with your hard-earned money. Armed with answers to both lists of questions, you will have a fairly good idea of the windvane's potential as a future crew member aboard your vessel. At the risk of belaboring the point, it is better to spend a bit more for a well-designed, solidly built unit than to wind up bemoaning a piece of junk you acquired for next to nothing.

1. Is the windvane from an established builder, or is it homebuilt? What company manufactured it? Does the company still exist?

2. What have you learned about the builder's reputation? Does the builder produce a reliable vane gear and wholeheartedly support its customers when they encounter problems with their units?

3. Does the vane gear meet the standards proposed in questions 1 and 3 to 9 of the New Vane Gear Checklist on page 72?

4. How old is the vane gear? If the owner is uncertain and the company still exists, jot down the serial number and ascertain the unit's age by contacting the manufacturer.

5. Has the builder discontinued this model? If so, what changes or improvements have occurred, and why? If the company still exists, this should be easy to determine and certainly worth your time if you suspect the unit was discontinued because of faulty design or manufacturing techniques.

6. Why is the unit for sale? Has the owner acquired a vessel too large or too small for the vane gear, or is the individual retiring from cruising altogether, reverting to hand steering or an autopilot for sailing in local waters?

7. Do you sense that the owner has been satisfied with the vane gear's performance? Thumbs up for "It's fantastic!" Thumbs down for "Uh, it's OK, I guess."

8. Has the owner used the windvane for an extended ocean cruise? Was the unit limited in terms of the wind strength and sea state it could handle? The vane gear should be able to handle more than a human can bear at the helm.

9. What is the general condition of the windvane? Do you see any broken welds, collision damage, or serious corrosion?

10. Did the owner ever have to repair the vane gear? What was the nature of the damage, and under what circumstances did it occur? How was the damage repaired?

11. If you see damage or corrosion, is it confined to one replaceable section, or does it affect a large portion of the vane gear?

12. Attempt to manipulate all the moving parts you see on the vane. Try to rotate the vane turret 360 degrees. If the unit is a servo-rudder system, swing the pendulum shaft through its full vertical and horizontal arcs. Do you feel excessive resistance or play in the movement? If so, can you determine the cause? You can rectify loose play by installing new bearings, snugging up a bevel gear, or tightening linkages. Undue resistance can be from either frozen bearings or a bent shaft.

13. If the windvane is damaged, do you think you can fix it?

14. Have you asked the owner or builder how you may order spare parts? If the model has been discontinued, do custom parts still exist? Who distributes them?

15. Does the manufacturer offer a spare parts kit for the model you are considering? If not, is the company willing to assemble a set of parts that are likely to need replacement during the life of the windvane?

16. Does the owner have the correct operator's manual for the unit? Make sure the manual is not for an earlier or later model. The manual should contain the builder's address and contact information, sketches or exploded diagrams, a parts list, and instructions for maintenance and repair.

Chapter 7
Installation

Lying on the dock in myriad pieces is your new windvane. If you have purchased a used vane gear, it is still new to *you*. The other yachties walk by and gawk, asking what this or that thing is for, how much you paid for the unit, and so on. After you have delineated for the eleventh time the purpose of the "flip-flop board" (horizontal-axis airvane) and how it controls the "big swingy thing" (pendulum shaft), pick one of the onlookers to help you through a day of installing the new gizmo. Your windvane steering system is your ticket to freedom—freedom from hand steering and freedom from relentless battery drain. This is a momentous occasion. Savor it!

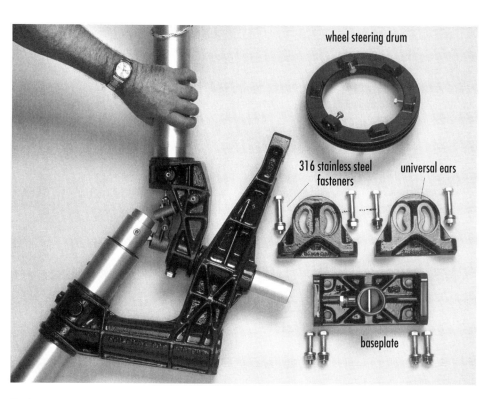

wheel steering drum

316 stainless steel fasteners

universal ears

baseplate

Sailomat 601 mounting system components. (Sailomat)

If you purchased a new vane gear, the manufacturer tailored the unit to fit your vessel's transom fairly closely, accommodating most of the constraints you anticipated in the windvane's installation. The unit may be very easy to install, as with a Sailomat, which requires you to drill four holes, insert and tighten bolts, and then run the steering lines through blocks to the helm. That's all there is to it. At the other end of the spectrum is the Cape Horn, whose sleek, understated appearance belies a somewhat more complicated installation process. With most of the remaining designs, your task at this point is mostly a matter of cutting tubes (if not precut exactly to required specifications), drilling holes in the transom, and installing the vane gear, making sure it is properly aligned.

Your owner's manual, packed with the unit, will be your best technical guide to installation. The objective of this chapter is to cover details that may not appear in the owner's manual, and to help those who have purchased a used windvane but may not have the proper manual for the unit. In any case, you will find guidance here on clearing airflow obstructions, prealigning the vane gear to measure mounting tubes, reinforcing the transom, installing steering lines and blocks, and related technical issues.

THINGS TO CONSIDER

Before pulling out the hacksaw and box-end wrenches, conduct a quick visual inspection of the transom and rear deck area. Installation will go a lot faster and easier if you start with a mental picture of how the vane gear and its steering connections will interact with obstructions in the vicinity of the unit. Even more effective is a sketch of the planned installation, which you may have received from the manufacturer. If you draft your own installation plan, draw it to scale with measurements calculated as close as you can get them. But do not start cutting tubes until later, when you have the opportunity to make an exact fit.

Overhead Clearance and Airflow

Ideally, an arch over the rear deck should allow at least a foot of clearance above the top of the light-wind airvane. This is an ideal measurement, and may not be practical in all cases. The less equipment and less acreage dedicated to solar panels aloft, the narrower the overhead clearance can be. Why? Because air current refracts the way water does when it passes around a rock or other solid object in its path. A vortex of wildly buckling air develops downwind of the solid object, adversely influencing the windvane's performance if the turbulence occurs too close to the airvane.

An obvious disturbance is any vertical surface blocking the air's unobstructed path to the airvane. Examples are weather cloths, solar panels, and radar domes mounted too close to the vane. Weather cloths, usually stretched between the toe rail and the stern pulpit, are not a problem as long as the vane yoke is above the level of the pulpit. Solar panels belong either very low, placed horizontally on the stern pulpit, or very high, over the arch, well above the top of the light-wind airvane, the longest of the vanes included with your vane unit.

If your vessel has a mizzen boom extending beyond the transom, no doubt you and the builder have worked together to see that the boom and vane gear do not interfere with each other. A used unit, not tailored for your ketch or yawl, can mean an accident waiting to happen if you don't plan the vane gear installation carefully. First see if there is some way to extend the mounting structure beyond the end of the boom. If not, make sure the boom's path is through the airvane, not through the main, stationary portion of the rig. At the same time, as with all servopendulum installations, you must ensure that the servo blade's or auxiliary rudder's length below the waterline falls within manufacturer allowances. In most cases, the top of the servo blade should be 3 to 6 inches above or below the waterline, depending on the model. Before you tack the mizzen, lower the airvane to its horizontal position, or remove it if necessary. After you have tacked and the mizzen boom has swung over, raise the airvane to the vertical position. I have been told this is a simple maneuver, a practice that soon becomes second nature. On long passages, several days may pass between tacks and jibes, so you should have plenty of time to think through your tacks before executing them. The worst that can happen in the event of an accidental jibe is a broken airvane, easily replaced from the spares you thoughtfully stored before leaving port. More likely, the boom will merely hold the airvane down, throwing the vessel off course until the helmsman corrects the situation.

Stern Configuration

Here again, the manufacturer may have furnished you with drawings of how the vane gear should sit on the stern, along with approximate positions of mounting brackets. Nonetheless, you will see that some judgment is still required to pinpoint where the unit and its mounting structure will join the transom. The wider the angle of the mounting tubes extending outward from the vane gear's main body to the transom, the more the whole installation will resist pressure from either side. Mounting the lower tubes as low as possible, yet safely above the waterline, gives the unit greater vertical support. At least one manufacturer recommends painting the name on the stern only after mounting the wind steerer to the transom so that vanity will not prevail over a solid installation.

Monitor mounted to the canoe stern of Doug and Valerie Crenshaw's *Satori* (Florida), a Pacific Seacraft 37. Note the long mounting tubes required for the reach to the hull.

Whether the unit is new or used, the installation is a simple matter on a vertical or slightly raked flat transom. "Flat," in this case, includes slightly convex surfaces. The ultimate challenge is a canoe stern with either a boomkin or a transom rudder. Manufacturers are accustomed to facing such challenges, and therefore most of the builders have lots of sketches and photographs of successful installations on hard-to-fit transoms. If you are attempting to install a used vane gear on a canoe stern, ask the builder to send you a few illustrations likely to indicate a workable solution. On a canoe stern, mounting tubes need to be much longer than on a conventional transom in order to achieve a wide enough pattern on the hull. With an extending obstruction on the canoe stern, the poles must be longer yet. It is critically important that mounting brackets be located low enough on the hull's sides to support the unit's weight and to prevent vertical movement of the structure, especially with heavier vane gears.

Sugar-scoop transoms may also pose a challenge, as Laurent and Beatrice Clarot of the 42-foot ketch *Banana Split* (New Caledonia) figured out when they ordered a Cape Horn from Yves Gélinas in Québec. Gélinas can communicate with the Clarots in French, making it easier for them to understand the many technical details attending the process of designing and installing the vane gear (by the way, his English is also impeccable). Laurent and I spent at least three hours devising exactly how we thought the vane gear would fit best—from the waterline to the Z-rod mounting tube over the sugar scoop, to the unit's quadrant in the lazarette, and to the position of blocks and steering lines, which connect to the vessel's own steering quadrant. We cut a cardboard wheel to ensure 360-degree clearance for the Cape Horn's quadrant, and then modified the whole series of

Where there's a will, there's a way: this complex mounting structure, marrying a Cape Horn to a boomkin, demanded some creative engineering. (Cape Horn Marine Products)

measurements, starting right back where we began at the waterline. Installing the Cape Horn requires a bit more thinking because of the through-transom mounting tube and the careful positioning of the quadrant, but other unconventional mounting situations also will require additional attention.

Blocks and Lines

Careful selection of blocks and steering, or control, lines will reduce friction and wear in these components and promote a more direct connection between the airvane's steering impulses and the helm. Low-stretch, double-braided polyester line, either $5/16$-inch or $3/8$-inch, is most often recommended in vane gear operator manuals for servopendulum systems. Spectra line is probably too stiff; I would recommend Sta-Set yacht braid from New England Ropes, or a similar product, which will render excellent service at a lower cost. There is always the temptation to pay more money, making us feel secure in having bought the "best" product. But some lines are so strong that they are inordinately hard and stiff, moving poorly through sheaves and exposing themselves to more abrasion. Sta-Set X, for example, has an inner wrap around a straight-filament core, making the line much stronger than regular Sta-Set and ideal for halyards and other semistationary applications. Steering lines need to combine high strength, low stretch, and a degree of suppleness if they are to survive jillions of rotations around a small radius without abrading or breaking.

Take plenty of replacement line with you when sailing in undeveloped countries. If you buy cheap, local rope, it might look like good stuff, but do not be surprised if it magically transforms itself into baggywrinkle at the sheaves within the first day of leaving port. This happened on *Saltaire* after I purchased a length of nylon-polyester combination braid in Tahiti. For running rigging, avoid nylon and, even worse, polypropylene line at all costs. Nylon rope has a lot of stretch, making it ideal for mooring and dock lines. In poor countries, you will see cheap, stiff, brittle polypropylene rope in virtually every kind of rigging on fishing boats: mast stays, halyards, sheets, anchor rode—even in unraveled strands for shoelaces. Because polypropylene floats, it is ideal for dinghy painters, which might otherwise get wound around the propeller. Avoid this type of rope for rigging unless you are being chased by pirates and could not schedule a trip to the chandlery before your untimely departure.

Blocks need to be light, but of strong construction with low-friction bearings. The blocks most likely to fit that description have Delrin cheeks, sheaves, and ball bearings, such as the blocks available from Harken and Ronstan. These pieces of hardware need no maintenance, save for an occasional dip in fresh water, or a heavy rain, to cleanse them of salt and grit. Blocks with aluminum sheaves or stainless steel bearings tend to be much stronger and heavier, but are designed for weight-bearing applications. They are perfect for halyards and mainsheets, but a slight oxide skin on the bearings can slow their action considerably. Try to avoid using blocks with sheave bushings or bearingless axles. Actually quite common in vane gear installations, these inexpensive alternatives are more cut out for boom vangs and preventer blocks because the blocks fail to provide the loose, sensitive action needed for transmitting sometimes weak steering signals from the vane gear to the wheel or tiller. Steering blocks need to be light because they generally extend horizontally from the stern pulpit stanchions and the cockpit coaming when the steering line is pulled tight between the pendulum shaft and the helm. A heavy block will pull the line down, absorbing steering tension rather than passing the energy along its path.

Your vane gear builder may be adamant about avoiding swivel blocks, preferring fixed blocks to reduce play. At first glance, this makes good sense, especially with a tiller. As the tiller moves back and forth, the angles of the steering lines coming from the coaming blocks shift to follow the tiller's path. The side movement of each block steals energy that would otherwise be passed onto the tiller, dulling the sensitivity of the system. In reality, it is difficult to install fixed blocks in such a manner that the steering lines never leave deep grooves in the block cheeks or become frayed. As you change the position of steering lines along a curved tiller, at some point the line may lie too closely against the side of the block. When not in use, fixed blocks pointing from the coaming inward toward the cockpit can jab someone in the back, spoiling a dinner party, or even

A less expensive alternative for control lines: two-inch bearingless swivel block by Ronstan.

worse, a romantic interlude—ouch! I have used fixed blocks at the aft stanchions and swivel blocks on the coaming for years, and while I have observed a slight loss of steering power at the swivel blocks, the fixed block cheeks are now a unique form of abstract sculpture. Experimenting with different fixed angles will alleviate most of your trouble, but swivel blocks should serve your steering purposes nearly as well. Another option is to employ oversized blocks, allowing for more deviation in the steering line angle at either cheek.

Scanmar recommends sheaves of approximately 2 inches in diameter for steering blocks. Most of the blocks I have observed in steering applications have been more diminutive, around 1 inch in diameter. The smaller blocks are visually less obtrusive, certainly less so than something resembling big, flat, burnt mangoes hanging over the cockpit seats. Those big blocks ensure three important things: less abrasion in your steering lines, less wear and tear on the block bearings, and less resistance in the steering system.

ATTACHING TO HULL

Preparation

Before you jump into this project with bolts, screws, and metal tubing littering the dock, you need to set up shop. You will need a hacksaw, a drill, a set of combination wrenches, a set of socket wrenches, some screwdrivers, and a few yards of old, stretched-out, double-braided polyester line. If you want to install wooden mounting blocks under the brackets on the transom, have them ready before proceeding. For an installation requiring permanent reinforcement of the hull, have ready some marine plywood, sandpaper, a saw, epoxy resin, fiberglass, and related materials. Read through the following section for a better idea of materials needed for transom reinforcement. To keep your vane gear looking new, find a tarp or an old sail for a work surface. A quick inventory of all the parts packed in the box will ensure you don't find yourself stuck in the middle of a project without the materials to complete the job. Be liberal in your time allowance for work completion: a solid day's work for a standard servopendulum or trim tab on a vertical or raked transom; a day and a half for a Cape Horn (to allow for fiberglassing around the mounting tube); and two days for any installation involving a boomkin or a transom rudder. Installing a simple four-bolt bracket mount, as for a Sailomat, should not take more than a couple of hours. However, reinforcing the inside of the transom, if necessary, will require at least a day for the epoxy or polyester resin to cure. You can perform some measuring and drilling from a dinghy, but you will have better results by rotating the vessel so the transom faces the dock. For difficult canoe sterns, your best bet might be to haul the boat onto dry land, especially if you need to drill close to the waterline. For most installations, you should have little trouble working with the boat in the water, unless you have slippery fingers and are afraid of dropping a wrench or a length of tubing into the drink.

Mounting Brackets and Backing Blocks

Backing blocks on the inside and outside of the hull distribute pressure from the bracket bolts over a larger area on the transom. In some cases, however, an extra heavy vane gear on a thin-walled transom necessitates additional reinforcement. For simple backing blocks on the inner side of the hull, cut a rectangular piece of $3/8$- to $1/2$-inch teak or marine plywood for each bracket, allowing the block to extend about an inch beyond the bracket's sides. Using the bracket as a template, drill bolt holes through the wood blocks. A coat of either penetrating epoxy or a 50-50 mix of linseed oil and turpentine helps plywood resist dry rot. Placing two fender washers against the inside backing block for each bolt will help to spread the load across the whole block. Teak blocks directly under the brackets outside the hull will protect the gel coat and make a more attractive, professional-looking installation. You may cut these blocks smaller and tailor them more closely to the shape of the mounting brackets.

A heavy gear with a small, single mounting area may require that you beef up the inside of a fiberglass hull with marine plywood and fiberglass. This job demands extra thought and diligence, since the mounting area is toward the center of the transom, where it is weakest. The method suggested here also applies if you want to install several permanent backing blocks to reinforce a weak transom. West System has oodles of literature that will guide you through every imaginable phase of marine epoxy work, so you may wish to consult some of their leaflets to ensure a top-notch job.

For really solid backing plates, cut pieces of $^3/8$- or $^1/2$-inch marine plywood, depending on the size and weight of the vane gear being supported, so that they extend at least an inch beyond the edges of the brackets. For a large single bracket in the middle of the transom, extend the edges at least 3 to 4 inches outward from the bracket. Bevel the edges about 45 degrees, and then round the edges of the smaller, exposed surface with medium-grit sandpaper. Sand the hull side, too, but leave the edges sharp. Also sand the mounting surface on the hull at least 3 inches out from the edges of the mounting block's position. Wipe the surface with a clean rag and acetone. Holding the block in position against the inside of the hull, draw a line around the edges of the plywood. Mix epoxy and colloidal silica into a thick paste, enough to cover the hull side of the mounting block. Press the plywood firmly against the hull, propping it in place with pieces of wood or whatever is handy. An alternate method for a deeply curved transom is to lay up sections of $^1/4$-inch marine plywood, applying epoxy resin and colloidal silica between layers.

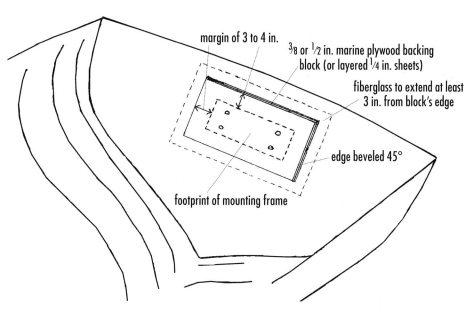

Figure 7-1. Backing block for a large, single mounting bracket on a relatively flat transom. For curved surfaces, lay up sections of $^1/4$ in. plywood to achieve desired thickness.

Materials for Backing Blocks

- Marine plywood ($1/4$, $3/8$, or $1/2$ in., depending on transom curvature and structural requirements)
- Teak blocks (1 to 2 in. thick) for mounting tube brackets
- Fiberglass cloth (6-ounce cloth and stranded mat), if required for transom reinforcement
- Sandpaper in varying grains of coarseness
- Epoxy resin
- Cleaning materials (rags, thinner, etc.)
- Linseed oil and turpentine

After the epoxy has hardened, sand the epoxy excess and the whole area again, finishing up with a rag and acetone. Mix a batch of clear epoxy, and apply at least three layers of fiberglass cloth—I prefer a sandwich of cloth, chopped mat, and another layer of cloth for a strong, relatively smooth surface. After the epoxy has cured, sand and finish the block according to your aesthetic needs. Now you can drill through the hull and block structure to mount the windvane. The obsessive-compulsive skipper may want to apply a coat of penetrating epoxy to the inner surfaces of the bolt holes with an artist's brush to ward off dry rot and guarantee the structural integrity of the block.

Mounting a unit to a steel or aluminum hull most likely does not require backing blocks, but you will need to use some form of dielectric between the brackets and the hull to prevent galvanism between the two surfaces. Electrical insulation applies equally when attaching aluminum brackets to an aluminum hull, since the odds are against their being precisely the same alloy from the same mill. The mere fact that the hull is constructed of rolled sheet metal and the brackets are probably cast suggests some difference in alloy composition. A pad cut from thin rubber sheet or gasket material should serve as an adequate dielectric.

Mounting Tubes

The steps outlined here are generic guidelines applying to any tube mounting structure. For specific instructions relating to assembling the vane gear and adapting its mounting tubes for proper installation, it is imperative that you consult your owner's manual. Most critical among the points you need to verify in the manual is the recommended clearance between the top of the servo blade and the waterline; some manufacturers are strict on this point, others are more lenient. Beyond that, as long as the vane gear's main body is perfectly ver-

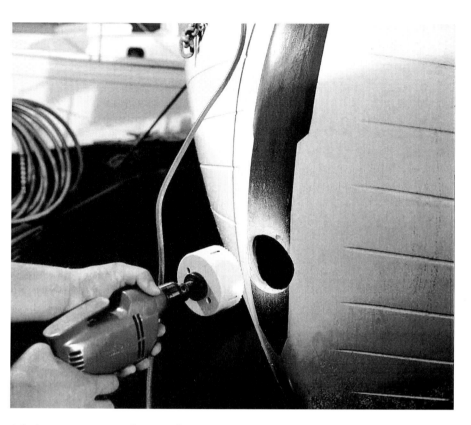

A hole saw prepares the way for a Cape Horn mounting tube on a canoe stern. The Z rod will pass through the tube and connect with a special steering quadrant inside the lazarette. (Cape Horn Marine Products)

tical in all directions and strongly mounted at the *center* of the transom, all should be well. A few models, such as the Sailomat 601, allow for off-center installation within strict manufacturer guidelines. Unless permitted by the builder, tilted or off-center installations can seriously compromise the vane gear's operation and durability. We can easily understand, then, why Scanmar International requests installation photos before signing off on warranties.

First drill the *upper* bracket holes *at the correct distance from the waterline*. Then drill the lower bracket holes, spacing them low and wide to support the windvane's weight and to resist side movement of the unit. Use a length of tubing to line up the tube end-fittings on the transom with those on the vane gear. You will need to hold the vane gear in place against the transom just long enough to make sure the brackets are properly placed. Then bolt the three or four mounting brackets to the transom, using a high-quality bedding compound between the bracket and the hull. Also squeeze sealant into the holes to keep water from dripping into the lazarette. Polysulfide sealant, available from BoatLife under the name Life-Calk, is an excellent, all-around sealant for use above and below the waterline, and is also removable. Be careful with polyurethane sealants, which can be next to impossible to remove. Because 3M's marine sealant 5200 forms a permanent bond, many sailors rely on 4200, similar to 5200 but easier to pry loose.

Next, measure the length of the center mounting tube or two upper tubes. A handy way to mark stainless or anodized alloy tubes is with a permanent marker or pieces of masking tape. With a fine-tooth hacksaw blade, cut the tubes, keeping as straight a line as possible. Strangely, though stainless steel is difficult to drill, it is easy to cut, even with a cheap blade. After you finish cutting, file off burrs and smooth out the tube ends with a piece of fine-grit emery paper. If the swivel joints require you to drill holes at the ends of stainless tubes,

Hydrovane snugly in place with a single lower mounting tube. Five different bracket designs are available from Hydrovane to fit the size and stern shape of your vessel.

first carefully mark the hole with a hammer and punch. The trick to drilling through stainless is to start with a small pilot bit, squirting a little cutting fluid (not machine oil) into the hole as you drill. Keep the bit rotating at a slow speed, so you can feel and hear the bite of the drill bit. Gradually enlarge the hole by increasing bit diameter, one size at a time. Bits should be tough and heat-resistant, preferably of cobalt or titanium steel. A word to the wise: keep a few carbide-tipped drill bits in your toolbox for tough jobs. They are appreciably more expensive than other bits, but when you see how carbide and cutting fluid bore through stainless, you will forget about the few extra dollars you spent on the little gems.

Now comes the tricky part. An extra pair of hands will make this phase of the installation a lot easier. Bolt all the swivel fittings onto the vane gear, and attach the upper tube or tubes to their fittings. The servo blade needs to be in place for proper results, but do not attach the lower tubes or airvane yet. Tie the old piece of double-braided line to the vane turret. Find a place to tie off the other end of the line so that you can adjust the fore-and-aft angle of the vane gear carefully. For a heavy windvane, it will be easier to use a couple of double-purchase blocks for careful adjustment. Improvise as necessary in order to align the vane gear properly. Adjustment lines on either side of the vane will be of considerable help in aligning the unit with the keel. Use the backstay or some other reference point to indicate the centerline. Pull the unit up until the top of the servo blade is within an acceptable margin from the water's surface, and the main body is vertical in all directions.

Look at the windvane from all angles. Is the servo blade at the correct depth? If the boat is out of the water, judge depth by the watermark at the stern. Is the main body vertical from all angles? Once you are satisfied that the unit is in its proper position, measure the lower tube lengths between the unit and each bracket, and cut the tubing accordingly. Cutting them an inch or so too long will give you an opportunity to adjust downward gradually. Mark each tube so you know which is which; they will be of different lengths, even if only slightly. Installing the bottom tubes concludes the main installation. If the unit has settled into a slightly backward tilt, you can raise it by removing the lower brackets and inserting thicker mounting blocks against the outside of the hull. On a canoe stern, you will probably have to cut a new, longer pair of tubes. After you have completed the installation, tie a line between the removable servo blade section and the frame just in case the servo blade separates from the upper shaft. Drill a small hole in each of your airvanes so you can attach them to the frame by a small lanyard. Are we having fun yet?

INSTALLING LINES AND BLOCKS

The two underlying issues in block arrangement for steering lines are friction and routing angles. Anyone can run lines in a creative, geometric maze here and there about the vessel, but we must remember this: every turning block and every angle away from a straight line in the steering lines produces more friction and more power loss, however so slight, in the steering system. The goal is to run steering lines in the most streamlined fashion possible, given the obstacles lying in their paths. To achieve that end, we attempt to use as few blocks as we can get away with, laying out lines in wide angles in order to conserve precious steering power.

Control lines emerge from all sorts of places on servopendulums, depending on the vane gear manufacturer and model. On the Aries, control lines rise up from long tubes extending down from either side of the unit, turning around blocks under the notched turret. Fleming lines bend around a block on the end of a steering arm above the mounting tube, emerging from a pair of blocks on either side of the main frame. Lines on the Monitor run from the lower pendulum shaft to blocks on the main mounting frame. If you have purchased an Auto-Helm, Hydrovane, or Windpilot Pacific Plus, there are no steering lines, so this discussion of blocks and lines is moot. Are you trying to figure out how to lay out lines for a Cape Horn? The rules are a little different, but we touch on them briefly later in this chapter.

A few more guidelines apply to all self-steering arrangements that incorporate steering lines. Again, use as few blocks as possible and the straightest, shortest run that you can negotiate reasonably between vane gear and helm. Use larger sheaves, say $1^{1}/_{2}$ to 2 inches for sharp turns, particularly at the cockpit sole or coaming where lines turn to connect with the wheel or tiller. Ensure that control lines do not chafe against LPG tanks, stanchions, PFDs, or other objects near the lines. Everything might look squared away in port, but when the boat heels over hard after you set sail, items stowed on deck can shift, pushing equipment against the control lines. This contact will cause line friction and interfere with helm trim. Another thing: do not leave dish towels, rags, or odd pieces of running rigging lying near or on the control lines, lest they get jammed in the blocks and halt steering action altogether. Control lines are not for drying laundry! As they say in Spanish, *la voz de la experiencia*.

Lines to Tiller

Arranging control lines and turning blocks for tiller steering is a hassle-free affair, as you will see by this logical approach. Alternate strategies are possible, but this will get your system up and running with little trouble. Starting from the lead blocks on the windvane frame, run the steering lines through a pair of fixed blocks mounted on the stern, aft pulpit, or other position near the transom. From that point, run the lines through fixed or swivel blocks on the cockpit coaming. Swivel blocks will serve this purpose well. The path between each fixed block and swivel block should be as straight as possible, averting the possibility of chafe between the line and the fixed cheek. On some models, steering lines originate on the pendulum shaft below the horizontal axis, so the installer crosses the steering lines between the unit and the helm (e.g., Aries and Monitor). Where the lines originate above the pendulum shaft's horizontal axis (e.g., Fleming and Sailomat), the lines are not crossed. Swivel block positions should be level with the point where they meet the tiller, or slightly below if you intend to have multiple attachment points on a curved tiller. Blocks placed too high will tend to pull the tiller up, causing excess slack in the lines. Opinions abound as to where exactly the control lines should meet the tiller. Some skippers prefer a system allowing adjustment, but more on that in the next section. The terminus should lie 20 to 30 inches from the center of the rudderpost; on 30-foot, full-keeled *Saltaire*, some experimenta-

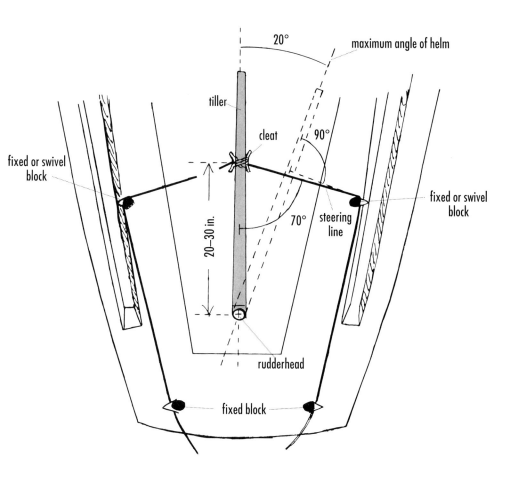

Figure 7-2. Control line placement for tiller. A 70-degree angle between the steering line and the tiller, in line with the keel, should allow a direct, 90-degree pull on the tiller when fighting extreme weather helm.

tion led to a fixed distance of 28 inches, but often I have thought of rigging a sliding system. Steering lines should emanate from the coaming blocks so that they meet the tiller at roughly 70 degrees, as measured from the boat's centerline (see figure 7-2). Using this layout, the steering line will be at a 90-degree angle to the tiller when the rudder is at 20 degrees, the probable maximum angle of helm. We want to reserve the direct, right-angle pull on the tiller for extreme conditions, particularly when the vane gear is fighting weather helm while beating to windward in a gale. These angles are based not on analytical design or theory, but on trial and error. Through a little experimentation, you may find other tiller attachment points and control line angles yielding results better suited to your vessel's steering demands.

Lines to Wheel

The same low-friction, straight-line principles apply to wheel steering but may not be as feasible as with a tiller. A large wheel is already a major obstacle, blocking passage to all but the most lithe when underway. Control lines extending horizontally from either side of the binnacle fortify the fence that much more. For this reason, some skippers prefer the lines to rise vertically from blocks on the cockpit sole. Others prefer to run lines through a pair of coaming-mounted sheaves at one side of the cockpit, allowing crew to pass on the other side without disturbing the control lines. Though wheel drum steering lines tend to be of smaller diameter, sheaves should still measure at least $1^1/2$ inches to ensure easy, sensitive steering response.

Cape Horn Control Lines

The Cape Horn's control line installation at first may be slightly intimidating, but it is really fairly straightforward. We will use quadrant steering as our example, since this is a common form of wheel steering, used by the company in its promotional materials. The Cape Horn's quadrant is supposed to have room for 360 degrees of rotation. Though less than half of that is quite sufficient for steering, when the pendulum is not in use the operator flips the blade out of the water, turning the quadrant upward at the same time. Allowing enough

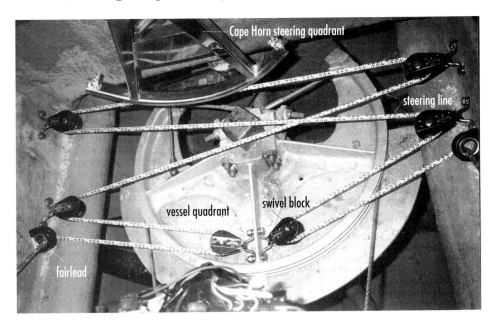

Cape Horn control lines running through swivel blocks to steering quadrant on Oceanis 39. (Cape Horn Marine Products)

vertical swing room for the quadrant will make life a lot easier. The paths of control lines from the vane gear's quadrant to the vessel's steering quadrant depend on which way the vessel's quadrant is facing. In Cape Horn's sample drawings, the vessel quadrant's angle faces aft on a horizontal plane, and the windvane's quadrant faces downward in a plane perpendicular to the vessel quadrant. Each one is a mirror reflection of the other. On some vessels, though, the quadrant faces forward, making the two parallel. Irrespective of the vessel quadrant's position, though, they rotate in the opposite direction. In other words, as with all servopendulum designs, when the servo blade swings to port, the trailing edge of the vessel's rudder should move to starboard. The two control lines should enter their respective grooves on the windvane quadrant in straight lines. However, the angle may vary up to 45 degrees above or below a horizontal line at the bottom of the quadrant (see figure 7-3). So that you keep the lines straight and lying properly in their quadrant grooves, be prepared to cut aluminum or stainless plates to fabricate mounting brackets for blocks. You may find it necessary to add an extra pair of swivel blocks to accommodate long runs or awkward control-line angles.

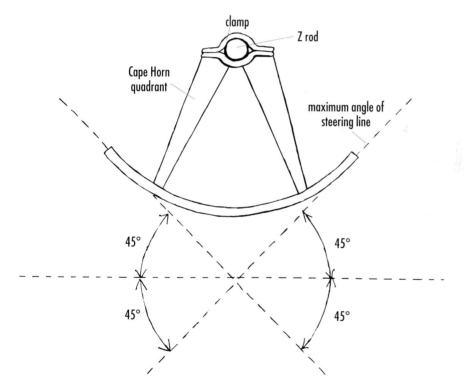

Figure 7-3. The dashed diagonal lines represent the maximum angles, up or down, for steering lines running through swivel blocks to the vessel's main steering quadrant.

ATTACHING LINES TO THE HELM

Tiller Steering

Line connections on the tiller may be either fixed or adjustable. On *Saltaire*, I installed a pair of plain, old-fashioned bronze cleats on the tiller, carved from a single piece of ultra-hard *ifilele* (similar to Hawaiian koa) by a local artist in Apia, Western Samoa. With cleats fastened by wood screws, always tie each control line to the opposite side of the tiller so that the screws bear a shear load rather than a pulling load. Otherwise, the lines eventually will rip the screws from their holes. The only other problem with cleats is the extra seconds required to untie the control lines while waves are breaking over your head. It is probably worth the extra few bucks for an Aries tiller connector, a small cast fitting that holds in place a short length of chain attached to the bitter ends of the control lines. In order to trim the rudder, you simply pull the chain from the small fitting, move the chain over a few links, and pop it back into the fitting. If you fancy an adjustable connector, you can lay a short length of track on either side of the tiller with a small, sliding fairlead on each track (figure 7-4). Secure the lines with a pair of cam cleats after running the lines through the fairleads. Bear in mind the servopendulum's mighty brute force in heavy conditions as you select hardware for this last system. While the boat surfs down

Bronze cleat for control line on *Saltaire*'s tiller, hand-carved from native *ifilele* in Apia, Samoa.

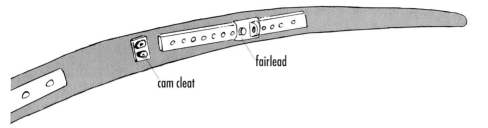

Figure 7-4. A sliding fairlead with a fixed cam cleat on the tiller allows you to adjust the angle of the steering lines and hence the degree of pull on the tiller.

12-foot seas for days on end, the pendulum yanks the tiller from side to side with hundreds of pounds of force in the vane gear's constant battle against yaw. Any hardware you attach to the stick as a connecting device must be heavily built and strongly fastened to withstand those forces.

Wheel Steering

Servopendulums work well with rack-and-pinion and cable wheel steering. However, servopendulums are not recommended for hydraulic steering or in cases where steering is made difficult by excess friction or play. Hydraulic steer-

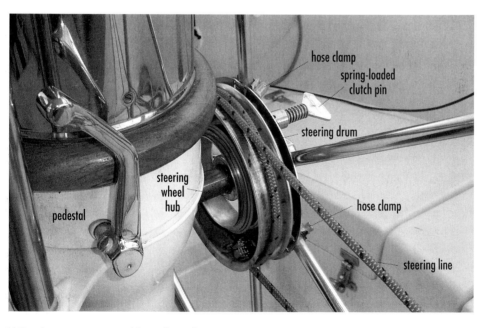

Wheel steering control line drum for Monitor.

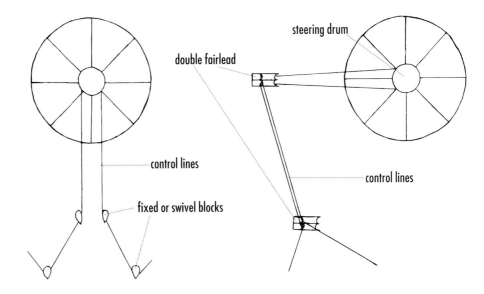

Figure 7-5. Control lines to wheel.

ing tends to be "soft"; furthermore, most hydraulic pumps have check valves, designed to keep the rudder from turning the helm in heavy seas. This protects the rudderpost, but renders vane gear and rudder trim about as solid as Jell-O. Worm gear steering tends to be a bit stiff, especially if not lubricated on a regular basis. For both hydraulic and worm gear steering, an auxiliary rudder type of vane gear is probably your best alternative.

Connecting control lines to wheel steering is made possible by a steering drum, usually sold as a separate kit by the vane gear builder. U-bolts are generally used to secure the drum to the wheel's spokes. You trim the helm with a rotating clutch, leaving the steering line connection intact at the drum—this is even easier than tiller steering. While you are planning the layout of the control lines, take into account where the lines will meet the drum. If the lines are served from one side of the cockpit—the port side seems to be the overwhelming favorite—one line will connect at the top of the drum, and the other at the bottom. These positions depend on which side of the cockpit the lines come from, and where the lines are crossed, either at the unit itself or between blocks mounted on the vessel (refer to the two examples in figure 7-5). Where lines arrive from either coaming, both lines will meet at the bottom of the drum.

The worst part of installing a vane gear is sitting around thinking about it. Set aside some time to figure out how you wish to proceed with the project. Reread the pertinent sections of this chapter and review your owner's manual. When you are ready for battle with all the equipment you need, start on the preinstallation work, like reinforcing the transom and cutting the upper mounting tubes, bright and early on a Saturday morning. Plan to work all day. If you finish by the time the sun is over the yardarm (beer o'clock), kudos to you, mate, for a lightning-fast completion. If it takes longer, you still have the rest of the day and all day Sunday to finish your work. The time and energy you invest in doing this job right will pay big dividends when you are, at long last, hundreds of miles offshore pursuing your dreams.

Chapter 8

Sailing with Windvane Steering

Windvane self-steering is a normal extension of the art of sailing itself, and a vane gear is nearly as necessary on an ocean cruising sailboat as sails and rigging. The windvane's mechanical principles are different from those of the sails, but their interdependent functions complement each other. It is common for the vane gear novice to complain about the steering system's inability to steer in certain conditions. "It's OK going to weather, but it can't steer on a beam reach." Or "The vane gear is great in all weather except on a run in winds under 18 knots." More than likely, what the sailor is really trying to say is, "I tried the windvane a couple of times for a few minutes, but I didn't really put in the time and effort it deserved." After more practice, that same sailor inevitably finds that the vane gear works well on all points of sail, but it has taken some practice to get the feel of how the system works. By the way, I was quoting my own initial reactions!

Where sailors seem to make their biggest initial mistake with vane steering is in assuming that the system will automatically steer a perfect course, regardless of sail trim. No form of steering, whether human, mechanical, or electronic, can do its job very well with an unbalanced rig. Therefore, a large portion of this chapter reviews basic sailing and the essential, underlying aero- and hydrodynamic forces governing a sailboat's behavior on the water. If you are an accomplished sailor, you may wish to skip the following two sections and move on to the section dealing specifically with vane gear steering.

REVIEW OF SAILING BASICS

True and Apparent Wind

For sailors, there are two types of wind: *true wind* and *apparent wind*. When you are standing still, facing the wind, you feel the true wind. If the wind is blowing 8 knots and you ride a bicycle directly into the wind at 7 knots, the air you feel on your hands and face has an apparent wind speed of 15 knots. As you turn your bicycle off the wind, true wind stays the same, but the apparent wind speed decreases. If you ride downwind at 7 knots with the true wind at 8 knots, the apparent wind you feel on your back is barely perceptible at 1 knot, since we have subtracted true wind speed from apparent wind.

The Points of Sail

Except when sailing downwind, the source of a sailboat's power is based on *Bernoulli's principle*: The pressure in a fluid drops as the speed of its flow increases. This principle is also called *lift*, which governs the flight of birds, aircraft, and yes, even those damned little no-no's in the jungles of the Marquesas. The pressure of air over the *camber*, or convex side, of a nonsymmetrical airfoil drops as the air rushes from the leading edge to rejoin air from the flatter opposite side of the wing at the trailing edge. The faster-flowing, lower-pressure area over the camber causes lift, enabling heavier-than-air objects to fly and sailboats to sail into the wind. The sailboat's keel, or submerged lateral plane, resists leeward *drift*, ensuring the vessel will be literally "sucked" forward. The principles governing windward sailing have been likened to squeezing a wet pumpkin seed: when you gently squeeze the seed between your thumb and index finger, the squeezing pressure forces the seed to shoot out from between your fingers.

There are four points of sail, which are best understood with the aid of a circular chart (see figure 8-1). Most boats cannot sail efficiently closer than 45 degrees off the wind while sailing *close-hauled* (also called beating). On this point of sail, the sails are sheeted in tightly, presenting a relatively flat wing to

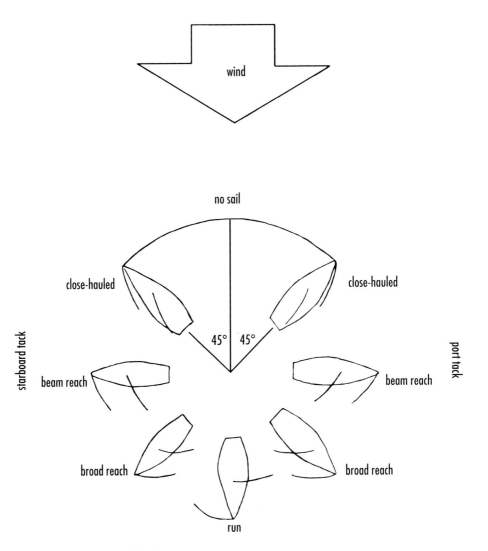

Figure 8-1. The points of sail.

the wind. Sliding the traveler to the *lee* (downwind side) allows you to ease the main without changing its shape. Employing a *boom vang* stabilizes the boom and keeps the main from dumping out too much wind as the boat pitches and rolls. A good rule for trimming the mainsail while close-hauled is to let out the boom (remember to loosen the vang first!) until the sail starts flapping. Then haul in the boom until the sail fills with air and becomes tight; at that point, bring in the boom just a little more so the main keeps its shape. The headsail should be sheeted in until the leeward telltales (strips of yarn or nylon cloth) are horizontal and the windward telltales are gently flicking up and down.

After the jib is set, air flowing off the sail may cause the main to flap again; haul in the main a little more until the flapping stops. In light winds, let's say under 8 or 10 knots, sailing close-hauled or on a close reach is generally the fastest point of sail because farther off the wind, the apparent wind is too weak to keep the sails full and to prevent the boat from rolling.

At a true wind speed of about 15 knots or more, a *beam reach* is the fastest point of sail. On flat water, it is also the easiest point of sail, ideal for kids taking their first dinghy sailing lessons. Unfortunately, it is also the point of sail on which people are most likely to trim the sheets incorrectly. Many sailors leave their sails close-hauled on a beam reach—some folks because they are lazy, others because they don't know any better. After all, the sails are tight and the boat is making headway, isn't it? Yes, but why are we doing only 4 knots with the rail in the water! The sail trim rules for a beat or a close reach apply more or less the same way to a beam reach. Let the main out until it flaps, haul in until it is tight, and then pull it in a little more. On a beam reach, the sails are trimmed out farther, with the boom extending over the water. A boom vang will add speed and stability to a beam reach in both light and heavy airs. If you are coming off a close reach, let out the jib after easing the main and adjust for best speed. Remember, as boat speed increases, the apparent wind's direction moves forward of the beam, putting the boat more toward a close reach. Watch the compass, decide on the best heading given your weather conditions and destination, and trim your sails accordingly.

Next is the *broad reach*, which for most practical purposes means sailing between 100 and 170 degrees off the wind. A sailing vessel will arc between 80 to 100 degrees off the wind on a casual, Sunday afternoon beam reach, 170 to 180 degrees on a *run*. The principle of lift really does not apply to downwind sailing, the hull's speed through the water depending directly on the wind's blunt force against the sails (although low pressure on the forward side of the headsail probably does generate a small amount of lift). On a broad reach, the sails are trimmed to a point between their close-hauled and beam-reach positions, though the main will be trimmed out a bit farther, the precise angles of both sails depending on sail plan and wind speed. Some sailors prefer to "tack downwind," or *jibe* back and forth between broad reaches rather than run. They say their time made good is faster than or equal to that of a run, and broad reaching allows them to continue using their genoas, drifters, or asymmetrical spinnakers instead of large, unwieldy conventional spinnakers. On a broad reach, both the main and headsail are used; also, the hull heels over and presents more length on the waterline. So the boat achieves greater speed than when running, knifing through the water instead of trying to climb up a large bow wave. One more thing: your best friend on a broad reach, or on a run if you are using the main, is a *preventer*, which keeps the boom from swinging over the cockpit in an accidental jibe. You can use the boom vang as a preventer by attaching the vang's lower block to a pad eye on the lee-side deck. Better yet, run two lines from a shackle on the bottom of the boom through blocks on either side of the house, and then run the lines aft to cleats accessible from the cockpit. This allows you to use the vang and preventer in unison, a technique that is also effective on a beam reach.

As long as winds are moderate to strong, most of us do not mind dousing the main, poling out the genoa, and proceeding downwind on a run. There we go, with the optimism of Sisyphus, lumbering up our bow waves, knowing that some hour, some day, or some week we will arrive at our destinations. Actually, we probably make the same time made good on a run as we do by jibing, although sailors argue over this question incessantly on the maritime ham nets. Much of this depends, of course, on the type of downwind sail employed. Today's sailors can select from a wide assortment of light downwind sails: spinnakers, cruising chutes, asymmetrical spinnakers, multiple-purpose spinnakers, gennakers, drifters, and bloopers—all of these available in different cuts and limitless color schemes. The bigger the headsail, the faster we go downwind. In addition to the standard assortment of headsails, you can set two headsails "wing and wing" or go the traditional route with the headsail and main set in opposite directions. The last method can be somewhat difficult and unnerving, even with a preventer to keep the boom from swinging, because of the constant backing of the mainsail or, on some boats, the tendency to round up. On some boats, the main remains furled during long periods of running on open ocean, especially with a poled-out genoa.

BALANCING THE RIG

Assuming you have done some sailing, by now you certainly have experienced the magic feeling that comes with self-steering. Have you ever dared take your hand off the tiller for a few minutes while your sails were trimmed just right, allowing the boat to sail to weather in 12 to 15 knots of apparent wind? Any properly designed hull and sail rig configuration will demonstrate this natural tendency to self-steer, given the right conditions. The phrase "natural tendency" needs some qualification: this tendency is achieved through a carefully balanced rig, eliminating as many of the interfering forces as possible, given the point of sail, wind strength, and sea state.

The aim of a windvane steering gear is to amplify a vessel's inherent ability to self-steer. A well-designed vane gear can tolerate a moderate degree of sloppy sail trim, but experience will show that the boat sails most effectively, with the least amount of strain on the rig and steering, when the sails are properly trimmed with the correct amount of canvas for the conditions at that moment. You may be lying in your bunk thinking the boat is sailing along happily under servopendulum steering on a close reach, even as wind speed creeps up. When you stick your head out the companionway to check the steering, you might find the tiller pulled hard to windward, struggling to keep the boat from rounding up into the wind. The novice may adjust the steering lines in this manner intentionally, being too naive to take proper corrective action. Obviously, you need to do something. One option is to set a "lazy man's reef" by simply letting out the main sheet. Better yet, put a reef in the main and adjust the vane to come off the wind a few degrees. Fine-tuning the steering lines at the helm is a normal part of the vane gear's operation as long as this practice is not meant to overcompensate for a severely unbalanced rig.

Interfering Forces

Sailors commonly cite five forces that work against a balanced rig: weather helm, lee helm, yaw, roll, and leeway. If you are an airplane pilot, you are already familiar with the last three. *Weather helm* is the boat's tendency to round up into the wind if the sails are hauled in too tightly or if the wind starts building up. Lift from the mainsail and other sails aft of the mainmast try to force the bow to windward while the headsail tries to push the bow away from the wind. If the main overpowers the headsail, the boat heels, losing lateral resistance from the keel. The boat then rounds up, and the sails begin to luff, or flog uselessly in the wind. An aircraft can experience a similar effect if it stalls and begins to fall from the sky. Ultimately, if left with sails set and no steerage, virtually any sailboat will eventually round up, irrespective of the other forces working on the vessel. One way to eliminate weather helm and restore balance is, again, to ease the main and possibly the jib. In heavier conditions, it will be necessary to reduce canvas, starting with the main, and to trim the rudder a bit to windward. So big a problem is weather helm that many cruising boats spend most of their time with at least one reef in the main, even in fair weather. In the tropics, a squall can form anywhere, anytime, in a matter of minutes. Every now and then we find ourselves beam reaching or close reaching with apparent wind speeds in excess of 20 knots. For most of us, that calls for a reef in the main. Some offshore sailors go as far as having their mainsails cut and resewn to the first reef point, eliminating unnecessary canvas and ensuring proper sail shape when the wind picks up.

The opposite effect, *lee helm*, occurs when the boat tends to steer itself away from the wind, commonly when there is insufficient air to power the sails. Rather than powering the boat, the breeze slowly causes the boat to drift to leeward. Adjusting the sails for the most lift may help, but the best remedy is obviously to do what the term suggests: trim the helm to the lee. The other cause of lee helm is a headsail overpowering the main. In this case, we make sure that we have shaken the reefs out of the main and hauled in on the mainsheet. Also, setting the boom vang will prevent the mainsail from dumping too much air.

Yaw, described in chapter 2, refers to a vessel's tendency to fishtail while the boat is running fast before the wind down the faces of tall swells and waves. As the bow plunges deeply into the oncoming water—a condition that can cause the vessel to *pitchpole*, or somersault, in extreme conditions—the bow digs into the back of the previous wave, impeding forward motion. While the boat surfs down the face of a wave, the buoyant, elevated stern tries first to overtake the bow, and then slides back in the opposite direction to repeat the process. The helmsman corrects the yaw by constantly pumping the rudder to offset each momentary swing of the stern, or turning to a broad reach so that the vessel surfs the waves diagonally. Now the boat is sailing faster and moving across a flatter cross section of the water's surface. The main objective here is to keep the boat from *broaching*, or suddenly turning broadside to the waves, a situation that theoretically can cause the boat to capsize if the waves are breaking and if their height is greater than the vessel's beam. Another means of correcting yaw is reducing canvas to depower the boat and, in very severe conditions, trailing a long line or a drogue off the stern to stabilize trajectory—like flying a kite with a tail. Sea state, wind speed, course, boat dimensions, and the crew's level of confidence will all enter into deciding how best to sail downwind in rough weather.

Rolling is the pendulum movement of a vessel along its fore-and-aft axis, becoming excessive either when a vessel on a beam reach has insufficient wind to remain comfortably heeled, or when a vessel is on a run, especially in light airs. For a beam reach in light winds, hauling in the main may offer some relief, but not much. If your bearing and time constraints demand that you stay on the same heading, the rolling will generate some forward progress. As the boat rolls to windward, the sails fill with air and power the boat. Unfortunately, the slatting is hard on the sails, rigging, and nerves. It is sometimes better in this situation to sail close-hauled for a while and resume course when the wind returns. Sailing to windward will also favor use of the vane gear, which is otherwise useless in near calms. For a run, using the main along with the headsail will resist rolling.

According to the *Pocket Oxford Guide to Sailing Terms*, *leeway* and *drift* are the same thing. Both words denote the angle between *bearing* and *heading*, or lateral movement away from the bearing, whether it is caused by wind, tide, or poor keel performance. A vessel may experience extreme leeway when close-hauled in a gale, a situation in which sails and rudder can lose much of their effectiveness. In such a case the skipper must choose among three options:

- heave-to under trysail or bare poles, making just enough headway to cleave the oncoming seas

- set a sea anchor off the bow
- drive downwind under reduced sail or bare poles with a drogue set off the stern.

Too little wind can also cause leeway because there is insufficient wind for propulsion. As in the case of rolling, sometimes the best remedy is to sail to weather for more speed. If water current or poor keel performance is the problem, the helmsman may steer the vessel back on its bearing by adding or subtracting the angle of drift, whichever applies. Occasionally a boat design incorporates a keel of insufficient area for effective lateral resistance. More often than not, the principal malfunction is a lazy skipper who allows the undersides to become a veritable biome of exotic flora and fauna. Unless cleaned regularly, the hull and keel eventually lose any semblance of their original hydrodynamic properties.

Sloop Rig

Balancing a sloop rig, or any sail rig for that matter, requires the opposing forces of wind and keel resistance to be properly aligned in order to generate optimum—which usually indicates *maximum*—boat speed. The interfering forces detailed in the previous section (with the possible exception of rolling) hinder a sailboat's progress by dampening the vessel's capacity to harness the wind's energy. Using our pumpkin seed analogy, forward movement of the seed occurs because the opposing forces of thumb and forefinger are equal. On a close or beam reach, the rig is balanced with no leeway when four forces are aligned for best advantage (see figure 8-2). First, aerodynamic lift forward and aft of the vessel's center of effort must be equal to eliminate weather helm and lee helm. Think of a sloop as a side-

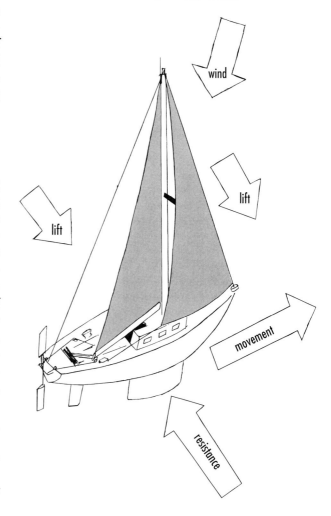

Figure 8-2. Alignment of forces in the balanced rig of a sloop on a beam reach.

ways scale: the jib, pushing the bow to lee, and the main, pushing the bow to weather, act like two weights teetering over a fulcrum. The other two forces are the tendency toward leeway from the lift created by the sails, and opposing pressure from the lee side of the keel. Lift energy not dissipated through the hull forces the vessel forward. These two latter forces also must be equal if the boat is to be propelled with no drift. In the real world, nothing is perfect. A sail rig is never balanced one hundred percent, and some leeway is normal, unless your vessel sits on rollers and zooms along a submerged length of track. What we try to achieve is the vessel's best performance, given its hull design and sail plan, and of course, the wind and sea state.

Split Rig

Balancing a split rig, usually a ketch or a yawl, is easier than balancing a sloop. On a ketch rig, the smaller main and fairly large mizzen spread the sails' effort more evenly along the full length of the vessel. A well-designed cutter-rigged ketch can be balanced so well that when you push the tiller to one side and let it go, it will snap back in line with the keel and resist turning until a gust or a lull causes the rig to lose its balance. We trim a ketch's or yawl's main and head-sail just as we would a sloop's, and we trim the mizzen more or less the same way as the main, but only after trimming the main and jib. The beauty of a ketch rig, especially a cutter ketch, is the variety of possible sail combinations. For example, if you are beam reaching in strong winds, you may hand the mainsail and proceed under mizzen and reduced headsail. You will enjoy a fast sail under a fairly balanced rig. When sailing to windward in a heavy blow, you can reduce weather helm by dousing the mizzen. Some ketches and yawls have a mizzen staysail, allowing extra canvas for downwind sailing in light airs. Most yawls are nothing more than sloops with small mizzens for added balance. As a matter of fact, many yawls are sailed as sloops. If you see a yawl daysailing in your local harbor, you may be fooled into thinking the mizzen is a radar mast— until you take a closer look and see the naked boom pointing aft. In cases where the mizzen is large enough to provide a measure of power, a yawl is trimmed in the same manner as a ketch.

Some ketches and yawls have mizzen booms hanging over the stern, making vane steering more difficult but still possible. Unless the mizzen boom is practically sitting on the stern pulpit, the airvane may be designed to fit below the boom while retaining enough surface area to operate the servo blade or trim tab. Scanmar offers an optional mizzen airvane with its Monitor vane gear. With a little experimentation, you can design an airvane in plywood or aluminum sheet that is just as effective on other vane gears (see chapter 10 for tips on making customized foils). A sailor I met on a Formosa 41 ketch in Pago Pago, American Samoa, didn't regard the mizzen boom as a problem at all.

When tacking, he would drop the airvane back to the horizontal position long enough to let the mizzen boom swing over, raise and adjust the airvane, and continue on his merry way. Since vane steering is used mostly for ocean passages with little tacking or jibing, his system appears quite practical.

More on Downwind Sailing

It is rather fun and easy to balance a rig when sailing to weather but quite a different matter when sailing off the wind. Rarely will a boat sail itself unaided on a run. However, we can take steps to ensure enough balance to satisfy our vane gear's needs. The best balance is achieved by sailing wing and wing or under a well-managed spinnaker (see figure 8-3). These two methods give the most nearly even spread of thrust forward of the mast for an even pull on the hull. Because spinnakers and twin headsails can be difficult to douse in sudden squalls, most shorthanded crews opt for more conservative downwind headsails, usually an asymmetrical spinnaker, a drifter, or a genoa set with a whisker pole. A headsail set on one side of the vessel exerts uneven thrust on the hull, which naturally tries to round up to the wind. This tendency is more pronounced if a gale blows out your headsail, forcing you to run under main only. Don't laugh—it happens. In this case, trim the helm, not the vane gear, slightly to windward in order to offset the bias.

An outboard Cape Horn keeps *Sarah* on course as she ghosts downwind in light airs. (Cape Horn Marine Products)

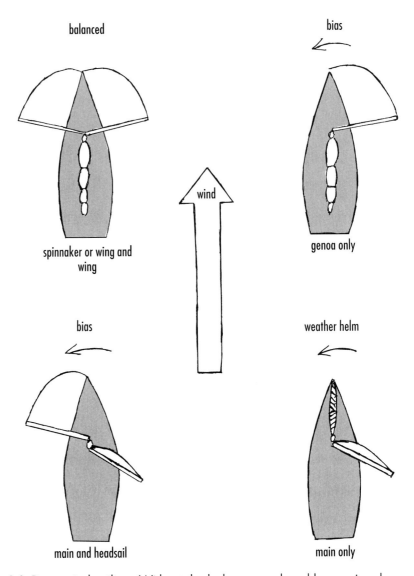

bias

wind

spinnaker or wing and
wing

genoa only

bias

weather helm

main and headsail

main only

Figure 8-3. Downwind sailing. Without the balance produced by a spinnaker or two headsails wing and wing, the vessel will experience some steering bias, corrected by trimming the helm slightly to windward to prevent the vessel from rounding up.

OPERATING THE VANE GEAR

Guidelines for sailing with either a servopendulum vane gear or a trim tab are quite similar. After all, they both incorporate an airvane that must be adjusted to account for shifts in wind speed, except on a run. As the boat moves faster and the apparent wind moves toward the bow, we compensate by rotating the leading edge of the airvane a few degrees aft to fight weather helm. The rest is largely a matter of sail trim. Therefore, the bulk of this discussion appears under Servopendulum Steering (next section), because to explain it again under Trim-Tab Steering would be redundant. The latter, shorter section covers only those procedures differing from the pendulum's operation. Despite their simplicity, trim tabs do have their own procedural quirks, and it is helpful to understand them before setting out under sail.

Servopendulum Steering

Before leaving your anchorage and setting out on a long passage, you need to verify that your self-steering apparatus is fully operational. First make sure the vane gear is tightly secured to the transom. Checking bolts with a couple of wrenches will help prevent undue working of the mounting tubes and other hardware. With the airvane standing absolutely vertical on calm water, see if the servo blade is parallel to the boat's keel. If not, you will need to adjust the pendulum bevel gear or push rod to correct the error. Push the airvane from side to side with one finger, making sure it swings easily. As you dip the vane, check to see that the servo blade rotates freely and in the correct arc. If the arc is biased to one side, adjust the main push rod extending from the foil carriage or realign the bevel gears (see chapter 9, Maintenance and Repair, for more details). From the stern or in a dinghy, make sure the servo blade swings freely from port to starboard.

After ascertaining the proper functioning of the vane gear, inspect the steering lines and blocks. The steering lines pass back and forth over the block sheaves thousands of times on a passage, and cheaply made double-braided line will begin to break down only hours or days into a voyage, snapping at the least opportune moment. Always carry replacement lines, precut with ends whipped, for quick replacement while on passage. Also see that the lines run correctly to the tiller or wheel so that if the foil dips to port, the boat turns to starboard. Do the blocks turn unencumbered? If they have Delrin or other plastic bearings, you may need to rinse the blocks in fresh water to dislodge caked salt and grime. Blocks with stainless bearings need to be disassembled, cleaned in kerosene or other solvent, and reassembled with light marine grease.

The easiest way to acquaint yourself with a vane gear's operation is to start close-hauled. If the apparent wind is below 20 knots, use the standard airvane provided with your unit. If the apparent wind is over 20 knots, use the storm vane. The shorter airvane will prevent oversteering and lessen the chance of breaking it. Balance the rig about 50 degrees off the wind and have someone take the helm. If single-handed, you can lash the helm before jumping back momentarily to the stern. Rotate the vane turret so that the airvane stands

Items to Have on Hand for Offshore Passage

- Spare airvanes of applicable sizes
- Spare steering lines, cut with ends whipped, for quick installation
- Set of spare parts, especially bearings, races, and fasteners (remember the set screws and circlips!)
- Spare breakaway tubes, connectors, or shear pins for servopendulum shaft
- Spray silicone lubricant
- Extra lubricants and adhesives, as recommended by manufacturer
- Owner's manual
- Copies of warranty certificate and receipt of purchase
- Items listed in the Tools and Materials section in chapter 9

straight up edgewise into the wind. The yoke's diagonal axle must be pointing *upward* toward the wind. Without wasting a moment, secure the steering lines to the helm, unlash the wheel or tiller, and study the steering. Is the boat rounding up? If it is, slacken the lee steering line a quarter inch or so, and then tighten the windward line to take up the slack. More steering line adjustment may be necessary to eliminate the weather helm. If you are offsetting the helm more than 5 degrees, the boat may be overcanvased or the sails improperly trimmed for that point of sail. Providing you have done everything more or less correctly, the boat should be sailing along happily on the correct heading, steering itself as you relax. But wait. Don't retire to the cabin quite yet. Even after you get to be an expert at this, you will want to babysit the operation for a while, making slight adjustments to the turret, steering lines, and sheets until you are satisfied with the vessel's overall performance.

Self-steering on a beam reach is much like sailing close-hauled, if not slightly more difficult. Boats do not balance themselves as easily on a beam reach. Broaching seas of only two or three feet easily toss a small vessel off balance during a beam reach, usually causing the boat to round up. This is not a problem for vane steering, even in much higher seas, as long as the vessel is trimmed properly for this point of sail. Let us assume you are sailing close-hauled. Leaving the steering lines and sails as they are for the moment, rotate the vane turret until the airvane is perpendicular to the keel, pointing the upper end of the vane axis toward the anticipated wind. As the boat turns off the wind, first let out the main to alleviate weather helm. Then let out the jib, using the telltales as your guide. Remember, though you know the vessel is supposed to be perpendicular to the air current, as boat speed increases, the angle of apparent wind moves forward of the beam. Trim the sails accordingly, keeping a keen eye on the compass. You may need to spend a few minutes retrimming the mainsail, vane gear, and steering lines so the vessel stays on course within a 10-degree arc. In rough weather, the arc may grow to 20 degrees or more. This is no reason for panic, as long as the bisection of the arc is the desired heading. Let's face reality: the vane gear is steering at least as well as you or I would under those conditions, actually better, since it can keep this up interminably without having to seek shelter from the elements. And in place of a positive terminal and a negative terminal, it has wind and water for its permanent, inexhaustible battery.

To repeat, beam reaching in heavy, broaching seas can be dangerous, particularly if the height of breaking waves is greater than the boat's beam. *Saltaire*, measuring 10 feet on the beam, was once caught in a three-day-long southeasterly gale while beam reaching from Vava'u, Tonga, to Suva, Fiji, around the southern end of the Lau Islands. During the worst part of the storm, sustained winds of up to 45 knots raised seas to 20 feet as we tore along under double-reefed main and only a small piece of roller furling jib, which shredded to ribbons during the second day of the storm. Every five or ten minutes, a huge wave would pick us up and throw us down on our beam ends. Books and galley ware flew about the cabin, the propane tank and other deck equipment shot off the deck in swirls of gray foam, and the skipper puked himself to the point of serious dehydration. How we managed not to capsize remains a mystery. Had there been a way to sail downwind without risking greater dangers, we gladly would have done so. We completed the last 250 miles of the trip under double-reefed main only, with the vane gear steering our little sloop perfectly all the way to the entrance of Suva Harbour.

Broad reaching with the pendulum vane gear will feel very similar to beam reaching, except for a loss of some of the apparent wind needed to deflect the airvane. The lost wind is a problem only in very light conditions. A broad reach is sometimes preferred over a run because a broad reach enjoys more apparent wind, generating more speed than a run without requiring a special downwind sail. The extra apparent wind offers the added benefit of more efficient windvane steering.

If you are changing your point of sail from a beam reach to a broad reach, first rotate the vane turret from its crosswise position to about 135 degrees off the wind; in other words, about 45 degrees from a dead run. Trim your sails for maximum boat speed. Since there will be very little weather helm on this point of sail, you will readjust the steering lines so that the vessel's rudder is trimmed more or less in line with the keel. Now you can adjust the vane turret for the best heading. If you watch the masthead weather vane carefully, you will notice that as the arrow points just inside the little black squares, the jib starts flapping. This occurs because the headsail is now in the mainsail's wind shadow. Constant flogging weakens sailcloth and drives crew to the brink of insanity.

Predeparture Checklist

For further information on maintenance, repair, and calibration, see chapter 9, Maintenance and Repair.

- Check to see that all fasteners are snug, particularly at the mounting brackets
- Inspect unit for cracks or excessive corrosion, especially in stainless steel welds and tubing
- Rotate airvane turret 360 degrees to verify easy movement
- Rotate airvane either vertically or horizontally, depending on design, to ensure unencumbered movement
- Make sure the airvane and either the servo blade or trim tab line up perfectly when deployed. If they don't, refer to the Calibration section in chapter 9 for further instructions.
- Check turning blocks, fixed blocks, and fairleads to verify that the sheaves turn easily
- Run the steering lines, if any, to the helm, removing any obstacles that may have crept into the lines' paths since the last voyage
- Make sure the steering line attachment system at the helm is firmly installed, with no play in the fasteners

The mainsail will momentarily produce just enough weather helm to pull the jib back into the wind, and then the jib will hide again behind the main to repeat this maddening yaw. Decision time! Either trim the airvane a few degrees closer to the wind in order to keep the headsail full, or douse the mainsail. Furling the mainsail liberates you to fine-tune the steering as you wish, and makes it easier to turn downwind or jibe if necessary.

As virtually all sailors know, a run is a whole different kind of sailing with its own specialized sails and tactics. This is also the most controversial point of sail with respect to self-steering. If you are a world-class offshore racer, your vessel's downwind speeds may be so near true wind speed that there may be insufficient wind to power a vane gear. This is where an autopilot–vane gear combination or, better yet, a large crew can be very effective. On garden-variety cruising boats, especially those under 40 feet LOA, there will generally be enough apparent wind on a run to manipulate the airvane. That's right, there is definitely an advantage to having a smaller, slower vessel. You can use the vane steering to your heart's content in virtually any strength or direction of wind, even on a run in 10 knots of true wind. On a 30-footer, that comes to about 3 knots for the vessel and 7 knots for the vane gear, which still means 72 nautical miles a day. Sometimes I have to remind myself, "Hey, it still beats the hell out of working."

Trim-Tab Steering

Your trim tab will sail more efficiently if you give it a thorough look-over before setting sail. Standing at the stern pulpit, check the airvane to guarantee it rotates freely through 360 degrees. A vertical vane turret may have a locking pin that sets into holes or notches spaced apart every 5 to 7 degrees. Lock and unlock the pin a few times to see if it needs oil. If the unit has a horizontal airvane, dip the vane through its full arc. Do you feel any resistance in the cables or linkage leading to the trim tab? If there is considerable resistance in the cables, they may need to be lubricated with silicone spray or replaced. It is unlikely that solid linkage will need any attention. Another cause of friction with a horizontal vane could be the trim tab itself. You may need to disconnect the steering cables or linkage to isolate the source of resistance. To complete the predeparture check, you will need to work from your dinghy. Visually inspect the rudder, be it the vessel's or an auxiliary, ensuring that it is free of growth and debris. The integrity of the hydrodynamic relationship between trim tab and rudder depends on a smooth flow of water around their surfaces. With the horizontal airvane linkage disengaged, or in the case of a vertical vane, with the vane unlocked, dip the trim tab back and forth with your hand. Also verify that the auxiliary rudder, if one is employed, moves easily through its full arc. Friction on the trim tab or auxiliary rudder could be due to corrosion. On the trim tab the problem is more likely due to small barnacles or coral growing on the tab's hinges. Time to don your diving mask and attack the job with a putty knife and a flat-head screwdriver.

Shipwright and highly experienced sailor Bill Bailey, who hails from Port Townsend, Washington, built the H-28 ketch *Noctiluca*, aboard which he sailed over 25,000 miles in the Pacific with his wife Lisa. For this he built a trim-tab gear based on Letcher's landmark self-steering treatise. In a long discussion regarding self-steering, Bill reiterated several times the importance of a balanced rig, especially with trim tabs. Servopendulums generate a huge amount of initial corrective steering thrust, oversteering at first, then tapering off as the airvane aligns itself with the wind. While this does not allow sloppy sail trim, a servopendulum does tolerate a degree of imbalance in the rig. In contrast, a trim tab, more notably one with a vertical vane, provides course correction only to the degree the airvane senses the wind, no more. The resultant steering power is inadequate to struggle against weather or lee helm in a hard blow. A wedge-shaped vertical airvane, an improvement over the flat vane, amplifies the wind's impulses, generating initial oversteering for more aggressive course correction. If you really want to sharpen your sailing skills, try cruising with a vertical-vane trim tab.

The first time you practice sailing with the trim tab, tune your sail rig and helm about 50 degrees off the wind. The airvane turret should be disengaged while you balance the rig. Even in a stiff breeze, you should be able to achieve near-zero helm, though this may necessitate reefing the sails below the wind speed at which you are accustomed to doing so; this could mean, for example, shortening the main at 15 knots of true wind rather than 18. Next, lash the main rudder. If using a vertical vane, the vane should swing around and line up automatically with the wind. Lock the turret clutch. With a horizontal vane, rotate the vane turret until the airvane stands straight up in the wind. If the trim tab is on the vessel's rudder, unlash the helm so that the rudder is free to respond to the trim tab's impulses. The helm obviously remains lashed with an auxiliary rudder. Though you may do your level best to balance the rig, no boat can sail a perfect course in rough seas, so you may need to fine-tune the main steering to offset a bit of helm. In order to adjust the steering for an auxiliary rudder, trim the main rudder while the windvane is in operation, and then re-lash the helm. There is no way to cheat with a main rudder trim tab. Your only recourse is to rotate the airvane a few degrees back off the wind for weather helm, or slightly toward the wind for lee helm.

You should have no trouble figuring out how to execute the other points of sail with a trim tab if you have read the foregoing matter in this chapter. Rotate the airvane into the wind, making darned sure you have the sails trimmed properly for that point of sail. (Yes, I know, a few pages back I was belaboring the point—now I'm nagging.) Compare a trim tab to the action of a servopendulum, and you will find that the trim-tab gear is more sensitive in light airs, steering with a greater degree of precision and smoothness. With an auxiliary rudder, you will feel additional stability on all points of sail by virtue of the extended plane of lateral resistance. On a run in heavy seas, however, nothing beats the yaw-preventing action of the servopendulum.

In this chapter, we covered a lot of ground in very few words. Proficiency in sailing and vane gear steering requires a modicum of reading, but most of all, practice. Sailing authors have written millions of words on how sailboats harness the forces of wind and water, and how crew tackle problems at sea. As you become more familiar with the behavior of your vessel, especially in offshore conditions, you will gain confidence in your ability to sail and to keep a course under vane steering. The interfering forces of weather helm, lee helm, yaw, roll, and leeway are all part of a boat's repertoire, for which the seasoned cruiser has learned a set of Pavlovian responses. Operating a vane gear gradually melds into that conditioned behavior, becoming as natural as sailing itself.

Chapter 9
Maintenance and Repair

E very boat, every piece of marine hardware, and every sailor eventually must yield in some way to the ravages of wind, wave, and sun. Your windvane self-steering system is no exception to this rule, regardless of who built it or what kinds of exotic alloys and low-friction polymers entered into its construction. Plastic bushings and sleeves wear out, stainless welds occasionally break, control lines fray and snap, and noninsulated stainless fasteners eventually eat big, ugly holes in aluminum. Though it is virtually impossible to anticipate when a weld will break, we anticipate wear and tear in plastic parts, and if careful, we get decades of service from aluminum extrusions and castings by inspecting them periodically and protecting them from dissimilar metals. So again, the totally inert, collision-proof, maintenance-free windvane has not been invented, nor shall it ever be. Most of us will never have great cause to worry about our vane gears. They shrug off storms, maybe losing a light-air vane that we were too lazy to exchange for a storm vane, and their constant motion ever so slowly erodes their plastic bearings, causing play in stainless and aluminum shafts. No one really knows how long vane gears can last—they have been in commercial production for less than 40 years—but it is safe to assume many will outlast the boats they are mounted on. Periodic inspections and maintenance will ensure that after 30,000 nautical miles of hard sailing, or a circumnavigation by way of two canals, you will enjoy the same performance from your vane gear as you did when you first installed the unit.

One of the comforting aspects of working with mechanical things is that there is always a logical way to pull apart and reassemble the apparatus. We lay out pieces in order, replace or repair defective parts, and then reverse the order to restore the machine to its proper state. This works when all the parts are close at hand so we need not work from memory at some later date. It is better to have both a detailed diagram of the unit and a complete parts list. The builder should be able to furnish owners with a parts list, including prices, in cases where one is not included in the owner's manual. If the unit is used, order a manual from the builder, or at the very least, photocopy one from another sailor who has the same make and model vane gear. The detailed sketch or diagram is probably drawn to scale, depicting every piece of hardware, down to the tiniest setscrew, going into the final assembly. Review the drawings before you start working on the unit so you can anticipate which tools you will need. Hand tools may include a set of combination wrenches, a Crescent wrench, a set of socket wrenches, hex keys, screwdrivers, circlip pliers (internal and external), Vise-Grips, and other tools, depending on the model and what you need to accomplish. Oh yes, and throw in a can of shaving cream. Read on.

INSPECTION

The predeparture inspections detailed in the previous chapter serve as fairly good maintenance checks. What you want to ascertain first is that all moving parts rotate through their full arcs with little friction and no play. Friction might be due to corroded stainless bearings or, in aluminum pieces, either surface corrosion under plastic sleeves or swelling of the plastic itself from constant exposure to water. Swollen plastic sleeves and bushings are most likely to be found in sections near or under the waterline. Play is evident if shafts and other moving parts wiggle through their rotational axes, with looseness owing to worn plastic bearings, races, spacers, etc. The surfaces of these components slowly give way to erosion caused by salt water and constant movement under pressure. Plastic bearings can be expected to last for three to five years of ocean cruising under normal conditions. Scanmar recommends changing them after every 15,000 miles or five years of use, and Fleming guarantees its Delrin bearings for the same period, five years. Again I stress the importance of a spare parts kit. If a volcano or coup d'etat suddenly erupts in your tropical paradise, you will be far more concerned with the proper functioning of your vessel's systems than with analyzing some subtle nuance in a warranty certificate.

Check metal tubing to make sure there are no unintended bends or dimpling. Damage not previously identified may indicate a collision with another vessel while you have been away from your boat. A slight bend in the tube mounting structure or, even worse, in the rudder shaft can seriously interfere with the vane gear's ability to steer. Also check stainless welds very carefully for cracks. If brown rust makes it difficult to see, first polish the area well, and then check for the telltale brown line through the weld. A small crack is nearly as bad as a totally severed section, which is what you will have the next time you use the vane gear if you don't fix the problem first.

Maintenance Tools and Materials

Not all these items necessarily apply to your vane gear. For some models and installations, you may need to add to the list.

- Metric and SAE combination and socket wrenches
- Socket extensions
- Crescent wrenches
- Vise-Grips
- Metric or SAE hex wrenches, whichever apply
- Screwdrivers
- Circlip pliers (internal and external)
- Plumb bob (may be improvised) to be suspended next to horizontal airvane during calibration
- 15–20 feet of old, double-braided polyester line
- Dowel rod ($^3/_4$ by $4^3/_4$ in. for Monitor, longer for some other models)
- Swaging tool with halyard wire, thimbles, and sleeves
- Assorted fasteners as needed, including circlips, set screws, cotter pins, etc.
- Can of shaving cream
- Lubricants and adhesives, as recommended by manufacturer

Checking the windvane's peripheral components, namely the control lines, blocks, and airvanes, should be as much a part of your routine as checking the wet exhaust every time you start the diesel engine. Double-braided control lines fray around sheaves, blocks occasionally freeze up, and a plywood airvane sometimes starts cracking just above the yoke long before it takes flight in a gale. Not a big deal, but definitely a pain in the posterior when it's 0200 and blowing force 8. If you discover a frozen turning block, look between the sheave and the cheeks to see if a length of string, fishing line, or hair has wound itself around the axle. Hanging stringy, frayed towels on the control lines could have the folks at Duncan worried about competition. Who knows? Maybe that's how the yo-yo was invented!

BUSHINGS, BEARINGS, AND SLEEVES

Before you disassemble the unit to remove bearings, sleeves, and related hardware, verify that you have on hand all the little pieces you will need to replace them. Also, you would be wise to remove the vane gear from its transom mounting brackets before reducing the unit to bits and pieces. If you do not have a spare parts kit and were not able to order parts from the builder, then you have no choice but to disassemble the vane so you can compare the hardware to other pieces that may fit. Plastic and stainless ball bearings are standard items found in well-stocked hardware stores. Roller, or needle, bearings will be a bit tougher to find. Some nylon bushings and sleeves are readily available at Ace, Home Depot, True Value, and similar retail stores in the United States, but you may have to cut or drill out the pieces to make them fit. For custom-machined Delrin or other plastics, order them from the builder. Otherwise, you will need to have pieces machined from whatever materials are handy. Try to use the same materials as the originals for replacements. Placing a brass bushing between an aluminum tube and a rotating stainless shaft is so insanely destructive, just typing this sentence is making me laugh! If you cannot find the same type of plastic, find another chunk of plastic that you can have milled as a temporary replacement. Bushings and sleeves should fit inside the larger, stationary component snugly. The inner, rotating shaft should move smoothly, but without play; allow enough room for some swelling from water and heat.

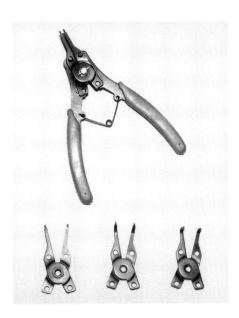

This inexpensive pair of reversible circlip pliers comes with four attachments in different sizes and angles.

Before attempting to remove plastic bushings or bearing races, check to see if they are held in place by setscrews; if so, remove the setscrews and set them aside. On some models, you will need to remove a *circlip*, or spring clip, with a pair of circlip pliers to free bearings. There are two types of circlips: internal, fitted in a groove inside a tube, and external, fitted in an outer groove. Note that each type of clip has its own corresponding pliers. Securing the circlip with a piece of string through one of the eyelets will prevent the piece from ricocheting through the mast orchard.

Remove bushings, sleeves, and bearing races from their tubes by pushing them out with a wooden dowel and a hammer. A section of broomstick should serve well for this purpose. If the dowel covers only part of the circular fitting, tap with even pressure as you move the tip around the edge of the plastic piece inside the tube. Avoid using pliers or screwdrivers, which damage plastics. Save old fittings for spares.

When disassembling pinion (bevel) gears to get at bearings, mark the alignment with a thin daub of brightly colored paint or an indelible marker; do not scratch the metal. Though bevel gears are cast in high-grade stainless or bronze, disturbing the oxidized surface makes it susceptible to pitting from galvanic action as the exposed metal develops a new oxidized surface. Check to see if either casting has a stamped mark to indicate proper alignment. While you are at it, check the gear teeth for breakage or serious pitting. If you need to disassemble rod linkage, first mark the proper calibration points of threaded rods with pieces of tape that will not fall off. Self-welding rigging tape and Teflon pipe thread tape are good choices for this purpose.

Reassembling bearings does not have to be a nerve-racking experience. A wooden dowel, such as the $3/4$-inch dowel included in the Monitor repair kit, makes this job a lot easier. If you do not have this tool, with a jackknife and a piece of medium-grit sandpaper you can whittle and sand that same broomstick (usually about 1 inch in diameter) until it is of the same diameter as the stainless shaft that passes through the bearings. Chances are, though, the local hardware store has a hardwood dowel in the exact diameter of the shaft. Another trick is to keep bearings in place with shaving cream—or whipped cream if you have a sweet tooth or don't shave. After reassembling the bearings and reinstalling the circlips, wash out the foamy mess by rinsing the bearings thoroughly with water. When reassembling bevel gears, be careful to adjust the thrust bearing or put the correct number of spacers, which hold either one of the gears in place, so that the two gears mesh properly, but not too tightly. Overtightening can impede smooth steering action and may even damage gear teeth. Use Loctite on setscrews and other fasteners to keep them from coming loose.

Some plastic sleeves and bearing races are held in place with a strong adhesive instead of a setscrew. After removing the hardware, clean the inside of the

Jack Dunn of *Fair Rose* installs new bearings and bushings in a Monitor vane gear.

tube with fine-grit sandpaper. Secure the new fittings in the tubes with the adhesive recommended by the manufacturer. Sailomat suggests using Super Bonder #415, manufactured by Loctite.

Plastic bearings require no lubrication. However, a fellow sailor once recommended a spray silicone lubricant that Sport Divers Manufacturing distributes for scuba diving equipment. It has worked wonders on the Torlon bearings in *Saltaire*'s roller furler and on the Delrin bearings in the vane gear. Avoid using grease or oil, which cause plastics to swell and dissolve—plastics themselves are petroleum-based products.

Caring for stainless bearings is fairly easy. As long as the bearings are not pitted, all you need to do is clean them, along with the races, in kerosene—never use gasoline as a cleaning solvent. Wipe them dry and reassemble them in their races. Diesel is OK, but take care to dry hardware with a rag instead of letting pieces air-dry, as diesel contains sulfur, which slowly eats stainless. Most "experts" recommend leaving stainless ball bearings unlubricated if they are exposed to water. Their logic is that grease emulsifies with salt water, becoming a thick paste, and then drying and hardening into a semirigid cement. On the other hand, stainless bearings left unprotected can become as crusty as an old sailor. A little marine grease will protect the bearings against oxidation and keep them moving smoothly, but do not put the grease in a spot you cannot access easily. Greased bearings require frequent inspection, cleaning, and regreasing.

BLOCKS AND CONTROL LINES

Permanently riveted blocks with polymer bearings and sheaves do not permit any sort of maintenance aside from washing in fresh water to dislodge salt and grime. When they finally wear out, buy new ones and save the old blocks for less demanding jobs. Inexpensive blocks with bearingless sheaves have a way of jamming up and then wearing away on one side. Time for the Dumpster. It is possible to disassemble some blocks with plastic bearings by removing the nut from the sheave axle, or from the bolts arranged around the sheave, and then removing the cheeks to expose the bearings. Expect to see at least two sets of ball bearings: some blocks have two sizes of bearings in concentric grooves on either side of the sheave. After you assemble one side, press the cheek into place over the bearings, turn the assembly over, and apply the other cheek. That's right, turn the other cheek. It is doubtful you will have occasion to use blocks with stainless bearings for the control lines, unless you employ them as fixed blocks, but even this is unlikely with the vast array of lightweight, smoothly turning plastic sheaves and bearings available in modern turning blocks. Clean the metal bearings in kerosene, and if you so elect, lubricate them in the same manner described in the previous section.

Steering lines can take quite a beating on rough passages, and cheap line inevitably fails before long. Vane gear builders recommend double-braided polyester line, ranging from $1/4$- to $3/8$-inch, depending on the model. Make sure the blocks you select match the size of line you are using. Line too thick for a given sheave size can lead to premature failure of the double-braided polyester covering. Your control lines will last longer if you cut them with added length, and occasionally advance them 6 inches or so along the path between the helm and the vane gear. This technique distributes exposure to sheave duty over a longer portion of the lines. After the lines have passed as far as they can go in one direction, remove and reinstall them in the opposite direction, repeating the rotation process to get maximum mileage from the lines. Leaving a little slack in the control lines provides some dampening against oversteering and adds to the longevity of their fibers. Experiment with this and see what works best for steering and for the durability of your double-braided lines.

Nylon, polypropylene, and three-strand rope have little place in a servopendulum steering system. Nylon has a high degree of stretch, making it great for dock lines and anchor rode, where the fiber acts as a snubber, or shock absorber. That is the last thing we want between the vane gear and the helm because the tiller or wheel needs to receive impulses from the servo-rudder with little dampening. Polypropylene is weak, brittle, and highly susceptible to attack by UV light. For cruisers, it is relegated to dinghy painters and wherever else we want cheap floating line. Some vane gears have a mechanism and trip line to disengage the steering function in case of emergency. A long piece of floating polypropylene line trailing off the stern permits a single-hander who has fallen overboard to pull the quick release line so the boat will round up and stop.

Three-strand rope is available in low-stretch polyester and is a favorite among those who want traditional running rigging with modern wear characteristics for classic vessels. However, while polyester three-strand line may work for a while as self-steering control lines, it does not hold up as well, or wear as evenly, as double-braided line when subjected to constant motion through sheaves. One exception to the prohibition on three-strand rope is when it is employed as an adjustment line for the vane turret. A line splice allows infinite movement of the cord through a small remote block and around the turret.

BENT TUBING AND BROKEN WELDS

Bent aluminum or stainless steel tubes on your vane gear require the services of a skilled welder. This situation may also call for a reputable practitioner of admiralty law because virtually the only way this damage occurs is by collision with another vessel. Unless you sail backward, we will assume that you are the aggrieved party. Do not just pocket the settlement money and attempt to bend the tubing back in place with a twelve-pound sledgehammer. Once tubing is bent into a particular shape, it can be bent into a more acute angle, but in most cases, it cannot be straightened. The metal is compressed on the inside of the curve, while the wall on the outer side of the angle is stretched. No amount of creative pulling or pounding will stretch the compressed side or compress the stretched side. If you try, you will end up with a frame and mounting structure as dented and crumpled as Gunga Din's bugle (in the movie, not the poem). The manufacturer should be able to rebuild the unit. If you are far from where the vane gear was built, ask the builder to ship you a piece of preshaped replacement tubing so a welder can refabricate the damaged section.

A broken weld, more common in stainless tubing than in aluminum, is definitely outpatient surgery, requiring only 10 to 15 minutes of the welder's time. For stainless, be sure the welder is using a TIG (tungsten inert gas) outfit to ensure a clean, professional weld. TIG is a method of melting the surrounding metals without use of a consumable rod. Brazing with a brass rod is not hot enough for proper adhesion, and this would only cause a bigger mess for the next welder to clean up and repair. Unshielded arc welding, or stick welding with regular steel rods, is also inadequate. Aluminum requires a great deal of skill in the welder. Excessive heat can cause *annealing*, or weakening of the surrounding metal, ultimately leading to structural failure under extreme loads. TIG is also appropriate for aluminum welding. For welding sections $1/4$-inch or more in thickness, the technician should use MIG (gas metal arc welding).

MIG incorporates a wire feed to fill in the deep crevice between the welded edges.

CARING FOR ALUMINUM

Unfreezing Oxidized Parts

Back in the mid-1970s, I had the opportunity to "be all I could be" in the U.S. Army at Fort Sherman, Panama Canal Zone. When I got myself into trouble with the military police, not only was I demoted, but I was also kicked out of my radio shop job and banished to the boathouse overlooking Fort Sherman's beautiful, palm-fringed lagoon. My fall from grace entailed unspeakable horrors: waking up late, living in swim trunks, working on outboard motors, testing rubber rafts and small motorboats on the lagoon, and figuring out how to dislodge aluminum hardware welded together by galvanic corrosion. One day, the section chief handed me a bucket full of frozen aluminum inflation valves taken from old fifteen-person inflatable rubber rafts (RB-15s). We had enough WD-40 (the army buys it in 5-gallon drums) to submerge and soak only about half of them. The others we left in a bucket of fresh water. After a few days, the valves soaking in WD-40 finally yielded to our twisting, but the oxides were still present. After soaking in fresh water a week or so, much of the white oxide powder on the other valves had sloughed away. We dunked this batch of valves in the leftover WD-40 for about an hour, and then persuaded them to open. The difference was that the water-soaked valves were cleaner and the threads seamed to mesh with less crunching. Both sets of valves returned to duty on the RB-15s. While my experiences with alloys in the boathouse helped catapult me back to the lofty rank of PFC, they would also help me later in life as a cruising sailor.

Most of us have not the money to purchase, nor the room to store, large drums of penetrating oil, just in case we need to soak the entire main body of a predominantly cast-aluminum vane gear for a week. But we will have no trouble finding a large plastic tub for a freshwater soak. Be careful not to attempt prying frozen hardware apart prematurely, or you could wind up breaking the very pieces you are trying to salvage. A common practice with automobile brake cylinders, which are made of cast iron but may contain aluminum pistons, is to boil the whole cylinder in fresh water in order to dislodge the frozen aluminum. Just in case you were wondering, petroleum-based solvents are harmful to the rubber hoses, diaphragms, and O-rings in brake systems, so penetrating oil is out of the question. Boiling could make short work of unfreezing vane gear pieces small enough to fit in a large pot. If you're in a hurry, gentle tapping with a hammer over the frozen area and liberal soaking with penetrating oil should eventually disjoin frozen aluminum sections.

Cleaning and Lubrication

There is a fairly simple method for cleaning and preparing surfaces of large, moving, bare aluminum fittings that come into close contact. These parts commonly include toothed gear castings and pawls, among other items. I use a stiff plastic or straw brush—not copper, a soft metal that can rub off and leave a harmful cathodic film—and fresh running water to remove as much loose grime and oxidation as possible. This leaves intact the protective oxide surface, probably the best guard the alloy has against further corrosion. Use the sharp edge of a hardwood stick to grind off stubborn oxide nodes. If a troublesome spot gives way to a large crater, you may need to replace the fitting. A welder can repair rolled aluminum sheet or extrusions, but again, it is probably wiser to replace the section. After letting the surface dry well, if it is absolutely necessary for the proper operation of the section, coat the contact surfaces with marine grease. Otherwise, leave the surfaces dry. It should be emphasized that grease is not to be applied to plastic hardware. Marine hardware manufacturers also warn us not to use oil on Delrin and other plastic bearings. However, a number of sailors have told me they break the rule, liberally applying machine oil and even 30-weight motor oil to the rock-hard, chemical-resistant Delrin and Torlon bearings in their vane gears. In chapter 10 you will find a method of modifying your old Aries or other aluminum vane gear to take advantage of this, shall we say, controversial method of lubrication.

Fasteners

When it comes to fasteners, there are numerous products and methods from which to choose, depending on application and personal preference. For screws and bolts threading directly into aluminum, some sailors prefer Never-Seize, a metal-containing grease that allows you to remove fasteners easily. The downside of this product is its tendency to run and smear after repeated dousing in water. This is solely a cosmetic concern, since a satisfactory coating of residual lubricant seems to remain on the threads for a long time. A number of other treatments act as dielectrics to prevent galvanism, but not all are lubricants. Duralac is popular because it electrically insulates the fastener from its host and also keeps the fastener in place until you are ready to remove it. TefGel and Loctite 242 are also effective dielectrics allowing easy removal of fasteners.

At some point you might strip out the threads from an aluminum fitting, leaving two options: buy a new fitting or employ some alternate method to reuse the hole. If the situation allows, simply drill out the hole and tap it for a larger bolt or screw. As a rule of thumb, drill the hole 1 mm smaller than the tap. Compare the threads of the new fastener with those of the die you are considering; mesh the threads together and check the diameters again. If in doubt about compatibility, drill and tap a hole in an old piece of aluminum or other soft metal and try the fastener in the new hole. Because the tap's threads are a wee bit wider than its corresponding bolt or screw, verifying the tap's size by attempting to screw a nut on it will not work.

Another option is to drill the hole out to a slightly larger size than the original and screw in a Heli-Coil, permitting you to use the original fastener. If you have spent much time working on old aluminum Volkswagen engines, no doubt you have already used these little humdingers. The directions on the package will indicate the exact size of drill bit and tap you need, and how to insert the coil with the special wrench included. Also, remember to use Duralac or similar treatment to act as a dielectric and keep the Heli-Coil more or less permanently in place at the base of the hole. Heli-Coils are appropriate for metals at least $1/2$ inch thick. For less depth, your best bet is to drill out and tap the old hole for a larger-diameter fastener.

Plastic Insulators

We have already covered this topic, so there is not much more to say about the role of plastics in protecting aluminum, or any other highly anodic metal, for that matter. The only other thing you may want to think of is the option of putting a plastic sleeve or bushing where perhaps there was not one before. This applies to the joining of any two solid materials where we want to reduce friction. Sometimes we find ourselves sliding a bolt through a hole and then into a threaded hole in a fitting on the other side of the first hole. If the unthreaded hole has too much play, it may be wise to insert a cheap nylon sleeve to firm up the movement and insulate the bolt. If all you can find is a bushing with a flange on one end, well, grab a hacksaw and cut the flange off. Voilà, a sleeve.

CALIBRATION

With any luck, calibrating your vane gear's linkage will be a one-time affair, when you first install the unit. Properly aligned bevel gears and threaded rod linkage should keep you in good stead until the unit's next major overhaul. Trim-tab cables probably will need replacement every few years, but calibration of the trim tab is a simple process. The exception, regardless of vane gear type, may be when the structure has incurred damage serious enough to require welding, straightening, or replacement of whole sections. A slight shift in the mechanism's shape might require an adjustment here or there to keep the air-vane and servo blade or trim tab properly aligned.

For accurate calibration, the vessel needs to be on calm water with no wind or even the slightest swell. The boat should be evenly weighted from port to starboard, and there should be no one walking around above or below decks disturbing the vessel's roll axis. Before starting the process, check over the mounting structure with a handful of wrenches, verifying that the mounting tubes are attached firmly to the transom and all other components are snug in their places. Also check for any bent or damaged sections, which will require complete repair before calibration is possible.

Servopendulums

Once properly assembled, most servopendulums need essentially no calibration. Their gears or other linkages are fixed into one position, remaining fairly stable if left undisturbed. The following procedures, like much of the other material in this book, are generic. And even if the servopendulum system rarely needs adjustment, these guidelines will help you ascertain whether the servopendulum has suffered some form of hitherto unseen damage resulting in misalignment.

Set the vane gear up as if you were going to use it for a sail, excluding the control lines, which may remain attached to the vane gear, but not to the helm. The standard airvane should be in its yoke, and the servo blade should be hanging freely in the water. Is the airvane absolutely vertical? Check with a piece of string and a fishing sinker acting as a plumb bob. If the vane is visibly off balance, adjust the counterweight downward, or depending on its design, slightly to the opposing side until the airvane stands up solidly vertical.

Now that the airvane is standing vertically while in line with the boat's keel, see if the servo blade is in line with the keel (see figure 9-1). You do not need high-precision tools for this—trust your eyes. If the pendulum is pointing in the wrong direction, even slightly, you will need to adjust the pendulum shaft bevel gear or push rod (on the Monitor, the actuator shaft) to correct the error. For rod adjustment, first loosen the lock nut where the threads meet the sleeve fitting, then make the necessary adjustment, and finally, retighten the nut. To realign the bevel gear, loosen and pull away the thrust bearing or other fitting holding the gear in place. Rotate the gear one cog at a time, until the servo blade is in line with the keel.

Even if the airvane and servo blade line up perfectly, there is still one more alignment that you must check. Dip the airvane from side to side with one finger, making sure it swings easily. As you dip the airvane, check to see that the servo blade rotates freely and in the correct arc. This is difficult to measure accurately, so find two symmetrical points on the unit's frame to compare the outer edges of the servo blade's arc. If the arc is biased to one side, adjust the main push rod extending from the yoke. You will probably make several ad-

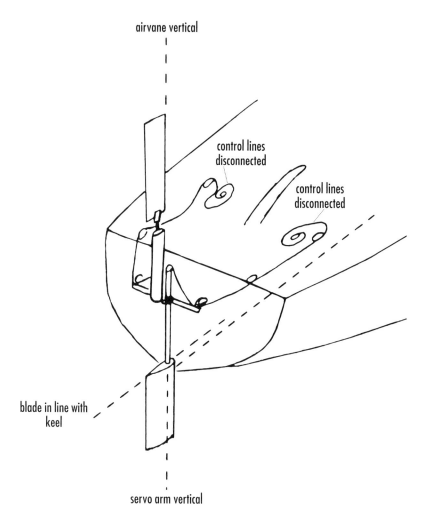

airvane vertical

control lines
disconnected

control lines
disconnected

blade in line with
keel

servo arm vertical

Figure 9-1. Alignment of airvane and servo blade.

justments and observations, but once you have fixed the problem, you should not have to worry about it again; that is, barring any future structural damage to the unit. A word of caution: your servopendulum may call for a certain degree of bias in the servo blade's vertical axis; refer to your owner's manual to verify the proper bias, if any.

Trim Tabs

Calibrating a trim tab is far simpler than calibrating a servopendulum. The rudder itself, whether main or auxiliary, requires no adjustment whatsoever because it is essentially a separate mechanism and rotates freely. The airvane, linkage, and trim tab comprise a separate device, which we superimpose on the rudder. If the system has a vertical vane, your work is already done. You calibrate your system every time you change course. Other than that, just make sure you tighten the appropriate fasteners and reduce as much unnecessary friction and play as possible in the hard linkage. If the vane gear has a nylon clutch or some other peculiar fitting, such as that found on old RVG vertical trim tabs, test the operation of the fittings to make sure they hold tightly. A worn, slipping clutch calls for the services of a machine shop to make a replacement. Also check the base of the vane mast for signs of bending or breakage at the weld.

If you have an Auto-Helm or other horizontal-vane trim tab, calibration consists of aligning the airvane and the trim tab itself. First secure the rudder so that it is perfectly in line with the keel. For the main rudder, simply lash it in place. To stabilize an auxiliary rudder, run a couple of lines from some point on either side of the rudder, and tie them to a couple of deck cleats. Disconnect the airvane from its cable or hard linkage, and check to see if it stands straight up. If not, adjust the counterweight downward until the airvane stays firmly erect. Avoid extending the weight down too far because doing so will reduce the airvane's wind-sensing ability, making it difficult to self-steer in light winds. Counterweight adjustment, especially on some homebuilt units, can become an art in itself. With the counterweight adjusted satisfactorily, reconnect the airvane to its linkage. Now observe, as well as you can from your vantage point, whether the trim tab extends straight back from the rudder. Have someone look from a dinghy or from dockside to help you with the adjustment. Adjust the cables or rod linkage until the trim tab points straight back while the airvane remains in the upright position.

BROKEN AIRVANES

Naturally, the best cure for a broken airvane is a new one. The cost of a piece of thin plywood is minimal, so it is simply a matter of purchasing another piece and cutting one or, even better, several new airvanes. An aluminum vane can only bend, and a plastic sandwich airvane is probably immune to any kind of wind damage, so your concerns will be limited to plywood. When a heavy blow hits a plywood airvane, initially the vane may only crack at the stress point a quarter-inch or so above the yoke. This is likely to happen if you forget to switch the light-air vane for a storm vane early enough after weather conditions deteriorate. In that case, obviously you will switch vanes, perhaps saving the damaged one to use as kindling at your next cruiser bonfire.

For now, though, a pair of splints cut out of spare wood from the Ship's Junk Box can restore the airvane until you have the chance to make a new one. Cut a piece of $3/8$-inch plywood or a similar thickness of wood plank into four strips measuring 1 by 6 inches (see figure 9-2). These are approximations only; thin aluminum straps are even better, but steel or thick wood sections will impose excessive weight on the airvane, disturbing its balance. Place the wooden sections on either side of the airvane, straddling the spot where the vane slides into the yoke. A couple of C-clamps make this a lot easier. Drill a $5/32$-inch or slightly larger hole at either end of each pair of splints. Fasten the two pairs of splints together with four size 8, $1^1/4$-inch machine screws. After a gale cracked *Saltaire*'s light-weather vane in the Gulf of Papagayo off northwestern Costa Rica, I anchored my boat in a small, uninhabited cove and splinted

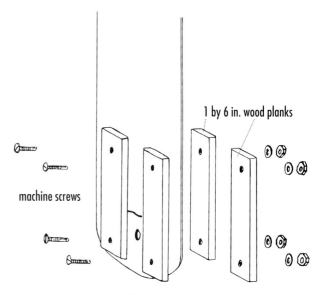

machine screws

1 by 6 in. wood planks

Figure 9-2. Repairing a broken airvane with splints.

the airvane using this method. The repair was so effective, the vane lasted another year, finally snapping off and flying away in a gale near Bora Bora.

An alternate method of repairing a foil is to fiberglass both sides of the crack with epoxy resin and 6-ounce glass cloth. The problem here is keeping the board absolutely flat while the resin sets. A set of temporary splints, as explained above, along with four C-clamps would hold the vane section more or less straight, but there may still be a slight warp above and below the crack itself. Lying flat, it may not seem like much, but when mounted, the slant could be a problem. Perhaps you can flatten the area with a block of wood and a few whacks with a hammer before sanding and glassing over the crack.

Maintenance, repair, and calibration of your vane gear will occupy only a tiny fraction of your cruising career. Well-built vanes can take a lot of abuse, certainly far more than a human being or an autopilot could ever endure. I have woken up after several hours' sleep to see the lee control line completely severed from fray, and the vane gear still steering on course, as if nothing had happened. And to tell you the truth, a vane gear slightly out of calibration will steer accurately with some offsetting at the helm. Nonetheless, we want the cleanest, most precise steering we can achieve for maximum speed and course control. It is a matter of pride, if nothing else. The repairs you have read about here are more serious issues. Always carry enough hand tools, fabrication materials, and spare parts to tackle any job likely to present itself during an extended cruise.

Chapter 10

Customizing Your Vane Gear

After having owned your windvane steering system for a while, you may identify certain aspects you would like to refine further. Does the airvane seem a little heavy, not rising up fast enough even with the counterweight adjusted out all the way? We will look at a neat trick for putting that airvane on a quick weight-loss plan. Does the vane gear always seem a little loose, twisting back and forth no matter how often you tighten the tube structure's bolts? Added struts or wire stays may be the only means of stiffening the whole ensemble, ultimately yielding better steerage and extending the life of the unit. Have you picked up an old Aries or some other aluminum vane steerer that has been neglected for many years and allowed to freeze up? After unfreezing the unit, as explained in the previous chapter, you may want to try a modification that will make lubricating bearings fast and easy. If you have purchased an Auto-Helm or Autosteer and need to build a trim-tab assembly, the notes in this chapter should help you sort out a workable method for completing the job. A note of caution: if the vane gear is still under warranty, do not permanently alter the system in any way without prior approval from the manufacturer, lest you unwittingly invalidate the warranty. Custom airvanes and the trim tab for an Auto-Helm or similar vane gear should not pose any problems, as long as you stay within the guidelines stated in your owner's manual.

REINFORCING THE MOUNTING STRUCTURE

Excessive twisting and play in your vane gear probably indicate a loose mounting structure. As you sail, spend ample time studying the unit's movement. You may hear a chafing or squeaking sound as the servo arm rotates. Try to determine the likely source of the noise—it could be worn bearings. If you see that the unit is shaking or twisting, regardless of how the pendulum shaft, linkages, and bearings are behaving, then the obvious solution is to reinforce the mounting architecture. It is probably better to change the plastic bearings, bushings, races, and sleeves first in order to get a precise picture of the frame's movement. After you have followed up with a stronger mounting structure, the vane gear's action should be like clockwork. There are two good ways to bolster the frame's attachment to the transom: adding solid struts to the existing mounting configuration, or firming up both sides of the frame with wire and turnbuckles.

Struts

Your first step with either struts or wire is to loosen the vane gear's mounting bolts and tie a pair of lines between the vane turret and two points on the stern pulpit. Adjust the lines until the vane gear frame is positioned exactly where you want it. Correct sagging in the structure by pulling the whole frame upward. Now determine where best to place the struts. Ideally, they should extend from two points at or near the center of the unit, perhaps the center tube where the main push rod passes through. The two struts should be of approximately equal length, meeting at symmetric points on the hull. A fairly wide angle be-

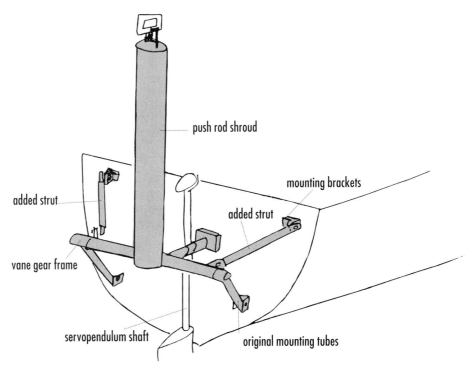

push rod shroud

mounting brackets

added strut

added strut

vane gear frame

servopendulum shaft

original mounting tubes

Figure 10-1. Additional reinforcement struts on a servopendulum vane gear.

tween the tubes, reaching to either side of the transom, will add considerable stability to the overall structure (see figure 10-1). If you have doubts, or if the unit is still under warranty, discuss this first with the manufacturer, who may already have drawings available to assist you. Hire a welder to attach two tangs with predrilled holes for fasteners to the frame or center tube. The technician should be using a gas-shielded form of arc welding, most probably TIG. Bolt on brackets at the appropriate places on the transom, using 3M 4200 or Life-Calk as a sealant. If the transom seems weak at the bracket points you have selected, reinforce the hull at those two points, following the method detailed in the previous chapter.

Internally threaded, thick-walled stainless pipe and eyebolts will enable you to fine-tune the unit's alignment on the transom (see figure 10-2). Each pipe will need only one tapped end, while the other end will have the eye welded in place. In order to produce these custom pieces of hardware, no doubt you will need to seek the services of a machine shop. No lock nuts are needed on the threaded eyebolts because rotation of the eyes and tubes is not possible once the struts are installed between the vane gear and transom. You should now have a mighty strong vane gear installation.

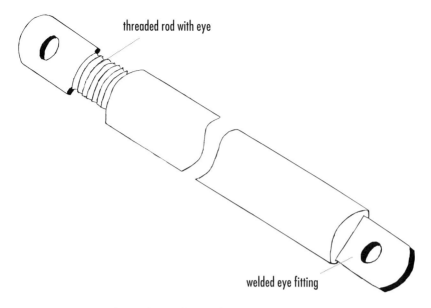

threaded rod with eye

welded eye fitting

Figure 10-2. Custom stainless tube with end fittings, suitable for use as an additional mounting strut.

Wire and Turnbuckles

Old stainless rigging, particularly halyard wire, has lots of great uses. I always keep a coil of used $1/8$-inch halyard wire in the lazarette and a handful of copper swaging sleeves and stainless thimbles in the toolbox, just in case I need to make a headsail pendant, a padlock cable, or some other little piece of wire rigging. Combined with small turnbuckles, you can fabricate all sorts of strong, yet inexpensive cables for securing semipermanent gear, including propane tanks, awnings, and vane gear mounting frames.

As explained in the previous section, the first step in stabilizing the vane gear is pulling the frame into position, employing a pair of lines made fast to a permanent fixture, more than likely the stern pulpit. Slide a swaging sleeve onto each of a pair of wire halyards, and then wrap the wires around the points you have chosen on the stern rail. To prevent abrasion between the wire and the stainless rail tubing, slide a piece of rubber tubing over the wire. Make a professional-looking swage with an inexpensive, through-bolted tool, such as the one in the photo next page, top. Cut the rigging wire at about one-third the distance between the stern rail and the wire mounting point on the vane gear. Open up a rigging thimble and push the round, or fixed, end of a small, hooked turnbuckle into the thimble. Swage the thimble, along with the turnbuckle eyebolt, at the bitter end of each wire you have swaged to the stern rail. You are done with the easy part.

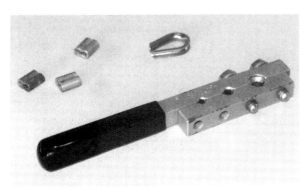

A swage tool, thimble, and sleeves can turn an old piece of halyard wire into a useful piece of rigging, such as a headsail pendant or an additional reinforcement for your vane gear.

Now swage a thimble into one end of each of two other pieces of wire, leaving more than enough length in each wire to wrap around and swage to the unit. Insert the turnbuckle hooks into the thimbles; a few wraps of masking tape will keep the hooks from falling out of the thimbles while you finish your work. Wrap each wire around its mounting point on the vane gear and swage into place. If you prefer, install the turnbuckles with their bolt eyes fixed to the vane gear instead; it makes no difference which way they face. Here, too, use rubber tubing over the stainless wire if you wish to protect the vane gear—this is a must if the contact point on the windvane is aluminum. Tighten the turnbuckles to align the frame, and then finish the project by tightening the lock nuts on the turnbuckle. This reinforcement system is not as firm as the addition of a pair of struts, but wire saves you money and time and

Wire-and-turnbuckle reinforcement between *Saltaire's* stern pulpit and the push rod shroud of a Fleming Global 301 servopendulum.

keeps extra weight off the stern. If you need to remove the vane gear, simply loosen the turnbuckles and pull out the hooks before pulling the unit from its mounting brackets.

LUBRICATING VINTAGE ALUMINUM VANE GEARS

Conventional wisdom, for what it's worth, dictates that plastics should never come in contact with petroleum-based lubricants. Spray silicone lubricant works well on acetyl bearings, but it eventually wears off from constant exposure to the elements. On passage, periodically leaning over the stern rail with an aerosol can to keep bearings moving with absolute minimum friction is difficult, to say the least. Deferring again to conventional wisdom, the occasional rain shower is generally enough to keep polymer bearings clear of grime and salt crust.

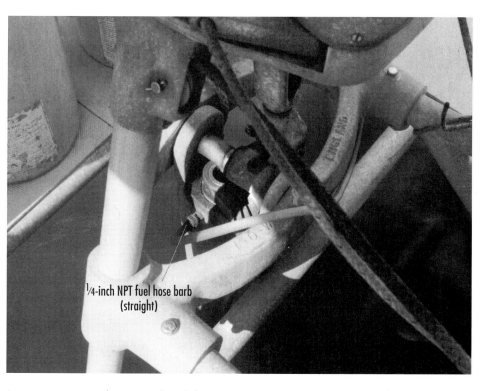

¼-inch NPT fuel hose barb (straight)

An unconventional approach to lubricating a vintage Aries: 30-weight motor oil is pumped through a rubber hose, entering the upper end of the servopendulum shaft tube via a ¼-inch NPT fuel hose barb.

Hose and ¼-inch NPT elbow fuel hose barb at lower end of Aries servo-rudder tube.

All this having been said, some owners of vintage Aries vane gears, and perhaps other aluminum windvanes, choose to keep their units moving freely with frequent, liberal oiling of all moving parts, including acetyl sleeves and bushings. Acetyl plastic (Delrin and Torlon) is extremely hard and resists swelling in water and oil, unlike nylon, another popular material for sleeves and bushings. Scott Bannerot, of *Élan* (Florida), installed a lubrication system on his vintage Aries, which he and his wife Wendy purchased at Sailorman chandlery in Ft. Lauderdale. Working with advice from another sailor, he drilled a ½-inch hole at the top and bottom of the pendulum shaft tube, right through the acetyl sleeves, and screwed a ¼-inch NPT fuel hose barb into each hole (see pictured installation). For the top hole he used a straight barb fitting, and for the lower hole, an elbow fitting turned upward. If you try this method, put a few wraps of Teflon tape around the threads to act as a dielectric between the brass fuel fittings and the aluminum host. After attaching a rubber hose to each barb, Scott pushed the tip of an oilcan spout into each hose and squirted 30-weight motor oil through the upper and lower acetyl sleeves, right onto the pendulum shaft. After putting a stopper in the end of each hose, he coiled both hoses up and tied them to the tube frame. Since the modification, the Bannerots have had no trouble keeping their Aries vane gear lubricated, and the machine has performed flawlessly through more than 30,000 nautical miles of Caribbean and Pacific cruising.

CUSTOM AIRVANES

Have you ever looked at a vane gear and thought to yourself what kind of interesting shapes you would like to try out for airvanes, just to experiment and see what happens? You are not alone. Maybe your curiosity is fueled by legiti-mate need, as in the case of an overhanging boom or some other obstruction, forcing you to compress a large amount of area into a short airvane. Or perhaps you want to add a little octane to the vane's light-air sensitivity, crowding on linear inches while trying not to add too much weight to the section. You will find a few ideas here, but the bottom line in custom airvane design is a three-way tug-of-war among perceived need, mechanical limitations, and creative flair.

Not only has Scott Bannerot figured out how to keep the Aries lubricated, but he and Wendy also have conducted extensive experiments with airvane

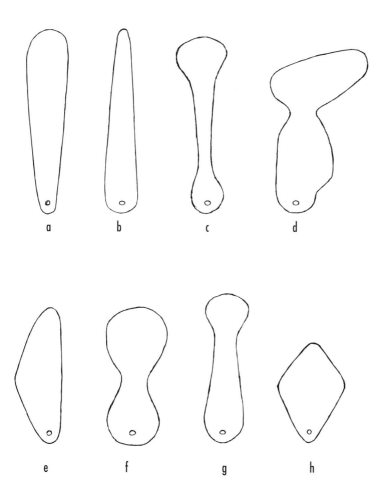

Figure 10-3. The Bannerots' foil shapes: (a) fair results; (b) nonreactive; (c) good reac-tion, but top heavy; (d) good in wind up to 25 knots. Further testing needed: (e) "sail edge," (f) "fat head," (g) "modified fat head," and (h) "diamond." (Scott Bannerot)

shapes for the unit. They have never had problems with the standard vane, but on a long passage from the Galápagos to the Marquesas, the couple entertained themselves with their artistic skills and an electric jigsaw, trying out at least a half-dozen new, exotic airvane designs. The Bannerots found that edges protruding too far forward or aft of the vane yoke flapped too much in the oncoming airflow. Also, they found that when they tried to put more area up high for better mechanical advantage, the resulting design put too much weight aloft. They roughly estimated center of effort and center of gravity, testing their designs to solve this elusive conundrum: what is the best shape, considering overall weight, leverage, and aerodynamic properties, for a horizontal-axis airvane? They finally deduced that either a conservative, straight-edged or elongated, oval-shaped airvane was the best choice; in other words, a standard vane. Figure 10-3 shows a sampling of Scott and Wendy's airvane shapes and a few notes on their findings.

For the vast majority of situations, the easiest thing to do is copy the airvanes illustrated for your vane gear model in the owner's manual. If you feel the urge to improve the design, go to your local lumberyard and purchase a 4-by-8-foot piece of plywood with a thickness that will fit your vane gear's yoke (usually about $1/8$ inch). You should have enough plywood to conduct quite a series of experiments. For initial testing, remain at anchor or in a marina if the wind is blowing well at your location.

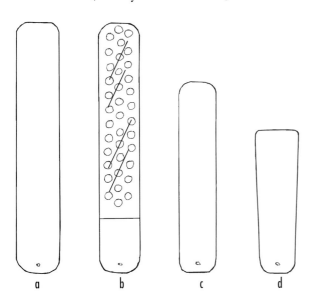

Figure 10-4. Conventional airvanes: (a) light-air vane with 60 percent more area than standard vane; (b) lighter version of light-air vane, holed out and covered with plastic shrink wrap; (c) standard vane; and (d) storm vane with same area as standard vane, but 20 percent shorter and slightly wider at the top.

Standard Airvane

Your main airvane, providing it has no obstacles to duck under, should be conservative in size and shape. If you do not know what dimensions to use, start with a straight-sided vane measuring 40 inches by 7 inches. Place it in the yoke, and watch it respond to the wind and counterweight while the boat remains stationary. Wind speed for this vane should fall between 12 and 20 knots. Does the airvane hang over too much to one side? Cut it down an inch at a time until you arrive at a length that seems to work. You may also need to cut an inch or so off the vane's width to reduce weight. Different vane gear models use different sizes of airvanes, so don't assume that a vane for one model will suffice for another.

Vane for Light Airs

The area differential between a standard airvane and a light-weather vane can be substantial. The Monitor's light vane, for example, has 60 percent more area than the standard vane. That does not mean 60 percent *longer*. A big portion of the light-weather vane's larger area is due to an inch more width than the standard vane. If you haven't a clue as to what size to start with, try a vane 48 inches long by 7 inches wide, and work the shape down from there. The apparent wind for testing should be no more than 12 knots.

Same Thing, But Lighter

Hans Bernwall of Scanmar International shared with me a really neat trick for lowering weight aloft while maintaining the high mechanical advantage of a long airvane. Starting from a point near the top of the vane, cut holes in the plywood with a $1^{1}/2$- or 2-inch hole saw. Then cover the holes on both sides with clear packing tape. Another cruiser told me he covered his holed-out light airvane with shrink-wrap plastic skin, the kind used for model airplanes. Either of these coverings should yield a lightweight vane with plenty of leverage on the servomechanism in light winds.

Storm Vane

The storm airvane will obviously be shorter, and not full of holes because of the strength required to withstand high winds. Fleming's storm vane is roughly 20 percent shorter than the standard vane, but the two vanes have approximately the same area. The storm vane is slightly wedge shaped, flaring outward from bottom to top. This keeps the center of effort high in an otherwise low-aspect airvane. If you are satisfied with your standard airvane design, try using Fleming's formula: 20 percent shorter, same area. Instead of plywood, some vane gear builders use anodized aluminum plate for the storm vane, but this practice is probably overkill. If you have purchased a big piece of plywood to try out different airvane shapes, you have no need to lay out more money for aluminum sheet. Test your storm designs in apparent winds of over 20 knots.

Mizzen Boom Vane

Designing an airvane for an overhanging mizzen boom is something like writing a sonnet: creating something new within very strict parameters. To begin,

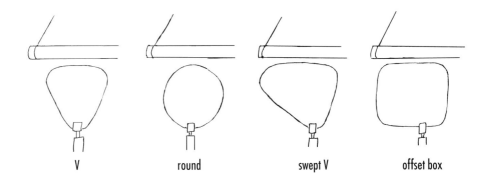

| V | round | swept V | offset box |

Figure 10-5. Possible foil shapes for mizzen. You will need to fit these or other possible shapes to the clearance between your vessel's mizzen boom and the vane yoke. Some experimentation will determine the best combination of shape and size.

if the boom slashes an arc only two or three inches above the vane yoke, I suggest dropping the vane to the horizontal position between tacks and forgetting about a custom vane. If the clearance is at least 20 inches or thereabouts, you may have some room to be creative. Begin with a design that pushes the leading edge no more than two or three inches forward of the front edge of the yoke but has a trailing edge extending well aft of the leading edge, perhaps more than 18 inches. Such a design will compress a lot of area into a short airvane, more than likely yielding a shape resembling a lopsided guitar pick. Other possible shapes are a circle, a square, and an inverted pyramid (see figure 10-5). Design, cut, observe results, and keep notes of your findings.

Cutting and Finishing

Always use a fine-tooth jigsaw or coping saw blade for cutting thin plywood in order to avoid splintering the fine end grains of surface veneers. After you have developed a shape that seems to work well for its size and purpose, sand the vane's surface and edges with fine-grained sandpaper. A good way to prevent the vane from breaking just above the yoke is to reinforce both sides of the bottom center of the vane with 6-ounce fiberglass cloth. Cut two pieces, 4 by 6 inches, and apply each one lengthwise to either side of the airvane, starting at the bottom edge. Use your preference of either epoxy or polyester resin. After the resin has set, redrill the bolt holes for the vane turret.

The best finish for an airvane starts with a coat of penetrating epoxy, such as Smith's or Git Rot. Epoxy resin seals the wood grains and provides an ideal surface for painting or varnishing. Let us remember, though, that an airvane is an expendable item, not likely to become a prized heirloom. You can achieve an attractive, weatherproof finish, plus save time and money, by coating the bare wood and fiberglass patches with a coat of one-part marine primer and two coats of whatever type and color of marine enamel you have lying around. The combined methods of fiberglass reinforcement and one-part primer and enamel have worked great for *Saltaire*'s vanes. Some really nutty sailors like to paint goofy pictures or epitaphs on their airvanes. If you want an off-the-wall medium to express some inner feeling, you have found your canvas.

TRIM TAB FOR TRANSOM RUDDER

Installing an Auto-Helm or Autosteer for a transom rudder will necessitate designing and installing your own trim tab. Do not take this "little job" lightly. It does not involve the same high-tolerance fabrication as its rich cousin, the aileron on an airplane wing, but it does deserve careful thought and construction. Your first stop in the design process should be with the manufacturer, which may have drawings of trim-tab installations adaptable to your boat's needs. Even with the builder's help, you will need to experiment a bit.

Design

There are two ways to approach the design of a low-speed hydrofoil, which is what you will be building. On the one hand, you could simply install a relatively thin plank of wood with rounded edges to do the work, or you can design a high-lift, NACA 0010 to 0022 hydrofoil (see Selected NACA Four-Digit Profiles in the appendix). Ratcliffe Marine Design in Pembroke, Massachusetts, has pointed out that the foil with the most lift is a flat plane. We can surmise, then, that the purpose of the more conservative NACA designs is to give operators a greater degree of control over lift. A principal advantage of NACA foils is far less drag than what we would experience with a simple $1/2$-by-3-inch plank rounded at the edges with a bit of sandpaper.

A number of years before I started reading up on NACA designs for this book, I had built a 16-foot open sailboat from study plans I had found in a public library. The plans were rough and sketchy, not intended as blueprints for construction. Acting purely on horse sense, I built the keel and rudder with rounded leading edges and tapered trailing edges, but not to any clear plan or design concept. The two hydrofoils were more or less straight-sided, save for the lumps of Bondo on the stack of old two-by-fours through-bolted to form the keel. *Flotsam* sailed like a witch, often passing larger boats on Balboa Harbor in southern California. Would she have sailed better with carefully tapered NACA foils? We will never know.

If you wish to design a NACA foil trim tab, first calculate its length and width, allowing for at least six inches of clearance above the waterline to permit

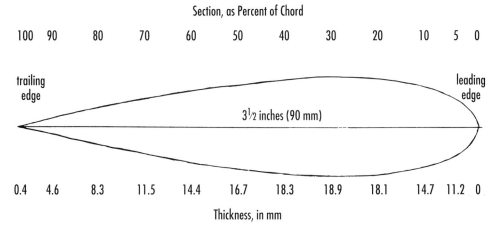

Section, as Percent of Chord

| 100 | 90 | 80 | 70 | 60 | 50 | 40 | 30 | 20 | 10 | 5 | 0 |

trailing edge

leading edge

3½ inches (90 mm)

| 0.4 | 4.6 | 8.3 | 11.5 | 14.4 | 16.7 | 18.3 | 18.9 | 18.1 | 14.7 | 11.2 | 0 |

Thickness, in mm

Figure 10-6. Sample trim tab cross section (NACA 0021 foil; chord = 90 mm). The chord is the distance from the leading edge to the trailing edge.

taking advantage of the stern wave. Once you have established the two dimensions, the width becomes the chord of the hydrofoil. Let us assume a NACA 0021 foil with a chord of $3^{1}/2$ inches for the purpose of discussion. We can convert that to 90 millimeters for easy calculation and subsequent measurement. The nice thing about metric measurements is that instead of having to turn fractions into percentages, we work strictly with whole numbers and decimals, which we can throw into the hand calculator without much thinking. Thus we come up with the ten sections illustrated in figure 10-6, rounded to the nearest tenth of a millimeter. Note that NACA four-digit foils are commonly displayed with ten equally spaced sections, not including the leading edge or the halfway section between the leading edge and first section. Some sources list many more sections to ensure precision. For our purposes, each section represents 10 percent of the chord.

Construction

For this particular trim tab, you would need to start with a half-inch piece of plank or marine plywood, working it down first with a plane and then sandpaper. I don't know about you, but my eyes cannot even see a tenth of a millimeter. My humble suggestion is to round to the nearest millimeter, or as close as you can get. Do not obsess with trying to achieve perfection. Even if you spend a week straining your eyes and hands with vernier calipers and 300-grit sandpaper, wood rarely allows such close tolerances. An easy, honorable way out of this formidable task is to dispense with NACA foils and round the edges of your flat wooden strip with sandpaper, tapering the trailing edge to a dull point. A trim tab that is too buoyant may not swivel properly when submerged. To alleviate the problem, drill a few $^3/4$-inch holes toward the bottom of the trim tab, and fill them with molten lead or fishing sinkers.

Now that you have carefully honed your trim-tab masterpiece to within a micron of tolerance, you get to slather it with fiberglass, epoxy resin, and antifouling paint. Apply two or three layers of 6-ounce cloth, sanding well between coats for a nicely faired-out surface. Afterward, you will need to fit a pair of pintles to the leading edge of the trim tab, one above the waterline, one below. It is better to use pintles that may be locked into place with pins, as long as they do not interfere with the tab's swinging arc. Cotter rings or receiver pins will prevent the tab from floating off the matching gudgeons that you install on the trailing edge of the rudder. Pick a strong set of $^5/16$-inch pintles and gudgeons; these will fit trim tabs for any size of vessel where a trim-tab steering system might be employed. Schaefer produces high-quality stainless pintles and gudgeons for a wide range of rudder sizes. If you have difficulty fitting the hardware to your trim tab and rudder, hire a welder to fabricate a set in 316 stainless steel.

Drill holes for the pintle brackets into the trim tab and rudder. Also drill holes for the cable brackets or hard linkage controlling the trim tab. Then soak the holes with penetrating epoxy and allow it to cure. After this, you can apply your choice of undercoat primer and antifouling paint. As a final safeguard against water intrusion, squirt a daub of marine sealant over the holes before attaching the hardware and securing it with fasteners. Refer to the Auto-Helm section in chapter 5 and the West End notes in chapter 12 for a visual concept of a completed trim-tab installation.

COUPLER FOR AUTOPILOT AND VANE GEAR

Motoring through calms or sailing downwind in light airs under spinnaker can present an untenable situation for a windvane. Nowadays, many skippers revert to the autopilot without a second thought under such conditions. While you are motoring, the alternator provides more than adequate current for the autopilot, but the autopilot is still subject to normal wear and tear. Running downwind, however, requires more power and increases chances of autopilot failure because of the constant battle against yawing. A popular technique, about which you might have already read in *Ocean Navigator*, *Cruising World*, *Cruising Helmsman*, and other sailing magazines, is to couple the autopilot with the vane gear. This integrated approach cuts down wear and tear in the autopilot and ensures ample steering power. On a run with a servopendulum gear,

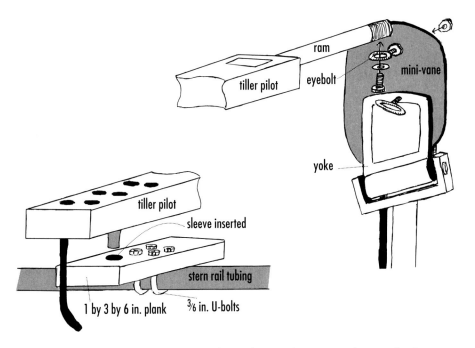

Figure 10-7. The coupling arrangement shown here is but one technique for harnessing both the steering power of a servopendulum and the accuracy of a tiller pilot, a very effective technique while motoring or sailing downwind in light airs.

the coupled system greatly reduces amperage draw while retaining the anti-yawing protection afforded by the servo blade.

The coupling method in figure 10-7 is but one way to achieve a marriage between your choice of tiller pilot and the vane gear. Cut a 6-inch piece of 1-by-3-inch wood plank to serve as the base. Drill four holes to accommodate two stainless steel U-bolts large enough to fit your stern rail tubing. For a 1-inch tube, you will want $^3/16$-inch U-bolts with a thread length of $1^3/8$ inches. Drill a hole large enough to fit the bronze or plastic sleeve provided with your tiller pilot. The position of the sleeve hole and, for that matter, the overall mounting design, depends on the juxtaposition of the stern rail and vane yoke. It may be necessary to elevate the tiller pilot by some contrivance to bring it more or less level with its connection at the yoke. There are numerous ways to connect the tiller pilot ram either to the yoke itself or to a small piece of material inserted in the yoke. Some skippers tie a piece of string or a rubber band around a screw in the ram's tip and some point on the yoke. Another method is to connect the tiller pilot ram to a small piece of plywood or aluminum plate in place of the airvane. Cut a piece of plywood of the same thickness as the airvane (you should have plenty left over from your airvane creations), making the mini-vane large enough to clear the upper edge of the yoke by 2 inches. Drill a

$^1/4$-inch hole in the center of the exposed plywood tab. Screw a nut onto a $^1/4$-by-2-inch eyebolt with a $^3/8$- or $^1/2$-inch hole, allowing ample room for the ram head to move. Then attach the eyebolt to the plywood tab. After mounting the autopilot to its wooden bracket, attach the ram to the tab eyebolt with a washer and a bolt of proper size to thread itself into the ram tip. Allow enough exposed bolt length to permit free swinging of the tab. A string or rubber band wrapped around the joint will reduce play in the connection.

A more sophisticated coupling system incorporates a Morse cable between the vane yoke and a below-decks autopilot. The cable passes through a grommet-sealed hole in the hull, well above the waterline, keeping the entire autopilot installation safe from the elements. A single cable between the hull and the vane yoke eliminates the extra clutter experienced with the above-decks coupling system and guarantees a sturdier, longer-lasting installation.

Customizing your windvane steering gear is usually elective surgery, intended to refine what we would hope is already satisfactory performance. As you have seen, none of these improvements requires a degree in engineering, rather a little mechanical understanding and a moderate dose of determination. An airplane pilot would shudder at the thought of ripping the wings off of a Cessna 172 and designing a whole new set from scratch in a hangar as a weekend project. That's one of the beautiful things about sailing—and vane steering, a natural extension of the sailing art. We as sailors enjoy the luxury of being able to experiment with different designs and modifications of our onboard systems with relative impunity. If the wire-and-turnbuckle reinforcement is inadequate, attach struts between the vane gear and the transom. You don't like the light-wind performance of your airvane? Then design a new one. Is the trim tab you built for your main rudder too small? Cut and shape another trim tab with an extra half-inch of chord. Etcetera. At worst, the modifications we have reviewed here will force us into a bit of chin scratching over our mistakes and going back to the proverbial blackboard. But one way or the other, the vane gear will still work!

Chapter 11
Emergency Rudders

N one of us wants to think about the possibility of losing the vessel's main rudder. A grim picture forms in our minds: the boat crashes about insanely in heavy seas while we frantically drill holes through dinghy oars and pieces of plywood bulkhead, hoping our jury-rigged rudder doesn't shatter into toothpicks after we tie the contraption to the backstay or the stern pulpit, using double-braided polyester line as a hinge. We hack away at the choppy brine as if trying to kill a floating bug with our big flyswatter. Somewhere I recall the phrase "pleasure sailing." If we leave port with an emergency rudder system ready for deployment, we eliminate one giant worry from our minds. An emergency rudder can take one of several forms: a convertible servopendulum blade, a trim-tab auxiliary rudder, or a separately hung rudder that we purchase as a kit or build on our own.

Some vane gear builders offer emergency rudders as modification kits to be adapted to the servo blade or auxiliary rudder, while other packages are sold as totally separate units. A few of the readymade units appear in this chapter, but since the windvane steering industry is quickly catching on to the growing demand for this type of product, we can expect the list to continue growing. A number of emergency rudder models already have served their owners quite well. If you wish to carry a spare rudder on your cruise and do not want to pay for a commercial unit, you may use the simple approach offered in this chapter, modifying it as needed to fit your vessel's size and transom shape.

THE NIGHTMARE OF RUDDER FAILURE

No rudder is immune from failure, but some are more exposed to grief than others. Any seasoned sailor will attest to this obvious fact. Modern "performance cruisers" and ocean racers have less wetted surface area than traditional cruising vessels of the same length. Another speed-enhancing feature of racing yachts is more length on the waterline for a given LOA, a factor contributing to some tracking ability lost to a fin keel and a spade rudder. The racing pages of popular sailing magazines are replete with stories about rescuing survivors of boats having lost their skinny keels or rudders while tearing across the seas at 20-plus knots. Professional, sponsored crew know they are putting their lives at grave risk when they leave port in ultralight racing sleds. In the Transpac, the nautical version of the Indianapolis 500, vessels are designed for absolute maximum speed and minimum weight. Unfortunately, some cruisers think they can safely combine the best modern racing features with a complement of liveaboard trappings and dub their vessels cruising boats—sort of like stuffing a Lamborghini full of camping equipment and calling it an SUV. Maybe they think their weather fax will always keep them safe from the gnashing teeth of sustained gales, or their depth sounders will somehow alert them to coral towers lying only two or three feet below the water's surface in the countless lagoons they will visit in the tropics. It is easy to see how the loss of a spade rudder or a weakly supported skeg rudder can turn a sailing adventure into an extreme sport.

Rudder loss is not the exclusive domain of spade rudders. When 41-foot *Stella di Mare* left Bora Bora for Penrhyn Atoll in August 2001, a strong northeasterly forced the vessel off track, so the crew turned downwind toward American Samoa. The 20-plus-knot winds on the starboard quarter provided for some brisk, manageable broad-reaching, nothing dangerous. One night, as skipper Gene Meleski recalls, "all hell broke loose." He and his crew noticed there was a serious problem with their steering, but they were too far in denial to accept what had actually happened. Donning his mask and snorkel in rough seas, Meleski found only a bare rudderpost protruding aft of the skeg. The crew seriously considered abandoning ship, but they put together a makeshift rudder with their Med-moor plank. The system barely provided steerage. After three days of experimentation, Gene's wife Pat remembered an emergency rudder design in Gary Jobson's book *Storm Sailing*, which they had onboard.

Following Jobson's guidelines, Gene and fellow crewman Chuck Roberts fashioned a rudder from a closet door, and then fastened it to the spinnaker pole with large C-clamps. They controlled the rudder by means of double-braided lines, blocks, and deck winches. Amazingly, they entered Pago Pago Harbor under their own power five days later.

Pago Pago Harbor has two hardware stores, one of which, The Tool Shop, sells fishing hooks, epoxy resin, yacht cordage, and a few other odds and ends for mariners passing through. Once in a while they might have a pair of wooden oars on display. Stella's Sewing Shop, located behind ABC Market, can repair sails, and while you wait, you can have lunch at her Filipino restaurant a block away. What the harbor does not have is a place to haul out a pleasure boat or to take on a large project like building a rudder. Torrential downpours and gale-force winds can occur any time, making it nearly impossible to undertake large fiberglass construction projects outdoors. The Meleskis recruited local diver Ross Weich of *Bear Cub* (Vancouver) to remove the rudderpost. Complicating matters, the yacht builder in Italy had lost the plans for the vessel, but a New Zealand shipwright agreed to develop new plans from photographs and build a replacement. The Meleskis and their crew lost nearly two months of valuable cruising time before finally leaving American Samoa and heading for Fiji. Fortunately, the crew of *Stella di Mare* had the combined advantages of nonstorm conditions and several individuals onboard to share ideas and help with emergency rudder construction. Their determination and resourcefulness saw them through what could have developed into a far worse scenario. Yet imagine the time they could have saved at sea between Penrhyn and American Samoa, not to mention the damage to the cabin's interior they could have averted, had they carried an emergency rudder.

Keel-mounted rudders on traditional, full-keeled hulls are not likely to disappear suddenly or bend their rudderposts in a knockdown. And they are naturally more resistant to damage from underwater collision with submerged objects. Nonetheless, a keel-mounted rudder, hinged snugly at the bottom in a heavy, cast-bronze gudgeon, can be put out of service by broken internal welds or a severed rudderpost. Well-known sailing guru John Neal, in his book *Log of the Mahina*, lost steerage on his Vega 27 when the rudderpost broke away from its internal fan bracing while sailing through the Cook Islands in 1974. Luckily for Neal, he was near Aitutaki Atoll, where by sheer providence he was able to anchor. He then arranged for a tow into the lagoon, and found someone at the local airport to arc-weld the stainless rudderpost back to its bracing. The repair held together throughout his remaining cruise to American Samoa and back to Hawaii.

Bronze rudder shafts on keel-mounted rudders are the least likely to break from crevice corrosion, the most likely cause of *Mahina*'s rudder failure. However, the lack of anodic protection in the area of the rudder eventually can lead to dezincification of the bronze and ultimate failure. In short, every offshore sailing vessel should have some form of emergency rudder, be it an auxiliary rudder employed as part of a vane gear system, or a separate, dedicated rudder that can be mounted easily in rough conditions.

SERVOPENDULUM CONVERSIONS

A few manufacturers offer conversion kits for their servopendulum vane gears. Scanmar markets the MRUD as an optional add-on to its popular Monitor vane, and Sailomat offers its BEST auxiliary rudder, which slips onto the pendulum (servo blade) shaft in place of the servo blade. Fleming also makes available a bolt-on rudder kit for its Global series vanes. With each of the three models, the helmsman first installs an enlarged version of the servo blade, and then stabilizes the shaft to act as a rudderpost. A tiller pilot can be connected to each emergency rudder, but the coupling technique will be different with each model.

BEST

Sailomat's BEST (Blade Extension for Emergency Steering) is a wing-like foil, which doubles the area of the servo blade. The operator disconnects the airvane-to-tiller linkage and connects a small, backward-mounted tiller to the unit. The operator controls the small helm by means of 6 mm control lines. The BEST system has been qualified as an emergency rudder in a number of ocean racing events where such a system is a prerequisite for entry. Each emergency rudder is made upon request, so allow a few weeks for construction and delivery after you place your order.

Fleming Optional Emergency Rudder

The Fleming emergency rudder assembly is comprised of an upper and lower epoxy-coated steel brace, fitted onto the servo blade by means of two stainless tubes and five bolts (see figure 11-1). A flat piece of weight-saving aluminum plate is butted to the servo blade's trailing edge between the braces, doubling the original blade's surface area. The operator ties the upper end of the servo arm amidships to stabilize the rudder assembly. Now this person can steer by means of the airvane yoke, taking advantage of the rudder's lift characteristics. In other words, as the rudder is canted to one side, it grabs the water the same way the vane's servo blade does when it is functioning as a servopendulum for

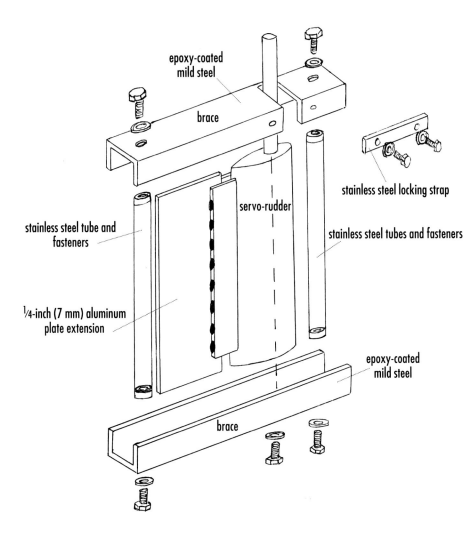

Figure 11-1. The Fleming optional emergency rudder is mounted onto the unit's servo blade.

self-steering. The operator may also attach a tiller pilot to the vane yoke to assume duty at the helm.

MRUD

The Monitor Emergency Rudder (MRUD) is a large, stainless, high-lift NACA foil that the operator latches onto the servo blade shaft in place of the standard servo blade. On the MRUD's leading edge are four eyebolts, two on each side, where double-braided lines are attached to keep the rudder vertically stationary. At the top of the emergency rudderpost is the same type of latch found on the servo blade shaft. Note that only Monitors built since 1991 can accept the MRUD assembly. The previous model must be retrofitted with a "strutguard" between the windvane's two lateral legs. Installation of the MRUD requires the operator to affix a special brace to the strutguard in order to stabilize the Monitor's upper pendulum shaft.

AUXILIARY RUDDER CONVERSIONS

An "auxiliary rudder conversion" on a vane gear that already uses an auxiliary rudder for steerage is an obvious misnomer, but hey, it got your attention, right? In actuality, there is nothing to convert. Remember, where such a system is in use, the auxiliary rudder is already steering the vessel independently of the main rudder, which is lashed during self-steering operation. While sailing downwind in light airs under spinnaker, trim-tab systems are known for their keen sensitivity to slight wind shifts. If you are motoring, you can steer the auxiliary rudder by manipulating the vertical or horizontal windvane as you would with a servopendulum. If the airvane yoke is out of easy reach, attach lines to the vertical vane's counterweight or the horizontal vane's yoke to make remote steering possible from the cockpit. The Hydrovane may be controlled by either the airvane or a tiller extension attached to the steering control handle extending from the transmission. A tiller pilot may be mounted easily to the Hydrovane or to a horizontal-axis vane, such as that on an Auto-Helm, but connecting it to a vertical-axis vane will take some creativity. Theoretically, you should be able to control the vertical vane's axis by attaching the tiller pilot to either the vane itself or, more likely, the counterweight. For this technique to work, you will have to build a tall bracket to hold the tiller pilot in place so that it may be attached to the desired spot on the vane gear. This is because the place where the tiller pilot and the vertical vane connect probably will not be very close to any other fixed structure. The Windpilot Pacific Plus, which features an auxiliary rudder, has a pin that accepts either an Autohelm or Simrad tiller pilot. In the case of the Auto-Helm, an airvane unit mounted atop a stern arch will allow easy attachment of steering control lines—just tie them through one of the holes in the aluminum airvane and run them to the cockpit through turning blocks. On an old Sailomat 3040, attaching lines to the yoke for self-steering should be a simple matter, since the unit's frame is close to the transom, and there is enough solid surface on the stern rail and on the unit itself to mount a tiller pilot bracket.

SOS RUDDER:
SELF-CONTAINED RUDDER KIT

Scanmar's SOS Rudder should appeal to the boatowner who either doesn't have a windvane for easy conversion to an emergency rudder, or whose windvane for some reason does not readily lend itself for use as an auxiliary rudder. Entirely constructed of 316L stainless steel, the SOS Rudder has a mounting tube structure custom-designed to fit the individual vessel (see figure 11-2). The rudder is similar in shape to the MRUD, concentrating most of the effort toward the top of the hydrofoil for less strain on the assembly. Totally self-contained, the package is complete with its own tiller and four mounting brackets, which are to be mounted permanently to their place on the transom before the vessel leaves port. The SOS Rudder is designed to steer a boat up to 50 feet long, though the foam-filled rudder and hardware ensemble weigh only 16 kilograms, or 35 pounds. And with a little inventiveness, you should have no trouble connecting a small tiller pilot to the tiller. You can store the SOS Rudder, along with its mounting tubes and other hardware, in its big orange bag, emblazoned with the letters "SOS." If you are interested in this unit, allow a space of 48 by 18 by 6 inches for storage. That may sound rather large, but let's face it: any emergency rudder you carry in your boat is going to occupy a large amount of space unless it is already hanging on the stern in the form of a servopendulum or auxiliary rudder trim tab. The standard SOS Rudder, with a depth of 35 inches, sells for $1,595; the XL model is 42 inches deep and costs $1,995.

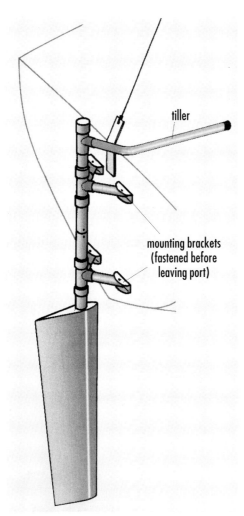

tiller

mounting brackets
(fastened before
leaving port)

Figure 11-2. Scanmar's totally self-contained SOS Rudder. (Scanmar)

BUILD YOUR OWN
EMERGENCY RUDDER

The Berkeley Yacht Club (BYC) has a website entitled Emergency Rudder Design and Construction, three pages of mathematical equations and two pages of building details that had my head swimming, but the cabernet probably had something to do with it too. Call me simple-minded, but I like pretty pictures with tiny dots for foam, squiggly lines for wood, and neat little arrows and numbers with double hash marks impelling me to build something. The BYC website is no doubt a good guide to calculating the thickness, total area, and lift coefficient of the foil, given the length and theoretical hull speed of a particular sailing vessel. And their concept for a lightweight, foam-filled section, essentially a surfboard, is definitely something that deserves serious consideration. It would weigh only a fraction of the plywood rudder I outline in this chapter. I did not see any mention of a NACA profile at the BYC website, but we needn't worry, since this is just an emergency rudder to get us to the next port, not a permanent installation intended for thousands of miles of service. With these thoughts in mind, and recalling the Meleskis' closet door and spinnaker pole, it seems as if almost any strongly built, firmly mounted, hinged vertical plane of sufficient area should serve the purpose well.

Since the emergency rudder is hung much farther aft than most main rudders, it exercises more steering leverage and therefore does not require as much area to do its job effectively. A flat-sided section of half the area of the main rudder should steer your vessel satisfactorily, as long as it does not have to fight weather helm while close-hauled. For that purpose, you will need a larger surface, but do you have enough room in your cabin or lazarette to store an item nearly as large as the main rudder? I don't either, unless it doubles as the table for the saloon. Instead of concerning yourself with NACA profiles or fancy calculations, concentrate on making your emergency rudder strong and, if possible, waterproof. Use $^1/_2$-inch 316 stainless pintles on the rudder and heavy gudgeons on the transom to bear the extreme pressure and cavitation imposed by the flow of water. Putting a long pintle at the bottom of the rudder and a short one at the top will make installation a lot easier than trying to line up two pintles at the same time in 12-foot breaking seas. If the pintles you buy do not have holes at their ends for retainer pins, drill a hole in each, just behind the beveled tip, allowing room for the gudgeon.

Figure 11-3 gives examples of rudders you can build from two $^3/_4$-inch pieces of marine or exterior-grade plywood laminated together with epoxy resin. The rudder's leading edge should be rounded, and the trailing edge somewhat pointed to reduce drag. If you cannot find a way to keep the whole plywood section under pressure for lamination, fasten the middle area together with stainless or bronze wood screws, and then follow up with large C-clamps around the edges. I have found this technique very effective in constructing several rudders of different sizes and shapes. After the epoxy has set up, you may leave the screws in place or remove them and cover the holes with epoxy filler. Finally, cover the rudder with two layers of fiberglass cloth to add strength, as well as water resistance. Building this simple emergency rudder

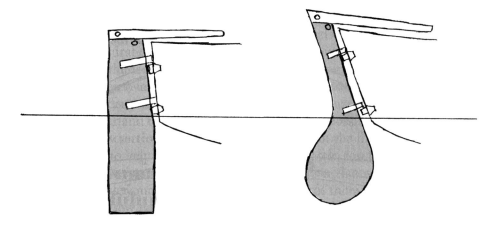

Figure 11-3. Emergency rudder shapes that you can build yourself: vertical or slightly raked transom *(left)* and raked transom *(right)*.

and stowing it before your next offshore passage will save you money and, more importantly, unnecessary worrying over what to do in the event of steerage loss.

INSTALLING AN EMERGENCY RUDDER

Deploying an emergency rudder in heavy seas will not be easy. Converting a servo blade into an emergency rudder may be especially difficult, possibly requiring someone to go over the side. If you have an auxiliary rudder, your work is already done—enjoy your trip. A separate rudder with its own gudgeons looks really simple to install on paper, but it is not quite that easy at sea, especially if the rudder is light and buoyant.

The first step to installing the emergency rudder is to either find a way to heave-to, or conserve your energy for moments when the boat turns its bow to the oncoming seas. Following seas are not only frustrating, but also dangerous. You and anyone helping you should be wearing a harness unless conditions are calm. Also be sure to make a lanyard fast between the emergency rudder and the vane gear frame. Although it is possible to attach an emergency rudder foil to a servopendulum while the pendulum shaft is elevated out of the water, the rudder's weight and awkward size could make this untenable. Prepare to have someone dive into the water to install the rudder. Each type of servopendulum emergency rudder has its own unique coupler. The Sailomat rudder slips onto the pendulum shaft and is secured with a pin, making the process easy. If you have an MRUD, the emergency rudder has the same hinge coupler as your standard servo blade. Since the blade is buoyant, it may be easier to let the blade float as you pull the upper pendulum shaft to one side and join it to the hinge. For the Fleming, first raise the servo blade up as far as it will go, and tie it to the main body of the unit. Remove the two bolts holding the servo blade, and remove it from the pendulum shaft bracket. Now you can assemble the add-on pieces in the cockpit before reconnecting the blade to the shaft.

A separate emergency rudder will necessitate your installing mounting brackets or gudgeons, whatever the design calls for. If the transom is thin and weak at the points where you want to mount the hardware, you might want to reinforce the transom at those points. See chapter 7, Installation, for tips on transom reinforcement. Drill the appropriate holes and mount the hardware to the transom, applying marine sealant around the bolt holes before tightening. When you deploy the rudder, place yourself directly over the mounting position and slip the rudder's pintles into their gudgeons. This sounds a lot easier than it is. A plywood or foam-filled rudder floats, so you will need to muster all your strength and coordination to keep the rudder from floating off to one side as you wrestle it into position. When you have the rudder in place, keep pressure on the rudderhead as you slide a receiver pin into the end of each pintle to keep the rudder in place. To install the MRUD, it will help to have an extra pair of hands. One person holds the unit in place while the other pops a clevis pin into place at each bracket. In rough seas, expect any emergency rudder installation to take quite a while. And always make fast a lanyard between the rudder and a strong point on the vessel or vane gear before you attempt emergency deployment. Practicing the installation procedure several times in calm water will give you the confidence you need if and when the occasion arises.

Losing the use of our main steering is one of the last things we want to think of happening offshore. It ranks right up there with capsizing and dismasting on our list of unpleasantries. Fortunately, though, preparing for emergency steering is a relatively simple matter. The BEST, the Fleming Emergency Rudder, the MRUD, and the SOS Rudder all appear to be good options for offshore boats, depending on the vessels' self-steering and main steering systems. If you want to save money, a separately mounted, homebuilt emergency rudder should get your vessel to the next port, as long as the destination lies at least 60 degrees off the wind. It is also wise to establish an emergency deployment plan, starting from stabilizing the vessel with the sails, and continuing through hanging the emergency rudder and steering by hand or with a tiller pilot.

Chapter 12

Build a Horizontal-Va.
Trim-Tab System

Overview of West End Concept

Design

Materials and Construction

This horizontal-vane auxiliary-rudder trim-tab system took its name from the West End of Catalina Island, a windy cape roughly 23 miles southwest of Los Angeles Harbor. West End lies near the popular yachtie hangouts of Isthmus Cove and Catalina ("Cat") Harbor, and is commonly the first waypoint for sailors passing through the lower Channel Islands on the 2,100-mile trek to Hilo, Hawaii. The stunning rock formations and deep caves around the point represent some of my best memories of California coastal sailing. *Saltaire* made twenty-eight trips to Cat Harbor and Isthmus Cove in the three years prior to her Pacific crossing.

One sees a creative array of manufactured and homebuilt windvane steering designs in the anchorages around Catalina. Some of those designs, plus others I have observed in the South Pacific, have contributed to the West End concept. Rather than being an original design, this vane gear is essentially a distillation of conventional auxiliary-rudder trim tabs. Feel free to take liberties with both the design and the materials used in construction. One important thing to conserve is the basic mechanical connection between the airvane and the trim tab. The linkages can take different forms, but their path of motion cannot change direction. Otherwise, you will wind up sailing in circles. Also potentially challenging is ensuring the airvane exerts sufficient leverage on the trim tab. You can achieve this by adjusting the elbow linkage and trim-tab arm for optimum purchase. Another strategy would be to forgo the recommended pintles and gudgeons in favor of partially balanced foils, using bronze or stainless rods for axles on both the auxiliary rudder and trim tab. Studying foil design and rudder balance further will enable you to formulate a vane gear with greater steering sensitivity.

Through experimentation and persistence, you will no doubt end up with a fairly original design of your own, and then you can dub the new model by a name of your own choosing. I hope you have as much fun and success with this project as others have had with similar vane gears.

OVERVIEW OF WEST END CONCEPT

I use the term "design" loosely. The more nearly accurate word is "concept." The sketches are not to scale, nor do they reveal much in the way of actual measurements. The drawings only give you an idea of how this mechanism may be constructed. Far from rocket science, this is a straightforward concept: a horizontal-axis airvane transmitting signals via solid linkage to a trim tab, which in turn controls an unbalanced auxiliary rudder. The vane gear's key features are welded, all-stainless-steel construction; adjustable linkage; and the use of standard pintles and gudgeons for both the auxiliary rudder and the trim tab to make removal of the two hydrofoils easy. The horizontal vane feathers to one side as the boat veers off course, plunging or pulling a push rod. A swinging L bracket, such as that used for reinforcing a wooden frame corner, converts vertical motion into horizontal motion via a connecting rod to a lever on the trim tab's axis. Let us suppose you are sailing to windward on the port tack. As the boat starts rounding up, the airvane dips toward port, pressing the push rod downward. The L piece swings outward, pushing another rod linkage, which turns the leading edge of the trim tab toward starboard via an adjustable arm at the top of the trim tab. The trim tab forces the auxiliary rudder to aim to port, causing the boat to turn off the wind and resume the correct heading.

DESIGN

This conceptual approach still leaves most of the specific engineering in your end of the court. I have seen designs similar to the West End that have sailed thousands of miles without a hitch. Some sailors build trim-tab systems out of carburetor linkages torn from wrecked automobiles, along with assorted bicycle parts, welding their mild-steel creations together with a simple stick welder. They lavish grease on all the bearings and linkages and then paint the rest with rust-resistant primer and boat enamel. You may snicker, but some of these machines have made incredible ocean passages.

For the auxiliary rudder and trim tab, there are three ways to go. One is to combine both foils into one contiguous shape: the trim tab becomes the trailing edge of its larger partner, the two forming essentially one complete NACA foil. However, with pintles and gudgeons separating the two foils, there may be too large a gap for the pair to behave as one. That is why I chose the second option, drawing the two as separate foils. If you want to use a NACA profile, plan on a shape ranging from a 0010 to about a 0020 foil. In other words, for every 10 inches of chord, the span will measure anywhere from 1 to 2 inches. The NACA 0010 profile is a popular "all-purpose" design for applications calling for symmetrical, high-lift submerged hydrofoils, but some servopendulum blades and trim-tab auxiliary rudders incorporate up to a 0022 shape for better lift control. Refer to figures 2-6 and 10-5 for sample sketches of NACA foils, and also the appendix for selected NACA four-digit profiles. Your last option is to ignore NACA designs, which is what a lot of handy-dandy sailors do, usually because they have never heard of NACA and probably wouldn't give a damn if you told them. If their foil sections work, how can we blame them? The simplest method would be to round the edges of both foils, making sure the sides at the trailing edge of the rudder are flush with the sides of the trim tab. Shave the trailing edge of the trim tab to a dull point to reduce drag. This last technique will almost certainly work, but you can expect NACA foils to function much better with less drag and smoother steering response.

MATERIALS AND CONSTRUCTION

The best material available to the average sailor for metal fabrication is 316L stainless steel. However, this material is expensive. An acceptable second choice is 304 stainless, and a marginal third is mild steel. The advantages with the last choice are extremely low cost and ease of construction. Aluminum is also a proven alloy for vane gears, but fabrication with this metal is not an easy feat for the hobbyist. Successful vane gear construction in aluminum usually involves custom castings and extrusions to achieve adequate structural strength. If you want to take vane gear construction seriously, experimenting with your own designs, mild steel could provide a great medium for testing different models at a very small investment. After you have developed something that seems to function well in all kinds of weather and on all points of sail, duplicate it carefully in your choice of stainless steel or marine-grade aluminum. Welded construction is probably not as strong as a combination of castings and thick-walled tubes or extrusions, but professionally welded stainless vane gears stand up to hard cruising conditions for many years.

The greatest challenge in this project will be to fit bearings to the vane yoke and the swiveling point where the turret drum meets the vertical push rod tube. An old trick for the yoke axis is to use the front-wheel hub from a bicycle. You would need to repack the bearings with light grease regularly, and then there is still no guarantee the mild-steel construction will hold up long in a saltwater environment. Nonetheless, the technique has worked for others. The best choice is Delrin or Torlon bearings and races, but you would have to have the races custom-machined to fit the tube diameter and bearing size you select. A possible low-cost alternative is to insert nylon or Teflon sleeves into either end of the yoke tube, but this strategy would not ensure the same low-friction action as that of ball bearings. For the main vertical tube, a plastic sleeve insert should suffice for easy rotation of a narrower tube welded to the base of the turret. One of the key reasons for building a vane gear rather than purchasing one is to save money. Bear this in mind as you are putting together a shopping list for construction materials.

Finally, there is the matter of building the auxiliary rudder and trim tab. You could have very light foils with adequate strength by fabricating them much like surfboards. Lastafoam medium-density urethane foam boards can be purchased in $1^{1}/2$-inch-by-4-foot-by-8-foot sheets. Though much more expensive than plywood, urethane foam is certainly much lighter and easier to shape. A span of $1^{1}/2$ inches (38 mm) gives you a chord of 15 inches (380 mm) on a NACA 0010 foil, resulting in a far bigger section than you will need, except on a very large vessel. Two pieces of Lastafoam laminated together yield a 3-inch-thick rudder, permitting a much stronger 0020/0021 foil with the same chord of 16 inches. Plan on a chord of about 300 to 360 mm (12 to 14 inches) for the rudder and 65 to 75 mm ($2^{1}/2$ to 3 inches) for the trim tab.

Plywood will serve the purpose well, but in addition to its greater weight (though it is still buoyant in water), it is harder to shape. An electric planer can make short work of this kind of project. For a thickness of $1^{1}/2$ inches (38 mm), the span for a 12-inch (305 mm) chord on a NACA 0012 foil, you will need to laminate together two pieces of $3/4$-inch plywood. After you have arrived at the shapes you desire, finish the surfaces with fiberglass and epoxy resin. Install the rudder on the mounting plates with $1/2$-inch pintles and gudgeons. For the trim tab, pintles and gudgeons are $5/16$ inch. Each pair of pintles should have one long stem and one short stem to make mounting an easier task. Schaefer pintles and gudgeons, available at West Marine and other chandleries, are perfect for this job.

Buoyant foils on the transom certainly sound nice, but it is better to eliminate some degree of buoyancy. You can add weight to the bottom of each foil by adding lead to the sections. If necessary for plywood sections, drill 1-inch holes in the bottom of the auxiliary rudder, $3/4$-inch holes in the trim tab, and fill them with molten lead or fishing sinkers. Foam sections are extremely buoyant, and therefore will need a greater amount of lead. An alternate method of dealing with the buoyancy problem is to eliminate the pintles and gudgeons and devise some other hinge mechanism—perhaps a straight rod running vertically through metal rings or tubes mounted onto the leading edge of the trim tab, and on the leading and trailing edges of the auxiliary rudder. Thus your creation retains its buoyancy while staying securely fastened in place.

Figures 12-1 and 12-2 give you a rough idea of how the West End trim-tab system is constructed. Missing from figure 12-2 is the lower mounting bracket, which would more or less duplicate the mounting plate and horizontal tubes you see at the bottom of the pictured structure. You will have to determine the lengths of the tubes from the turret to the upper mounting plate, depending on the size of your vessel and the shape of its transom. The lower mounting bracket should be devised as a separate fixture to reduce weight. I have intended for all of the metal structure, including the gudgeons on the mounting plates, to be TIG welded of stainless steel. In the case of a mild-steel vane gear, you would

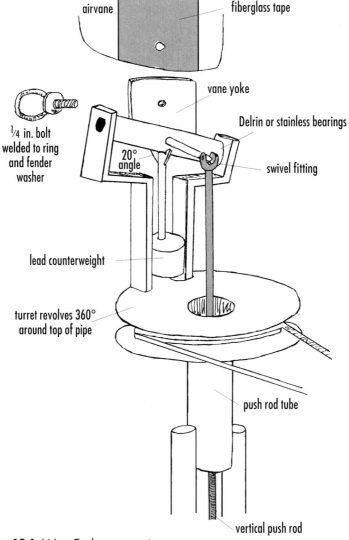

Figure 12-1. West End upper unit.

drill through the mounting plates and bolt the stainless gudgeons in place, using a dielectric, such as gasket material, to insulate the two metals from each other.

For details on designing, cutting, and finishing airvanes, refer to chapter 10. Dimensions for the West End airvane will be approximately 35 by 6 inches, but this will depend on the sizes of the trim tab and lead counterweight. As a general rule, the airvane's weight should never be more than about 28 ounces. A weight of 21 to 26 ounces is more acceptable.

I wish you the very best of luck with your project and with all your sailing endeavors. Fair winds and following seas!

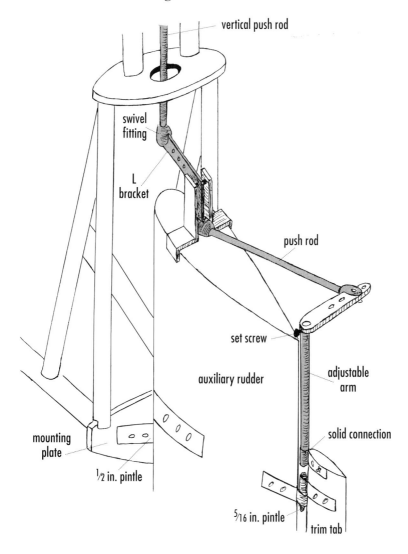

Figure 12-2. West End lower unit.

Appendix

MANUFACTURERS, DISTRIBUTORS, AND ONLINE SERVICES

AIRFOIL SELF STEERING
Manufacturer of Airfoil
  servopendulum.
South Africa
P.O. Box 336
Gillitts, 3603
Durban
South Africa
+27 (0) 31-7671064
info@selfsteering.co.za
www.selfsteering.co.za

United Kingdom
+44 7732-69-50-27

ARIES
Manufacturer of Aries
  servopendulum.
Denmark
Aries Denmark
Mollegade 54, Holm
DK 6430 Nordborg
Denmark
+45 7445-0760
Fax +45 7445-2960

aries@email.dk
www.selfsteer.dk

Germany
Shipshop
Georg Seifert
Schulz-Hohenstein Söhne
  Nachfolger
Geibelstraße 9–11
D-47057 Duisburg
Germany
+49 (0) 203-352044
Fax +49 (0) 203-355432
aries@shipshop.de
www.shipshop.de

South Africa
Action Yachting (Pty) Ltd.
P.O. Box 370
Paarden Eiland 7420
Cape Town
South Africa
+27-21-4194835
Fax +27-21-425-2459
actyot@iafrica.com
www.action-yachting.com

U.S.
Aries Gear USA
Guy M. Carlson
15 Korbel Way
Belmont, CA 94002-2218
650-591-3791
USAries@aol.com

Parts for Aries built in England
Aries Spares
48 St. Thomas Street
Penryn
Cornwall TR10 8JW
United Kingdom
+44 (0) 1326-377467
Fax +44 (0) 1326-378117
enquiries@ariesvane.com
www.ariesvane.com

CAPE HORN MARINE PRODUCTS INC.
Manufacturer of Jean-du-Sud,
    Joshua, Spray, and Varuna servo-
    pendulums.
316, Girouard St.
Oka, QC
Canada J0N 1E0
800-CAP-HORN (800-227-4676);
450-479-6314
Fax 450-479-1895
mail@capehorn.com
www.capehorn.com

FLEMING SELF STEERING SYSTEMS
Manufacturer of Fleming 201 and
Fleming Global 301, 401, 501, and
601 servopendulums; also Fleming
Optional Emergency Rudder.

Australia
Fleming Marine Engineering
P.O. Box 2065

Port Lincoln, South Australia 5065
Australia
+61 8 8684-2161
kevin.flemingselfsteering@
    bigpond.com
www.flemingselfsteering.com

U.S.A.
Water and Power, Inc.
1273 Scott Street
San Diego, CA 92106
877-4-FLEMING (877-435-3646);
619-226-2622; 619-795-7079
Fax 619-226-1077
sales@flemingselfsteering.com
www.flemingselfsteering.com

HARKEN AUSTRALIA PTY. LTD.
Distributor of Navik servopendulum
    by Plastimo.
Unit 6, 224 Headland Road
Dee Why
NSW 2099
Australia
+61 2-9905-9400
Fax +61 2-9905-9455
harken@deckhardware.com.au
deckhardware.com.au

HYDRA ENGINEERING
Manufacturer of AutoSteer servo-
    pendulum and trim-tab systems.
Warren Road
Indian Queens Industrial Estate
Indian Queens
St. Columb TR9 6TL
Cornwall
United Kingdom
+44 (0) 1726-862000
Fax +44 (0) 1726-862008
info@autosteer.com
www.autosteer.com

HYDROVANE
Manufacturer of Hydrovane VXA
  2D.

Canada (administration)
Hydrovane Self Steering Inc.
Unit 15, 636 Clyde Avenue
West Vancouver, BC
Canada V7T 1E1
604-925-2660
Fax 604-925-2653
info@hydrovane.com
www.hydrovane.com

England (manufacturing plant)
Haywood Engineering
18B Mansfield Road
Daybrook
Nottingham NG5 6AA
United Kingdom
+ 44 (0) 115 920 4170
Fax +44 (0) 115 920 4170

NORKA INDUSTRIES INC.
Manufacturer of Norvane
  servopendulum.
P.O. Box 130273
Carlsbad, CA 92013-0273
760-929-9884
Fax 760-929-0021
norvane@selfsteering.com
www.selfsteering.com

SAILOMAT
Manufacturer of Sailomat servopendulum and BEST emergency
  rudder systems.

**Design Office and Factory-Direct
International Sales**
Sailomat International

Attn: Dr. Stellan Knöös
P.O. Box 2077
La Jolla, CA 92038
858-454-6191
Fax 858-454-6696
info@sailomat.com
www.sailomat.com

SCANMAR INTERNATIONAL
Manufacturer of Auto-Helm trim
  tab, Monitor servopendulum,
  MRUD emergency rudder, Saye's
  Rig servopendulum/trim tab, and
  SOS Rudder. Distributor of
  Navik servopendulum.
432 South 1st Street
Point Richmond, CA 94804-2107
510-215-2010
Fax 510-215-5005
scanmar@selfsteer.com
www.selfsteer.com

WINDHELM
Manufacturer of WindHelm
  servopendulum.
3 Strezlecki Avenue
Sunshine, VIC 3020
Australia
Mobile +0412 444 359
Fax +61 3 9311 1531
crew@windhelm.com.au
www.windhelm.com.au

WINDPILOT
Manufacturer of Windpilot Pacific
  Light, Pacific, and Pacific Plus I
  and II servopendulums.

Germany
Bandwirkerstraße 39-41
D-22041 Hamburg
Germany

+49 (0) 40652-5244
Fax +49 (0) 4068-6515
windpilot@t-online.de
www.windpilot.de

U.S.
Doro and Greg Kruegermann
2226 Maurice Avenue
La Crescenta, CA 91214
877-2WINDPILOT (877-294-6374); 818-541-9321
Fax 323-662-7616
windpilot@ns4.usinter.net
www.windpilot.com

USED WINDVANES
U.S.A.
Minney's Yacht Surplus
1500 Newport Boulevard
Costa Mesa, CA 92627
949-548-4192
Fax 949-548-1075
sales@minneysyachtsurplus.com
www.minneysyachtsurplus.com

Sailorman
350 East State Road 84
Ft. Lauderdale, FL 33316
800-523-0772; 954-522-6716
Fax 954-760-7686
shop@sailorman.com
www.sailorman.com

Sea Chest Marine
1320 Scott Street
San Diego, CA 92106
619-225-1339
Fax 619-225-1523
steve@seachestmarine.com
www.seachestmarine.com

Australia
Rockbottom Marine
443 Esplanade
Manly
Queensland 4179
Australia
+61 7 3893-0555
Fax +61 7 3396-9726
rbmarine@ihug.com.au
www.workin4u.com/rockbottom/

Online Services
AuctionSail.com (www.auctionsail.com). Deals primarily in yachts, but also auctions used boat gear online.

John's Nautical & Boatbuilding Page (www.boat-links.com). The Mother of All Maritime Links: John's Nautical Links List is exactly what it claims to be. If it's nautical, it's in here somewhere.

Boat TraderOnline.com (www.boattraderonline.com) is the flagship of a company that publishes a variety of national and regional boat magazines throughout the U.S. Purchases are made directly through the seller, not online.

Crocker's Boat Yard Inc. (www.crockersboatyard.com) Links for Boat Lovers will lead you to yacht clubs, marine manufacturers, chandleries, government agencies, and nonprofit organizations related to boating.

Cruise News (www.cruisenews.net). Within this site is a section called Windvane Forum: Design, Construction, and Use of Self-Steering Gear, which invites comments from vane gear builders and users. Read input from designers cited in this book and owners' positive and negative points about different models.

Latitude 38 (www.latitude38.com). A popular racing and cruising magazine published in Northern California, also has a monthly online version. Click on Classy Classifieds.

Mariners guide.com (www.mariners guide.com). This site advertises Hasler/Aries self-steering spares, and invites comments and questions from visitors. Consult this site if you need to find spare parts or find answers to questions about these classic vane gears.

Public Domain Aeronautical Software (www.pdas.com). Ralph Carmichael's website is chock-full of information and software options for anyone planning to design airfoils or hydrofoils, whether for aircraft or waterborn craft. His foil coordinates are refined versions of old NACA data.

Sail Classifieds (www.sailclassifieds. com) lists rigging, electronics, sailboats, and such used equipment as sails and the occasional vane gear.

SailNet (www.sailnet.com). Receives articles and comments from contributors on all aspects of sailing. You will also find links to many other sailing websites.

SELECTED NACA FOUR-DIGIT PROFILES

NACA 0006

X	Y
5	1.78
10	2.34
20	2.87
30	3.00
40	2.90
50	2.65
60	2.28
70	1.83
80	1.31
90	0.72
100	0.06

NACA 0010

X	Y
5	2.96
10	3.90
20	4.78
30	5.00
40	4.84
50	4.41
60	3.80
70	3.05
80	2.19
90	1.21
100	0.11

NACA 0008

X	Y
5	2.37
10	3.12
20	3.83
30	4.00
40	3.87
50	3.53
60	3.04
70	2.44
80	1.75
90	0.97
100	0.08

NACA 0012

X	Y
5	3.55
10	4.68
20	5.74
30	6.00
40	5.80
50	5.29
60	4.56
70	3.66
80	2.62
90	1.45
100	0.13

X = percent of distance along chord, starting from leading edge of foil
Y = distance from lengthwise center line of foil to edge of foil, expressed as percent of chord
Note: Y coordinates are rounded to nearest hundredth of a percent.
Source: Adapted from Public Domain Aeronautical Software (see www.pdas. com on previous page)

NACA 0015	
X	Y
5	4.44
10	5.85
20	7.17
30	7.50
40	7.25
50	6.62
60	5.70
70	4.58
80	3.28
90	1.81
100	0.16

NACA 0021	
X	Y
5	6.22
10	8.19
20	10.04
30	10.50
40	10.16
50	9.26
60	7.99
70	6.41
80	4.59
90	2.53
100	0.22

NACA 0018	
X	Y
5	5.33
10	7.02
20	8.61
30	9.00
40	8.70
50	7.94
60	6.85
70	5.50
80	3.93
90	2.17
100	0.19

BEAUFORT SCALE

Force	Wind Speed in Knots	Description
1	<1	Flat calm
2	1–3	Slight rippling on water's surface
3	4–10	Small, glassy waves
4	11–16	Waves 1 to 4 feet; some whitecaps
5	17–21	Waves 4 to 8 feet; whitecaps with some spray; first reef
6	22–27	Waves 8 to 12 feet with white-capped seas and spray everywhere; second reef
7	28–33	Near gale: waves 12 to 18 feet; streaks form on breaking waves
8	34–40	Full gale: waves 14 to 18 feet; trysail or storm jib
9	41–47	Strong gale: waves at least 18 feet with dense streaks of foam; some reduced visibility from foam and spray; sail boats hove-to
10	48–55	Storm: waves 20 to 30 feet; heavily rolling seas covered with white foam; sailboats sailing downwind under bare poles, towing a drogue
11	56–63	Violent storm: waves 30 to 45 feet; greatly reduced visibility from foam and spray
12	64 and over	Hurricane/cyclone: waves over 45 feet; air filled with foam and spray; very little visibility

Glossary

Note: The following definitions were written within the context of sailing and windvane self-steering. For broader definitions, consult a standard dictionary. Italicized terms appear elsewhere in the glossary.

Airvane: the flat section of plywood, cloth, or aluminum plate that senses the wind and controls the vertical rotation of the *servo blade* or *trim tab*.

Annealing: process of heating and cooling metal to harden or soften it; excessive heat from welding that weakens the surrounding metal, especially aluminum.

Anode: a negatively charged substance sacrificing electrons to a *cathode*.

Anodization: act of protecting a metal through the strategic placement of a sacrificial *anode*, such as zinc; usually refers to the protective anodic coating applied to aluminum through electrolysis.

Apparent wind: wind felt or measured onboard a moving sailing vessel.

Arc welding: metal fabrication technique using either a consumable or non-consumable electrode.

Aspect ratio: in this text, ratio of *chord* to *span* in a *hydrofoil*, or ratio of length to width in an *airvane*.

Austenitic: type of stainless steel, including grades 304 and 316.

Autopilot: electronic steering device capable of directing a vessel along a selected compass course, to a *GPS* waypoint, or to a selected angle to the wind.

Balance: juxtaposition of center of lift and rotational axis in a vessel's sail rig, hull, rudder, or self-steering servo *foils*.

Beam reach: point of sail in which the wind is at a right angle to the vessel.

Bearing: compass direction between a vessel's location and some fixed point, such as a waypoint or the vessel's destination.

Bernoulli's principle: law governing *lift*: as the rate of flow of a fluid increases, the fluid's pressure drops.

Bevel gear: gear with beveled, or angled, teeth allowing the gear to mesh at an angle with a similar gear.

Block: device containing a round, grooved *sheave* on an axle between two cheeks; employed to route lines on a sailing vessel.

Boomkin: frame or platform extending horizontally from the transom of a vessel, usually held in place by the backstay and a bobstay.

Boom vang: see *vang*.

Braze welding: similar to *brazing*, the welder fills in a large gap between two metals by filling in the crevice with a brass or bronze rod.

Brazing: process of joining the edges of two metals through heating the two surfaces with an *oxyacetylene* torch and melting a brass or bronze rod into the seam through capillary action.

Brinnell Method: test of *hardness* for metals.

Broach: act of a vessel's turning broadside to a wave.

Broad reach: point of sail in which the apparent wind passes over a vessel's port or starboard quarter.

Camber: the convex side with greater distance between leading and trailing edge on a *foil*.

Casting: a solid metallic object with coarse, yet consistent grain structure formed by pouring molten metal into a mold; may take the form of sand casting, centrifugal casting, permanent mold casting, or die casting.

Cathode: a positively charged substance receiving electrons from an *anode*.

Chord: on a *foil*, the distance from the tip of the leading edge to the tip of the trailing edge.

Circlip: circular clip placed in an external or internal groove on a cylinder, usually to keep bearings or rotating fittings in place.

Clevis pin: cylindrical piece of metal with one flanged end, used to lock hardware, such as bolt eyes and standing rigging, in place.

Close-hauled: point of sail in which the *true wind* crosses the bow at roughly a 45-degree angle.

Coaming: low, vertical walls surrounding a boat's cockpit; also the sides of the cabin rising above deck level.

Control lines: rope, usually double-braided polyester, leading from the *servopendulum* shaft to the helm to transmit steering impulses.

Cope: in a mold, the side with an opening to receive molten material for casting; also refers to the one alternative left to crew whose only self-steering mechanism, an *autopilot*, has just broken down a thousand miles from the nearest port.

Corrosion: decomposition of metals through mechanical or electrochemical processes.

Cotter ring: springlike coil, similar to a key ring, inserted into a hole on a bolt or *clevis pin* to prevent the fastener from slipping out of its seat.

Crevice corrosion: a form of *intergranular corrosion* occurring along a thin line through stainless steel.

Cutter: a sailboat with fore-and-aft rig, a single mast, and two headsails.

Dezincification: intergranular stripping away of zinc through galvanic action (see *galvanism*).

Dielectric: nonconductive material used for the electrical *insulation* of dissimilar metals.

Drag: the closed side of a mold used for casting; also, friction or opposing force that retards movement.

Drift: angle between *bearing* and *heading*.

Drogue: large object, such as a plastic or fabric cone, towed behind a vessel by a long line to slow a vessel's downwind speed in a storm.

Ductility: a measure of how much cold plastic deformation a material can withstand through stretching, bending, or twisting.

Duplex stainless steel: a combination of *ferritic* and *austenitic* stainless, with higher tensile strength and corrosion resistance than 304 or 316 stainless.

Electrolysis: similar to *galvanism*, but induced by stray current.

Electrolyte: electrically conductive substance, such as salt water, in which *ions* carry electric current.

Erosion: sloughing away of particles from rushing water or other source of friction.

Extrusion: continuous, uniformly shaped structure formed by forcing molten material, such as metal or plastic, through a die.

Ferritic: type of stainless steel containing a high percentage of carbon and iron, including 400-series grades.

Foil: as used in this book, a hydronamic shape, such as a rudder, servo blade, or keel.

Galvanism: loss of particles from an anodic metal to a cathodic metal through an electrolyte.

GPS: global positioning system; electronic navigation system that calculates latitude and longitude, speed, drift, etc., by processing signals received from satellites.

Hardness: a measure of a metal's resistance to scratching or scarring, such as that employed by the *Brinnell Method*.

Heading: actual course of vessel over the ground.

Heave-to: to cause a sailboat to become nearly stationary by backing the sails and locking the helm to *leeward*.

Hydrofoil: on a sailboat, refers to keel or rudder; on a windvane steering gear, refers to an auxiliary rudder, *trim tab*, or *servopendulum* blade.

In irons: condition in which a sailing vessel has rounded up too close to the wind and has not the momentum to fall onto either tack.

Injection molding: practice of forcing molten plastic into a mold.

Insulation: protection of anodic metals from cathodic metals by means of a *dielectric*.

Intergranular corrosion: a form of *galvanism* in which anodic particles deteriorate in the presence of cathodic particles within the same piece of alloy when an *electrolyte* dissolves the alloy's oxide coating, invading the piece of metal as it produces a fissure.

Ion: atom or group of atoms carrying a positive or negative charge.

Isolation: protection of anodic metals by keeping them distant from cathodic metals.

Ketch: two-masted sailboat on which the rudderpost is located aft of the *mizzen*.

Lazarette (also lazaret or lazaretto): space in hull immediately forward of the transom; storage space between deck and hull for provisions or equipment on a vessel.

Lee, or leeward: opposite of *windward*.

Lee helm: tendency of vessel to steer itself away from the wind when *close-hauled* or on a *beam reach*, usually due to undercanvasing or an unbalanced sail rig.

Leeway: see *drift*.

Lift: aerodynamic or hydrodynamic force acting perpendicular to a *foil* when a low-pressure fluid passes over one side of the foil and a high-pressure fluid passes over the other side; see also *Bernoulli's principle*.

LOA: length overall; a vessel's length, usually measured from stem to stern.

Malleability: the degree to which a material may be hammered, pressed, or rolled without rupturing.

Mannesmann Process: the practice of passing a rod billet through nonparallel rollers under high compression until the center of the rod ruptures into a narrow opening, forming a tube.

Martensitic: type of stainless steel low in carbon and nitrogen.

MIG: gas metal arc welding; the process uses a gas-shielded, wire-fed filler material to join edges of metals, especially stainless steel and aluminum, $1/4$ inch or thicker.

Milling machine: apparatus with a rotating cutting bit that can turn in different angles and cut laterally, not just vertically; used to shape metals, plastics, and other solid materials.

Mizzen: short mast aft of mainmast on a *ketch* or *yawl*.

NACA: former National Advisory Committee for Aeronautics, replaced by the National Aeronautics and Space Administration (NASA).

Oxyacetylene: compressed gas burned with oxygen for torch cutting or torch welding, performed with or without a welding rod.

PFD: personal flotation device.

Pitchpole: capsizing of vessel stern over bow.

Preventer: line attached between boom and side deck to prevent the boom from swinging over the deck during an accidental jibe.

Push rod: solid shaft, usually adjustable with swivel end fittings, used as linkage between *airvane yoke* and central transmission device in *windvane* steering apparatus.

Quadrant: quarter section of a *sheave* connected to vessel rudderpost or *windvane* gear to provide steering leverage.

Receiver pin: similar in appearance to a bobby pin, U-shaped stainless wire with one straight side and the other with zigzags so that the pin stays in place when inserted into the hole of a pintle or *clevis pin*.

Rolling: process used to manufacture sheet metal and *tubing*; also, boat's rotation through fore-and-aft axis.

Run: to sail 180 degrees off the wind.

Schooner: two-masted sailboat on which the foremast is shorter than the mainmast.

Servo blade: submerged foil (paddle or oar) on a *servopendulum* vane gear.

Servopendulum: shaft and *hydrofoil* section capable of rotating through vertical and horizontal axes simultaneously as it receives impulses from an *airvane* and sends steering force to the helm on a sailboat; also refers to the apparatus based on this principle.

Sheave: wheel with grooved edge for routing rope.

Sloop: sailboat with fore-and-aft rig, a single mast, and one jib.

Span: widest point of a *foil* cross section.

Split rig: sailboat design with two masts; for example, a *ketch*, *schooner*, or *yawl*.

Spring clip: see *circlip*.

Stick welding: fabrication process using a fixed (as opposed to wire-fed), consumable metal rod electrode as filler material.

Stress corrosion: *corrosion* resulting from stretching or bending of metal, allowing an electrolyte to permeate the metal's surface and inner structure.

Tensile strength: a measure of a material's resistance to being pulled apart.

TIG: tungsten inert gas; welding technique using a gas shield to insulate a nonconsumable electrode from the surrounding air; used especially for thin sections of stainless steel and aluminum.

Tiller pilot: similar to an *autopilot* except that the whole unit is installed above decks, via a steering ram, directly to the tiller.

Toughness: a measure of a metal's resistance to repeated applications of force without failing through permanent deformation or breakage.

Trim tab: *hydrofoil* hinged to trailing edge of main or auxiliary rudder, forcing the rudder to turn for course correction as the *trim tab* receives steering impulses from an *airvane*.

True wind: wind felt or measured on the deck of a vessel that is standing still.

Tubing: hollow cylinder of metal formed by rolling a long rod billet until the center ruptures into a hollow space; also see *Mannesmann Process*.

Turret: round fixture, usually of cast stainless steel or aluminum alloy, holding the *airvane yoke* and capable of turning vertically 360 degrees for course adjustment on a vane gear.

Vane: *airvane.*

Vang: rope or solid, telescoping fixture connected between the boom and the base of the mast to keep the boom stationary.

Weather helm: tendency of vessel to steer itself into the wind, usually due to an unbalanced or overcanvased sail rig.

Windvane: any one of a large family of devices that harness the wind's power in order to steer a vessel at a selected angle to the wind.

Windward: sailing with the wind forward of the beam.

Yaw: tendency of a yacht to fishtail in following wind and seas.

Yawl: two-masted sailboat on which the rudderpost is located forward of the *mizzen.*

Yoke: horizontally rotating fixture that holds the *airvane* on the turret of a vane gear.

Z rod: Z-shaped stainless steel rod used as transmission device in lieu of rod linkage or *bevel gears* in the Cape Horn *servopendulum* system.

Bibliography

BOOKS AND PERIODICALS

"Aries: The Vane That Takes You Everywhere." Promotional flyer, Peter Matthiesen, Nordborg, Denmark: Aries Denmark.

Aries Vane Gear (owner's manual). Isle of Wight, England: Marine Vane Gears.

Bannerot, Scott, and Wendy Bannerot. *The Cruiser's Handbook of Fishing.* Camden, Maine: International Marine, 2000, 2004.

Belcher, Bill. *Wind-Vane Self-Steering: How to Plan and Make Your Own.* Camden, Maine: International Marine, 1982.

Calder, Nigel. *Boatowner's Mechanical and Electrical Manual: How to Maintain, Repair, and Improve Your Boat's Essential Systems*, 2nd ed. Camden, Maine: International Marine, 1996.

Carr, Michael. "Windvanes and Autopilots." *Ocean Navigator*, July/August 1997.

Chapman, Colin, and Mel Peace, with Gerry Denston and Val Charles. *Working with Materials: Wood, Metal, Plastic.* London: Collins Educational, 1997.

Dear, Ian, and Peter Kemp, eds. *The Pocket Oxford Guide to Sailing Terms.* New York: Oxford University Press, 1987.

Donaldson, Sven. "The Inner Life of an Autopilot," *Ocean Navigator*, March/April 2002.

Fenger, Frederic Abildgaard. *Alone in the Caribbean.* Belmont, Massachusetts: Wellington Books, 1958.

Fleming, Kevin. *Fleming Self-Steering Systems: Installation, Operation, and Maintenance Manual.* San Diego, California: Fleming Self Steering Systems, 1999.

Förthmann, Peter Christian. *Self-Steering Under Sail: Autopilots and Wind-Steering Systems.* Camden, Maine: International Marine, 1998.

Geary, Don. *Welding.* New York: McGraw-Hill, 2000.

Gélinas, Yves. "Yves Gélinas on Self-Steering," *Sailing Canada*, May 1988.

Gilchrist, Don. "The Self-Steering Dilemma," *Cruising Helmsman*, June 2003.

Henderson, Richard. *Singlehanded Sailing: The Experiences and Techniques of the Lone Voyagers*, 2nd ed. Camden, Maine: International Marine, 1988.

Holden, Frank. "Windvane Self-Steering," *Cruising Helmsman*, March 2000.

Huff, Robb, and Michael Farley. *Sea Survival: The Boatman's Emergency Manual*. Blue Ridge Summit, Pennsylvania: Tab Books, 1989.

Jones, Tristan. *One Hand for Yourself, One for the Ship: The Essentials of Single-Handed Sailing*. New York: Macmillan, 1982.

Kettlewell, John J. "Elegant and Efficient: For Low Impact on Your Batteries, Wind-Vane Self-Steering Gear Is the Way to Go," *Ocean Navigator*, March/April 2002.

Knöös, Stellan. *Sailomat 601 Manual: Mechanical Self-Steering for Sailboat*. La Jolla, California: Sailomat, 1998.

Letcher, John S., Jr. *Self-Steering for Sailing Craft*. Camden, Maine: International Marine, 1974.

Maloney, Elbert S. *Chapman Piloting: Seamanship, and Small-Boat Handling*, 63rd ed. New York: Hearst Marine Books, 1999.

Meleski, Gene. "*Stella di Mare*'s Mid-Ocean Improv," *Latitude 38*, February 2002.

Merriam-Webster's Collegiate Dictionary, 11th ed. Springfield, Massachusetts: Merriam-Webster, 2003.

Minick, Joe C. "Versatile Vanes." *Sail*, November 2002.

Morris, William V. "With the Wind in Their Vanes," *Afloat*, March 2003.

Neal, John. *Log of the Mahina: A Tale of the South Pacific*. Friday Harbor, Washington: Pacific International Publishing, 1995.

Nicholson, Darrell. "Self-Steering—With No Strings Attached." *Cruising World*, February 2002.

———. "Sorting Out Self-Steering Options." *Cruising World*, January 2002.

Pack, Geoff. "Autopilot and Windvane Together? The Best of Both Worlds?" *Yachting Monthly*, May 1995.

Pritchard, Derek. *Soldering, Brazing, and Welding: A Manual of Techniques*. Marlborough, England: Crowood, 1996.

Ratcliffe Marine Design. *General Instructions* (windvane owner's manual). Pembroke, Massachusetts: Ratcliffe Marine Design, 1976.

Reck, Marcia. "Steering True and Straight: Windvane or Autopilot?" *Cruising Helmsman*, December 1988.

Scanmar International. *Monitor Windvane Manual: Installation, Operation, Maintenance*. Point Richmond, California: Scanmar, 1999.

Seipel, Carl. *Self-Steering: Notes on Autopilots and Vane Gears.* Sausalito, California: Scanmar Marine Products, 1989.

Skeates, Nick. "Fitting Wind-Vane Steering." *Practical Boat Owner*, no. 242, February 1987.

Slocum, Joshua. *Sailing Alone Around the World.* New York: Dover Publications, 1956.

West Marine Master Catalog 2003. Watsonville, California: West Marine Products, 2003.

Woas, Lee. *Self-Steering Without a Windvane: A Comprehensive Manual of Natural and Sheet-to-Tiller Steering Systems for Sailboats.* Newport, Rhode Island: Seven Seas Press, 1982.

WEBSITES

AP Technologies. Manufacturers of plastic materials. www.aptechno.com

Aries Vane Gear. Products. www. ariesvane.com/products.html

Berkeley Yacht Club. Emergency Rudder Design and Construction. www.well.com/user/pk/ PCrudder.html

Boats.com. Day, George. The Silent Crew: Wind Vanes and Autopilots for Cruisers. Article by George Day. www.boats.comcontent/default_detail.jsp? contentid=1411

Bronze and metals information. www.nbm-houston.com/bronze/

DuPont Heritage. Delrin acetal resin. www.heritage.dupont.com

Engineer's Edge. Injection Plastic Molding Design and Data. http:// engineersedge.com/molding_guidelines.htm

Hydrovane Self Steering Inc. www.hydrovane.com

John Ward's Web Pages. Sheet-to-Tiller Self-Steering. Article by Al Gunther and John Ward. www.jsward.com/steering/index.shtml

Marine Survey Online. Corrosion: A Boatman's Primer on the Essentials. Article by David Pascoe. www.marinesurvey.com/yacht/corrosion_1.htm

Polymer Plastics Corporation. Transparent clear Lexan. www. polymer plastics.com/transparents_lexan.shtml

Public Domain Aeronautical Software. www.pdas.com

Scanmar International. www.selfsteer.com

Sea-to-Summit.net. The Ship Would Not Travel Due West. Article by Peter Marsh. www.angelfire.com/or/petermarsh/ostar.htm

United States Coast Guard. Aluminum Fracturing. www.uscg. mil/d13/units/ msopuget/al_fracturing.htm

U.S. Vintage Model Yacht Group. Free-Sailing Model Yachts. www.swcp. com/usvmyg/freesail/freesail.htm

Index

About the Author

Jack Dunn

Bill Morris, a native of Los Angeles, received his first inspiration to sail the world's oceans at the age of twelve when his father offhandedly suggested selling the house and circling the globe aboard a large yacht. The proposal was soon tossed aside, but the idea had been inexorably planted in Bill's imagination. Serving as a radio repairman and later as an outboard engine mechanic during a stint in the U.S. Army in the mid-1970s, he picked up valuable skills that would help him later in life as a cruising sailor. He went on to earn a doctorate in educational administration from the University of California, Los Angeles, spending nearly twenty years teaching technical and business writing in vocational schools and community colleges in southern California and southern Florida. Over the years he also has published dozens of articles in professional, academic, and mainstream publications. Bill acted on his childhood dream when he sailed out of Los Angeles Harbor in October 2000 aboard his 1966 Cal 30 *Saltaire* and crossed the Pacific to Australia. He plans to continue sailing the tropics and writing about cruising life.